777

THE LOST BLOOD

777

THE LOST BLOOD

EVE WOODSON

TATE PUBLISHING
AND ENTERPRISES, LLC

Published by Tate Publishing & Enterprises, LLC
127 E. Trade Center Terrace | Mustang, Oklahoma 73064 USA
1.888.361.9473 | www.tatepublishing.com

Tate Publishing is committed to excellence in the publishing industry. The company reflects the philosophy established by the founders, based on Psalm 68:11,
"The Lord gave the word and great was the company of those who published it."

Published in the United States of America

ISBN: 978-1-63122-116-3
1. Biography & Autobiography / Religious
2. Body, Mind & Spirit / Supernatural
14.02.04

DEDICATION

This book is dedicated to the Father, Son, and the Holy Spirit. Without whom my story would have been impossible to live and write about. Father, thank you so very much for all the wonderful things you have done for me and are still doing for me. You are an awesome God indeed, and I love you very much.

ACKNOWLEDGMENT

Special thanks to the people whom had helped me along the way. Honorable Cyrus S. Cooper, my dad; Sumo G. Woodson, my husband; Julie Hofer, my God sent mom; the Prophetess Annie Wolo Johnson; Yatta and Leleah Woodson; Dr. Kelly Collins; Grandma Kabbeh Jentzen; Lacey Romo Smith; Grandma Odessa George; Abu Bakarr Sillah; Gwen Fedema; Julia Cooper Grear; Munah Cooper; Therese Nearangarten; Blake Peterson; Lori Kaspner; Pastor David Sheriff; John E. Jefferson; Ellen Ledum; Nyemah Wisner; Beth Sheik; Dontra Rolands; and everyone else who is not listed here. Thank you very much for your help, and I appreciate all of your efforts in making me and my family life easier. God bless you!

CONTENTS

Preface 11

Chapter One: The First Fourteen Years of My Life 13

Chapter Two: My Time in the Ivory Coast 39

Chapter Three: Getting Pregnant with the Twins 57

Chapter Four: My Dark Days. 75

Chapter Five: Moving in with Sue and Sam. 113

Chapter Six: Meeting My Hubby. 125

Chapter Seven: My Time of Despair 171

Chapter Eight: Meeting Prophetess Annie Wolo Johnson. . . 217

Chapter Nine: The Return of Pasei 229

Chapter Ten: The Conclusion of My Story 241

"The Great Boss" 251

PREFACE

The names of the characters in this book have been changed to protect their identities except for me.

This autobiography is one you will find extremely odd, disturbing, and difficult to forget. Please do not be frightened. In 1997, my life as I knew it was very nice, and I was happy. That was until I woke up in the twilight zone. And it all started with a voice that I heard saying I was going to write a book telling everyone that he was alive and well. He wanted me to expose a secret society to you firsthand. It has not been an easy assignment. It took me fifteen years of pure torture, life and death, day and night to get this story to you in time when mankind's faith will be the only key to their survival. With the presence of light, darkness disappears. No matter whom you are or what you do, this book will speak to you personally, and you will experience the love of God. And have no fellowship with the unfruitful works of darkness, but rather expose them. Eph. 5:11

I must boast, not that it is profitable, but I will go on to visions and revelations of the Lord. I know someone in Christ who, fourteen years ago—whether in the body or out of the body I do not know, God knows—was caught up to the third heaven. And I know that this person—whether in the body or out of the body I do not know, God knows—was caught up to paradise and heard ineffable things which no one may utter. About this person, I will boast, but about myself, I will not boast, except about my weaknesses. Although if I should wish to boast, would not be foolish, for I would be telling the truth. But I refrain so that no one may think more of me than what he sees in me or hears from me (because of the abundance of the revelations). Therefore, that I might not become too elated, a thorn in the flesh was given to me, an angel of Satan, to beat me, to keep me from being too elated. Three times I begged the Lord about this that it might leave me, but he said to me, "My grace is sufficient for you, for strength is made perfect in weakness." I will rather boast most gladly of my weaknesses in order that the strength of Christ may dwell with me. Therefore, I am content with weaknesses, insults, hardships, persecution, and constraints for the sake of Christ, for when I am weak, then I am strong" (2 Corinthians 12:1–10).

CHAPTER ONE

THE FIRST FOURTEEN YEARS
OF MY LIFE

Today marks one of the happiest days of my life. Someone called to tell me that my mother just died. This is the best news I have gotten in a long time. Yes! I screamed out loud from excitement. I know what you are probably thinking. *Why is she happy about her mother's death?* You have to read my story to understand why I am very relieved about this. *Am I a murderer?*

Hello, my name is Eve Woodson formerly known as Evelyn Nyoundah Cooper. I was born in Grand Gedah County, Liberia, West Africa. This is my autobiography. My father served in the House of Representatives, and my mother was an uneducated self-employed businesswoman. We lived a life of privilege in Zwedru the capital of Grand Gedeh. My father was the first educated man of his Krahn tribe. Being born with a silver spoon in my mouth, I was spoiled rotten, and I knew it. But I never ate with the darn spoon. Everybody catered to me whenever Mom or Daddy was in town. My parents called me their love child because they were separated for twenty something odd years before they had me. They had my eldest sister Anastasia and my brother Hamilton before their separation. While separated, they both had children with other people. They probably never thought that they were ever going to get back together again, but they did, and now here I am. They treated me like a princess every day, all day. My mother always told me how she fainted immediately for eight hours after giving birth to me. She said I was the only child born in the hospital out of the twelve children she gave birth to. She said that she was not expecting me for another month or so. Mom said the minute she went into labor, it started to rain with lighting and thunder. The instant I came out, there was a very loud thunder, and the ground shook as if it there was an earthquake, and then she fainted. She said everything surrounding my birth was very odd and unusual. For this reason, she took me to a witch doctor a few days later to ask who I was and what my purpose was in this world. The witch doctor told her that I have come to work for God and be a very powerful prophet. Little did I know that this fact was going to be kept from me until thirty something years later. One day my stepmother told me how she prayed for thirty years the same prayer every day. She said it was "God, please let this wicked woman have a child that is of yours, who would have the gift of sight to expose her evilness to the world one day." Little did she know her prayers were answered 35 years ago. Here is my story the devil did not want me to write. But I did anyways.

I always thought everyone could see the same things that I did. I thought they could hear what I heard. I did not understand what I had was a gift. As a child, I used to see this man dressed in all white who would visit me all the time. He would take me on the mountaintop where we would talk for what seems to be hours. He would always tell me, "Sit on my right side," whenever I went to sit down. He said his name was Jesus. I was about to find out that there was more to life than I knew and that this Jesus person was not just anybody. He was the Prince of princes. My life has been in danger since the day I was born.

When I was two years old, measles almost took my life, but I lived. When I was four, I caught on fire from a candle that was lit and set on the floor, and my night gown burned and melted onto my body. I should have died, but I lived. Around six years of age, I woke up at the crack of dawn to get the fallen mangos as I did every morning. This particular morning, the drinking well was overflowing, and there was water up to my waist under the trees. That should have been impossible, but it happened. I heard a voice tell me, "Don't go there this morning or you will die." "This is not ordinary water. If you go near it, you will get sucked into the well, and it will look like you fell in. Go back in the house now!" I turned around and went back to the house. Little did I know that this was the voice of the Holy Spirit.

There was a group of people in Zwedru who wore all black that would hold night meeting at my parents' house. My mother told me that they were the ones responsible for the disappearance of others. They abducted people, killed them, and ate their vital organs to gain spiritual strength .With all the supernatural things I could see, I never thought anything of it. I thought that human sacrifice was normal because Mom was a part of it. These people were friends with my parents and sometimes held the meetings at the house with all of them wearing their black long robes with the hood covering their heads as they chanted. They held hands in a circle as I watched them. I was about five or six years old, maybe younger. Whenever Mom was in town, I would follow her everywhere she went. That made me to see a whole lot of things not meant for children. But I was never a kid that got scared easily, and Mom was the toughest woman I knew. I was a loner and had no friends even though I was a friendly child. Mom told me that when she was giving birth to me, she did not birth me with friends attached to me. She would not permit it therefore. No friend ever visited me nor did I visit friends. The only friend I had was the guy that called himself Jesus.

There was a girl who visited me that looked like my identical twin. She always had on whatever outfit I had on when she showed up out of thin air. She was not very nice to me, and I did not like her very much. She used to float and never touched the ground. She was always trying to pull something out of the top of my head. Sometimes my feet would leave the ground as she was pulling this transparent thing out. Whatever she was trying to pull out must had been very strong because it wouldn't come out until she got frustrated and vanished in thin air every time. No one at the house really liked me, so I did not tell anyone anything until Mom came home. She was always asking me who came to visit me while she was away and what they said. That was the only time I would talk about anything. She would ask me what I saw people doing in the future and what I did with my life in the future, and I would tell her in details everything I saw. She told me not to tell anyone anything and not to trust anyone at all. So I never did. I spent most of my time on the property we lived. There were many trees of all sorts. We had coconut trees, grapefruit trees, potatoes that we ate raw because they were so sweet right out the ground, different kinds of mango trees, apple trees, palm trees, papaya trees, lime trees, and a tree that oozed some sap that turned into gum, and we would chew it.

Being in the yard was my getaway. I would disappear all day until dinnertime especially if Mom or Daddy was not home, and I would take my little sister Pasei with me. I was only one year older than her so we were very close. She was very, very quiet and did not talk much. There were a lot of people living at the house doing all kinds of different tasks whom I did not care for much. I could just look at people and tell whether they were good or evil. I could tell the people in the house were either afraid of me or wanted nothing to do with me. Except my cousins Gus, Win, and Alice, they were very nice to me. Brittany was there too, my younger sister, but I did not like her much because she talked too much and was too hyper for me. My brother was the biggest jokester, so when he was not around, it was cool with me. You could never tell what mood he was going to be in when he showed up. He was not nice and was a big bully. Funny he only misbehaved when Mom and Daddy were away.

Then there was my very beautiful sister Josephine (real name) whom all the guys wanted to date. She had the prettiest smile and silky long hair that reached her bottom. She had a small waist, big butt, chest, and was about five eleven in height. One day Josephine and I went to the neighbor's yard where her friend lived. She was supposed to be cooking, but when Mom is not home, everybody do their own thing. Unfortunately for her though, Mom came home from wherever she was, and my sister was not there. "Uh-oh!" We could hear her screaming from where we were down the road. Josephine started running back to the house, and I ran right along with her. Not that I was going to get in trouble or anything. Mom treated me like an egg that shouldn't touch the ground before it cracked. Josephine ran into the room to make it seem like she was in her room the whole time. I ran in there with her. I hid under the bed. Mom had a temper that was out of this world, and everybody knew that. I could see Josephine, and she was so scared. Mom came in the room and grabbed Josephine by the neck with one hand and lifted her off the ground. She started chanting something. I could not hear Josephine make a sound. After my mom got done chanting, she dropped Josephine on the bed and walked out. Wow, she lifted Josephine with one hand, and my sister is not heavy, but she isn't light either.

Josephine was uncontrollably shaking. I came from under the bed and sat next to her; the whole time, she couldn't talk. After that incident, Josephine ran away from home. She was gone for some months. My mother went to Monrovia, the city, to find her. As soon as she came back, Josephine died a few days later. They said she had no blood in her body, and the doctors refused to give her a blood transfusion because she did not have the money. Any doctor would have been happy to hear that they were treating the Honorable Cyrus S. Cooper's daughter. Josephine was my mother's daughter and not my father's. Daddy treated her just like his own. But to her were none available to help. They brought her body back to Zwedru. As she was lying in the coffin, I had seen her ghost walking all over the place even after she was buried. One day my mother sent me in the house to get her a glass of water. Josephine's ghost was in there, and it was angry. She broke every single glass in the cabinet. She told me I was not going to get Mom any water. She said, "Mom killed me!" I was so afraid

I ran out. Mom heard all the commotion and came running in. She asked me,

"Did Josephine hurt you?" I told her no. She could see my sister as well.

She asked my sister, "Why are you scaring your sister like this? Don't you know she can see you?" A few days later, I was sitting outside with Mom when I saw Josephine walking back and forth just looking at my mom in an angry way. Mom looked at me and said, "Don't be afraid of her. She can't do anything to you. So I tried to pretend like she was not there, and she was just walking back and forward in front of the outside kitchen. Josephine's friend showed up at our house in Grand Gedah from out of town one day and asked for her. Mom told her that Josephine was dead.

She said, "But she was just with me a few days ago and she left her clothes at my house. That's why I am here to return them." I started to panic. I was so scared. Mom could tell that I was scared. She immediately screamed at my sister's friend and told her to leave and don't come back because my sister was dead and gone and there was no way that she could have seen my sister. I knew right away that I was not supposed to say anything to an outsider about her ghost being here. I kept quiet as Josephine watched the whole thing take place, and there was nothing she could say or do. But I was still very frightened. So Mom took us far away to the farm so I could get out of there for some days. Josephine's ghost followed us there. Mom knew I loved the farm because there were more fruits and trees there. It was really huge and about the size of seven football stadiums put together. I loved it even more because there were only two caretakers there and not a lot of people like our home in back in town.

That night upon our arrival while Mom and I were lying on the bed, someone started to knock on the door. I knew it was her. Mom tried to ignore her, but she just kept knocking harder. So Mom reluctantly asked, "Who is there?"

She said, "Josephine," and told mom to let her in. I heard her loud and clear. I was so scared and knew that the farm was not far enough from her. Mom told her that she is dead and she needed to go away because she was scaring me. I did not sleep that night. Of course I did not understand at the time why she was hunting Mom. I knew Mom killed her, but I didn't really understand why she was mad about that at that time. She was considered the bad seed, not knowing she had the brightest star and needed to be sacrificed so Mom could live and keep her powers and be stronger in what she did. I realized that the farm was of no use, so we went back to town after I told Mom I was ready to go home. Even though Mom screamed and yelled at everyone else, she never ever screamed or yelled at me. Mom to me was the best mother and I loved her because she loved me dearly.

We went back home to Zwedru. I don't know what happened to Josephine's ghost, but I did not see her anymore. I know Mom did something for that to stop happening. One day while in the kitchen with my cousin, I heard a really loud noise on the roof. Rushing toward the kitchen door to see what it was, right in front of me something really big and green started falling and coiling at the same time. It was a huge overgrown python that dropped off the roof and landed right in front of me missing me by inches. "Oh my gosh." We are going to die in this kitchen! My cousin Roberta got so confused when I started screaming my lungs out. She didn't know what happened. I tried to tell her that the loud noise was a snake that dropped off the roof. She thought that I was overreacting about something, and she did not want to get in trouble with Mom. She tried to get me out the kitchen and in the open for everyone to see that she was not harming me. She tried to push me outside, but the snake was so big it covered the entrance. No one could come in or go out. I got out of her way, and she was able to see the snake; then she started to scream along with me. By then, everyone came running to our rescue. We could hear them screaming from the other side.

But the snake was knocked out cold from the fall. My cousin Roberta grabbed me and held me really tight. I guess the noise from everyone screaming woke the snake up. It slowly crawled out of the yard. It left a big imprint in the grass. It crawled across the street in the neighbor's yard where it was later killed, I heard. Mom looked after me the rest of the week very closely because she thought someone was trying to kill me in witchcraft. She knew who was and who was not a witch. Apparently, I did too.

My cousin Alice told me I was born that way, and they had to hide me when certain people were coming to visit my parents. My mom would tell them to take me in her room the minute I started to cry because they said I never cry unless a witch or wizard was approaching. Because of that gift, my life was in danger, she said. And evil people wanted me dead. My mother was extremely overprotective of me, and that was one of the reasons she would take me everywhere with her. I remembered before the late President John Black became president in 1980, he came to my mother and asked her to help him. He was in an army uniform with a red hat. He said to her, "I want to be president, but I need you to help me."

She said, "If I help you, you have to appoint my husband to have an important position in your government." He said that he would do that. She told him to get on his knees; he did that, and then he held her feet. This was the way to bow down suggesting the one standing to be the superior one. He was very submissive to her. She chanted something while holding his head. My father was also there. She told him, "Rest assured you will be the president of Liberia, but if you don't keep your promise, you will have me to deal with." He became president shortly after that. I remember Mom asking him what was taking him so long to hire my father. He told her that these things took time and that he was going to keep his promise. He later appointed an important position to my father in the House of Representatives. Not that my father was not educated enough to hold such an important position, but in African politics, sometimes corruption overthrows credentials. My mother always boasted about how she is the child of the Satan himself, that her mother was a powerful witch and her father a powerful wizard and needed a child to carry on their legacy. A daughter needed to bare a daughter and so on. They went to this place in Grand Gedah where the devil himself resides under this mountain. When you get there and tap on the ground in a synchronized tap, it would open up, and you would meet with Satan in person. Satan put his spirit in my mother as she was in my grandmother's womb. He told my grandmother that the child would be extremely evil and kill a lot of people and would only work for him.

He said, "When you give birth, you will see that she only has nine toes, and that would be the sign that she is the one. I heard there is one general butt naked who has a video out describing this same place. I have personally never seen it, but Pasei, my younger sister, told me she watched it. I also heard that he has now given his life to Christ and goes by the name Joshua Bleyhi. He also talked about how he killed and ate people just like my mother did in order to be more powerful. I read an article on him recently that said he is preaching the word of God after having an encounter with our Lord and Savior Jesus Christ. Amen to that. I don't know whom all my mother had killed as she was growing up, but I know she killed her older sister among others. The ghost of her older sister came to me in a dream and told me this. When I described her to someone who knew her, the person started to scream and cry. Saying to me how my aunty was dead long before I was born and that there were no cameras in the interior then for her to have left a picture behind.

I had never met my aunt nor seen a picture of her before. Nor did I see any of my four grandparents who all died before I was born. But I have seen my mother's parents on several occasions later in life trying to kill me. This python almost killing me would be just the beginning. It was as big as the one that crawled in and out of the walls in our house in Zwedru. Except this one is solid and not transparent. My mother's dragon used to be in the house with us crawling in and out of the walls. I thought that was normal. I thought everyone else seen it too being that it never left. But it never bothered anyone to my knowledge. The only time I can remember Mom talking about it was when the neighbor granddaughter died and Mom told me it was her grandmother's dragon that killed her, and she told me it needed to feed. After the python incident and my sister's death, Mom started making preparation to bring us to America. Only Jasmine and I were allowed to come. What I knew was Alice and Josephine were the ones coming to America originally until Josephine died and then the status quo changed.

Mom said that if she didn't take me out of there, they were going to kill me. We were not allowed to tell anyone we were going to America; I fear they might kill us before that took place. A few months later, it was time to leave, so we went to Monrovia to Daddy. He took us to the airport a few a weeks later. When we got to the airport, they told my dad that we were too young to travel by ourselves. We needed to travel with an adult. So Mom came to Monrovia, and we were able to leave. I was thinking how much I was going to miss my father and Pasadena (Pasei). We landed in New York. Mom told me that I should be very careful here in America and not get in any trouble. My sisters in New York took care of us until we got to Minnesota. Then Anastasia and her son picked us up from the airport. It was cold, but she brought us winter jackets, and we put them on right away. That was my first time seeing such big jackets. The ground was covered in snow. It looked so weird. I couldn't stop staring out the window on the drive to her house. When we got to her house, everything seemed strange, and the smell was different. It took a good while to get used to.

She had a pretty home. She put us in school right away. It was fun. Except she lived in Maple Grove Minnesota, and that was odd not seeing any black people at all. When I asked her why she lived among all white people. She said it was because she was black and already knew black people's behavior. Now that she was living in America, she needed to know the white people's behavior. She said the best way to do that is to live in their mist and see how she could get along with them. That made a lot of sense, and she told me that I was going to thank her one day for that. She was very right about that by the way. One day, Mom told me that she was leaving the next day. We had been here for some months already. So that morning, she said, "When you come from school, I would be gone." I was sad, but I knew she had to go back to take care of my little sisters and her business. When I came home from school, she was gone. So I guess Anastasia was going to be the one in charge of me now.

After Mom left, I was doing real well in school. Anastasia was proud of me. She was my role model. She was also in school getting her degree in accounting. I used to make her bed every day and put little notes under her pillow, telling her how proud of her I was and how she was going to make it. Then she would say, "What will I do without you?" Her husband was never home. He would leave very early in the morning and come back late at times. I believe he was probably working. There was something about him that did not sit well with me, but I did not know what it was. We went to church every Sunday. I remember when I first became suspicious of him. He kissed me on the lips in the garage right before we went to church. I thought it was kind of weird. I said yuck to myself and wiped my lips. But I never said anything. I thought maybe that's how it was done in America. Until this day, I have a problem with men kissing me on the lips.

One time, we went to church and on our way back home in the middle of winter, Ana's (Anastasia) car crashed. It spun around on the bridge and got stuck on the guardrail. Down below was the highway. If anyone had moved, the car was going to fall onto the highway below and that was going to be the end of us. So

Anastasia and her son crawled into the backseat, and we all got out. Her husband was not with us that day. I remembered people speeding past us on the bridge and not stopping. This African American family stopped for us and took us home. We almost died. There was no way we were going to survive that crash if we had landed on the highway below. I felt so bad for her. She was so hard working. But I think the stress started to get to her.

I remember one day she was mad at me about something, and she said to me, "Your parents may have treated you like a princess, but I will make sure you don't get any of that royal treatment here. Jasmine is the princess in this house now." I just looked at her, looked at Jasmine who was standing right there and I didn't say anything, I smiled and just walked away politely. For some reason I didn't expect anything out of her. One night I was up late, and her husband came home and met me up. I was the only one awake, and I was in the bathroom curling my hair like I did all the time. It was very hard for me to sleep at night, and I had been that way ever since I can remember. He lay down on the couch and told me to get on top of him. I was so scared, and I did not want to, so he grabbed me and pulled me. He played with my body all kinds of ways and put his fingers in me. He tried to put his penis in me, and it couldn't go. *This is not happening*, I kept telling myself as the tears were rolling down my eyes. Anastasia was upstairs sleeping. He told me not to make a sound.

He said, "You know your sister hates you, and she would never believe you if you told her anything." It was clear to me that she didn't like me very much, so I couldn't scream for her help; she would probably think I was the bad one. The sad part is that he knew that. I felt so bad. I knew it was true what he just said. My sister's husband molested me at the age of twelve. Anastasia treated me poorly after Mom left, and Jasmine, I believe, had a lot to do with our older sister not liking me. She would always tell lies to Anastasia so she could get angry with me. Anyways, he had his way with me. Then he told me to go to bed. My legs were shaking underneath me. I was so confused. When I got in the room, I couldn't lay down in the bed. I sat on the bed next to Jasmine who was sleeping. I knew she didn't like me, so how could I tell her? But I woke her up and told her anyways.

And she sat up, and I explained to her what happened, and when I got done, she asked me, "Is that why you woke me up? You better take your ass to sleep." I had never felt so lonely in my life. I didn't know what to do after that. I was up the whole night just shaking a pouring tears silently so Ana won't wake up. The next morning, my sister Anastasia came in the room to tell us to get ready for school. She was so busy getting ready for work and picking up after us. She didn't notice me shaking and sitting on the bed. Jasmine got out of bed and went into the bathroom. When Anastasia noticed that I was not moving and was just sitting there, she looked up at me. She noticed tears rolling down my face, and I was still trembling. She got concerned. She came closer to me and started to ask me what happened.

"Did you have a nightmare?" I shook my head no. Then she started asking what's wrong. And the more she asked that question, the more tears rolled down my cheeks. So then she finally hit the nail on point and asked me the big question. "Did he touch you?" Then the floodgate of my tears opened.

And I said, "Yes, but he told me not to tell you because you won't believe me."

She said, "Oh I believe you." I told her right away I was sorry and I didn't mean to stay up late. She said it was not my fault and that I should not worry that I would never have to see him again. She did not send us to school that day. We went over to her friends' house. She believed me. I was relieved. I never was the kind of child that will tell you if something was wrong with me. My parent knew me for that. They kept a close eye on me all the time. Her husband was already at work when she found out. She said, "It's okay. He was cheating on me anyways, and it was just a matter of time." I had never felt her love more like I felt it that day. She made me feel much better after she found out and did not beat me. She actually hugged me. I could tell Jasmine was not happy with me. She just looked on. She did not talk to me the rest of the day. But as a child, when you sense someone doesn't like you, you tend to stay away from that person. And that was what I did with Jasmine even in Africa. Jasmine was one of those that illuminated hatred toward me whenever I looked at her. Therefore I never took to myself to get to know her. This experience will really be my first time being near her. She is another half sibling, my mothers' daughter whom my father also considered his own.

Anastasia's husband denied the whole thing after she confronted him. Sister, as we called Anastasia, I think kicked him out. Hell was already breaking, but this was when all hell broke loose for me. I don't know who was telling her what. Like I said, I did not talk much unless I was joking to make someone laugh or caring for someone when they were sick. Than I would say and do stuff to make them feel better and forget that they were sick. I noticed she was getting angrier with me as the weeks went by. I started to get scared. She started beating me in the house for everything. She would ask me if she thought I did something, and then before I explained, she would just jump on me and start beating me. She thought of me as a liar, and I was not and still am not. On a weekly basis, she started taking me to her friend's house at 4:00 in the morning before school started. They would strip me naked, and both of them would beat me with a belt. They whipped me at least twenty-five lashes total. They would wear gloves, mash some habanero peppers in a bowl, which they rubbed in my wounds. Then she would drive me back home about forty-five minutes away while my body was on fire from this extremely hot pepper. I didn't cry because I did not feel the need to. It wouldn't have made a difference and it would have given her some sort of weird satisfaction.

Back at the house, she would sit in the bathroom and make sure that I took a hot shower so the pepper would burn even more. All this would happen before I left for school in the morning. Never once did I tell my school counselor. I did not want to get her in trouble. One time she was mad because I took her sweater and wore it to school. She beat me until she sprung my wrist. While I was in class trying to take my spelling test, I noticed my wrist couldn't move up or down. My teacher noticed me and seen that my wrist was swollen. She asked me what happened, and I didn't want to say. So she took me to the counselor's office where I was questioned. I was concerned about my sister getting in trouble. The counselor assured me that my sister was not going to get in trouble. The counselor lied to me. She did, and the police and social services came to the house to question her.

Going to school was something I looked forward to; it was my getaway. She stopped beating me, but she started to punish me in other ways. She would buy a five-subject notebook and make me write in it for hours. I had to always write "I will not call Jasmine stupid." Because that was what I called her every time she did something to me. But what I got out of that was good handwriting skills, oh well. One day Jasmine started getting really froggy on me and decided to jump (she was bullying me). I waited for Anastasia to go to work. I beat Jasmine up really bad and put her head in the toilet where I almost drowned her before school. She was very lucky. The voice told me to stop. She never ever tried to fight me again after that. She's four years older than I, but I had to show to her that she couldn't punk me out, not because Sister was always on her side.

Then something odd happened. One day Sister came home and told me she wanted her husband to come back home, but he told her that I had to apologized to him first. So she was asking me to apologize to him. My heart, I think, fell out of my chest that day. All I could think of was him doing this to me again. She said, "I am going to call him, and this is what you are going to tell him." So I did everything she said to do.

And he asked me, "Did Anastasia tell you to apologize to me?"

And I said yes. He told me to put her on the phone, so I did. When she got done talking, she said he was not coming home as long as I was in the house. I knew my life was about to take the turn for the worse. She started to get even angrier. She started purposely doing things to make me feel bad. At this time, I was about thirteen years old. I only had two pairs of jeans, two skirts, and exactly five blouses for school.

One time she told me that I could spend the weekend with my best friend, and when the weekend came, she said, "I lied to you. You are not going anywhere. I wanted you to know how it feels to be lied to." And in my mind, I couldn't figure out why she always felt like I was lying to her. The person that was lying to her all the time was the one she considered truthful. I was not a snitch, so I wasn't going to say anything. She had to find out for herself.

Another time was when she went shopping and bought a lot of clothes and came home with bags. Her son, Jasmine, and I were all happy to see the clothes. I started looking in the bags for stuff for me, and she looked me in the eyes and asked me, "What are you looking for? There isn't anything in there for you. Why would I buy you anything? You are a liar." I knew from that day on, my sister hated my guts. Jasmine was very sneaky, and like I said, she had a lot to do with all of this. By now, I was asking Anastasia to please send me back home to my mother.

I painted this self-portrait in school that she was so proud of and that was one of the only times I had seen her smiled with me since the incident with her husband. That semester I decided not to concentrate on school anymore. I started doing things that would make her mad so she would send me back to Africa to my mom. It was a nightmare living with Sister. I felt so out of place and did not feel love, something that was so used to. We celebrated Christmas over at her friend's house one year. There was this boy that I knew at the party, and I took him into the bathroom purposely when I had seen my sister's friend looking at me. I knew she was going to tell her. That's why I did it.

Jasmine was upstairs in the attic with her boyfriend when she heard Sister banging on the bathroom door. The boy and I were in there, and he was saying sweet nothing to me. She kept banging louder, and she said, "Evelyn I know you are in there. Open this door right now!" So I did. Nothing at all happened between this boy and me. But I knew that was going to make Sister so angry that she would send me to my mom so that I won't have to take this abuse anymore. There is no feeling like being somewhere you know you are not wanted. Jasmine was not happy with me for that. She said she did not want me to go back home to Mom. I looked at her and knew that she was not going to have anyone to lie on anymore. She never wanted me here. She just wanted me around so Anastasia could tell her how she looked like a supermodel and how I was short, fat, and ugly. I did not know than what I now know as an adult.

Anastasia was trying to break my spirit. The voice would always tell me, "Don't listen to her. You are a good person." And I would feel so much love from within me that nothing else around me matter. The warmth and comfort that I felt inside me was the Holy Spirit, which I was not aware of yet. They say the Holy Spirit only visits you when you have received Jesus Christ as your Lord and Savior. I have being seeing Jesus since I was a kid. He would always visit me and take me places. He has been my best friend since I can remember.

Anyways, I have been baptized three different times in my life that I can remember. When I was a little girl, my dad took me to church with him, and I was then baptized around the age of three or four. Another time was when I was about eleven or twelve. The third time was after I had my last two children. I baptized the third time because I believe it to be by choice and not as a kid.

So the Holy Spirit has been visiting since I was a child. He was the great comforter that made me not to take anything to heart. I just looked at everything and knew as long as I could take a deep breath and breathe in and out, life still went on, and there was always going to be hope. One day Anastasia picked up the phone and called my mother to tell her that I was coming home. I was so happy. Anastasia sent me to my mother in the Ivory Coast at the age of fourteen. Here is what happened next.

My sister drove me to Chicago where I caught the flight to the Ivory Coast, which is not my country Liberia. First we stopped in Yemen. On the flight, the guy who sat next to me must have been drunk because he was very talkative, with slurred speech, and a little too friendly. He fell asleep right when the flight took off. He kept leaning on my chest, and every time I woke him up, within seconds, he would be sound asleep again. He and I did this over and over until I got tired and just let him sleep. He drooled on me for hours, and my blouse was soaking wet. When we landed and he realized what he had done after sobering up, he decided to clean my blouse while it was still on me. He attempted wiping the drool off, but instead it smeared even more. I was so annoyed with him. I just politely told him, "Don't worry about it. It's not that big of a deal. It will soon dry up."

Of course I could have told the flight attendants, but as a child traveling this long of a distance, you don't want to make any enemies for yourself. It was a fourteen- to fifteen-hour flight, and I was tired by the time I got there. To my disappointment, my brother did not show up. I waited for him all day, and there was no sign of him. There was a man who worked there that kept asking me if I was okay. He spoke English when everyone else spoke French. He took care of me while I was waiting. He bought me food and water. He kept my bags in a safe place so I won't draw attention to myself. He was very nice to me. When it was time for the airport to close, he became concerned and told me that I needed a place to stay. I did not have any money to catch a cab anywhere. Even if I did, I didn't speak French, and it was my first time in this country. They announced the closing of the airport, and everyone had to be out of the building. I was so scared. I went outside, and I swore I caught whiplash from looking around for my brother.

The man told me that I was going to get robbed if I stayed out there all night. The thieves could even rape and kill me. He offered to take me home with him. What choice did I have? It was either him or the strangers of the night, in a big African city. He told me that he would bring me back in the morning when he was coming to work. I took my chances with him. Whenever I'm in trouble, that's when the Holy Spirit would direct me on what to do next and what was going to happen. I did not know yet at that time that God had given me certain gifts. I was naïve and very trusting because of this voice that would help me out of every bad situation. I could trust this voice even though I did not see the person speaking. I just knew to trust it, and that's what I did. Not once was it ever wrong when it told me things to come. We took the cab to his house that night. He put my entire luggage in his place and told me to wait inside for him. He came back with a bucket of water so I could bathe.

After I got done bathing, we walked to the road where people were selling food. He asked me if I liked fish. I said yes, so he bought me fish and something that looked like rice but not really rice. It tasted really good. He started talking to me so he could find out more about me. He seemed really nice. After we got done eating, we went back to his place. It was very late, and I was tired. "Oh my gosh, where will I sleep?" I asked. He only had a room and a twin-sized bed. The floor had no carpet; it was concrete. I was not about to change into a nightgown. I did not know him, and he was not related to me. This man was a stranger even though he seemed nice. He could be like my sister's husband. He told me to sleep on the bed. I said, "No, where would you sleep?"

He said he would also sleep on the bed. I said, "Oh no, it's okay. I will sleep on your floor!"

He said, "Centipedes, millipedes, spiders, and other stuff crawl on the floor, especially at night."

"Okay, those things are nasty, but if I sleep on your bed, it's not going to be anything sexual." He agreed, and we lay down with our clothes on. At some point in the middle of the night while I was asleep, he started feeling on me. But he looked like he was sleeping, so I woke him up and told him no! He fell back to sleep. Not too long after, he started to do it again. I realized then and there that I was in deep trouble. He started touching me more and more. Being so scared, I started to cry. I told him, "Leave me alone and stop that, or I would take my bags and leave!"

He said, "But it is in the middle of the night. It's too dangerous out there."

I told him I didn't care about it being in the middle of the night. What can they do to me out there that he, Mitchell, wasn't planning on doing to me inside his house? I told him that I took a chance by coming with him, and now I am disappointed in his behavior.

He got up and looked at me and seen how frighten I was, he asked me, "How old are you?"

"I am only fourteen years old, so please don't rape me!" After telling him that, I had a flashback of the night I lost my virginity, almost a year earlier, to a buddy of mine named Shawn. I decided to have him de-virgin me because I didn't think it would be bad. It was. All my buddies at school were no longer virgins, and I felt like I was the only one left, so I did it. Shawn slept with my best friend the very next day, and I caught them red-handed. I wasn't mad. I just said, "Oh cool, I see how it is." And I walked away feeling sorry for my best friend and thinking, *Oh well, this is just another betrayal.* I felt sorry for her because I really did like hanging out with her. I did not make a big deal out of it when she told me that it just happened in the heat of the moment. She started getting angry with me as the days went by, and Shawn was trying to apologize to me. I dogged him, and in return, he dogged her, which made her mad enough to jump me at the bus stop one morning. She pulled a good chunk of my hair out, saying the reason Shawn liked me was because of my long hair. I was angry with her but decided to avoid her. Knowing that I was about to be shipped back to Africa was preoccupying my mind. At this moment that thought was where I was drawing my happiness from.

Anyways, now that I am here on some stranger's bed, pleading with him not to rape me, I realized quickly that I was in a real bad situation.

He looked shocked when I told him my age. "But you have big breast, and you look way bigger than a fourteen years old."

I said, "Yes, I know, but I am only fourteen." I understood what he meant because grown men have always looked at me funny since I could remember. He gave me a hug and assured me that he won't touch me anymore. Then he said he will not leave me alone until I find my brother and if I confirmed that it was my brother. After that, I lay back down and told myself that I believed him. I was really tired from being awake for almost twenty-four hours. I fell asleep.

The next day, I got up and remember the nightmare of a situation I was in. I looked at myself, and I still had all my clothes on; he kept his word. This man's name was Mitchell. We got ready and went back to the airport where he had to start work. He bought me breakfast and told me to sit and wait for my brother and that he would keep an eye on me. He was pretty much babysitting me. I told him sorry for spending his money on me. "But when we find my brother, he would pay you back."

He said, "Okay," and smiled. It was lunch time, and I still have not seen my brother. Mitchell bought me lunch and kept his eyes on me like he said he would. Whenever he seen a guy talking to me, he would come over and say whatever he said in French, and they would leave me alone.

I was worried that I will be stuck in a foreign country without my family if I don't find my brother. Mitchell told me that he would bring me back to the airport every day until I find my brother. He asked me, "Where in Ivory Coast is your mother?" I told him she was up in the interior in a place called Guiglo. He told me that if my brother does not show up at the airport, he would take me to Guiglo himself and look for my mother there. By now, I was comfortable with him because of his efforts in making sure that I was safe. It was evening time, and I still have not seen my brother. Mitchell bought me dinner. After we ate, we went outside of the airport to get fresh air. I had been sitting and waiting all day. As I was looking around in the distance, I had seen someone approaching. Mitchell noticed that I was looking with curiosity; he turned around to see what I was looking at.

"It's my brother," I yelled. "That's my brother!" I ran toward him. I was so happy. I hugged him really tight. At that time, I thought that was one of the happiest days of my life. I introduced Mitchell to my brother. I told my brother how I have been here for a day and a half. He was shock; he told me the date he was given to pick me up was today at this time. So he got the wrong date. I was not surprise in the least bit. Then he immediately asked me if I was hungry. "No, Mitchell had been feeding me." He was so grateful to Mitchell.

He kept telling him, "Thank you for taking care of my sister." He told me sorry for what happened. He was given the wrong date, he said. I believed him. He and Mitchell went and got my bags.

My brother Hamilton asked me if Anastasia gave me any money. I told him no. He said, "No, she had to have given you money." So I remember the brown envelope she gave me and told me not to open. I reached in my bag and took the envelope out and give it to him. He opened it; there was money in it. He asked me, "Did she tell you that she was putting money in here?"

"No." Then he turned around and took some money out and offered it to Mitchell for taking care of me. Mitchell refused the money. He said it was his pleasure. So I told him, "Thank you very much for everything." He told me that he would come to Guiglo one day and check on me to see how I liked it there. I said thanks, and we left. My brother was not happy with the fact that Anastasia did not tell me that I had money on me just in case. Then he said, "Suppose this nice man was not going to help you? I could tell not even him wanted to imagine what would had happened to his little sister." Hamilton and I spent some days in Abidjan before leaving for Guiglo. He showed me the city, which was the capital of Ivory Coast. It was very beautiful. When it was time to go to Guiglo, Hamilton told me not to expect it to look as nice as Abidjan.

We got on an old bus to go there. The ride was also very long. The whole way there, I was looking around until I fell asleep. I had so much fun hanging out with my big brother. We arrived very early at the crack of dawn that morning. Pasadena and Brittany were so happy to see me. They looked like they lost a lot of weight. They didn't look as good as they did in Liberia. Then my mom came out, and she looked even worse. I was surprised. I guess they are refugees and did not live the life they were used to living. The war in Liberia seemed to have taken a toll on them. They really looked strange. Pasadena seemed to have been the happiest to see me. She'd remember how close we were.

Mom just wanted the bags open so she could see everything that belonged to her. She hugged me and asked me how I was doing, and then she was off to the side with the bags. "Yep, that's her," I said, "and this is really happening. I am with my mom and siblings, and I am already happy." Among the things were some clothes Anastasia put in there for our half-sister Cellia. She is my father's daughter who is about three or four years older than me. Later that morning, Cellia came to see me. It was my first time seeing her. "Oh my gosh, you are so beautiful," I said. I immediately knew the clothes were not her type. But she took them anyways. She spent some time with me before leaving. From there on, she made sure she came looking for me every day. We became close.

A lot of people came to see me, and some of them were speaking our dialect. I couldn't understand it at all. That's all Mom spoke to me. She told me she was not going to speak English to me. She spoke Krahn. I have been here for a few weeks now. And the mosquitoes and the flies are bugging the crap out of me. I kept getting malaria. And on the side of my hip was a huge cyst-like lump that was filled with puss but was not yet ready to pop. It hurt like hell. On my finger was another one that had popped because Mom roasted a huge spider and palm oil, mashed it together, and rubbed it on my finger. The well water is so bad that my legs broke out into boils which the flies wanted to eat. I spent most of my time trying to swat the flies away. Being riddled with boils from the waist down was not my idea of the way I wanted to look. After my body got used to the water and the boils started popping and dried out, finally the flies stopped chasing me. And my mom told me to go to the interior and see my aunt. And I did just that. All the town people came to see me. And my aunt looked even older than I remember. But she was strong. My favorite cousin Alice took me to see my aunt.

I had so much fun with Sister Alice. She had a calm spirit, and since I was a kid, I just took onto her and loved her with all my heart. I remember when I was younger I used to cry when she was leaving for school in the morning. She was my sweetheart, besides my dad. The whole while I was in the interior, I slept in Sister Alice's bed, and not once did I sense evil out of her. She was a pure soul. At the time, I didn't understand why I liked her more than my birth mother. After being there awhile, it was time to go home, back to Guiglo, to Mom. Sister Alice took me back, and she noticed the tears in my eyes right before she was going to leave. It made her stay with me two extra weeks. I was happy. I felt free around her. That was more than I could say for a lot of people.

CHAPTER TWO

MY TIME IN THE IVORY COAST

After I came back from the interior that's when I started hearing some of the horrible stories. My sister Pasadena told me how Hamilton's leg had just healed. I remember seeing the pictures of his leg in America before coming to Africa. You could see his bones; there was no flesh on them. I remember Sister crying when she received the photos. "Is that why he has a limb in his walk?"

"Yes," she said. She told me how she was the one that healed my brother's leg when the doctor's gave up on him. She said her gift of sight was making people in the neighborhood concerned. As the days went by, she started telling me the different dreams she was having through the night. What I noticed was every time she had a dream, whatever she dreamed about would happen later that day.

She was dreaming of the witches in the area that were killing others in the spirit realms. She started to expose them. Every time a witch killed someone in her dreams, that person would die the next day from an unknown cause. She could even predict the day the person would die. So the witches threatened our mother to put her daughter under control before they kill her. What I know about witches and wizards is that they do not like to be exposed; it weakens their powers and can even cause death for some of them. So a witch or wizard will never admit what they are. That is like repentance to them. And that is very rare for a witch or wizard to repent. I was afraid for my sister's life. We were so very close. I started disliking all the people she told me were witches. She told me about this witch doctor, and we went out to meet him. She told me we had to hide from our mother because she was also a witch. At this time, I had not realized that Mom had wiped me of all my memories of these things.

Jasmine always used to ask me when I was still in America, "How come you can't remember anything from your childhood?" I was in some sort of a zombie trance and had not figured it out yet. When we met the witch doctor, he gave her a protection ring for her to keep on her at all times. As long as she had the ring on her, they would not be able to harm her. He looked at me and asked me, "Do you know why you are here?"

I said, "Because my sister Anastasia wanted me to come here."

He said, "Your mother sent for you an African sign so when you get here she could sacrifice you to the underworld. I looked at him in a funny way, but I did not dismiss what he said. Sometimes in life even if you don't believe what you have heard or seen, it does not mean that it's not real or true. You just got to give yourself time to process it. With time comes new information, and that can change everything. What he said made a lot of sense later on in life. My spirit was too strong for her mom and Anastasia. I was being watched over by God, and I was not even aware of it. I found out later in life, whenever you sleep with someone, they take a part of you with them spiritually. That is why it is good to only have one partner. Anyways, while Pasadena was bathing one day she took the ring off and put it next to the outside bathroom. The bathrooms were just a little room made of planks and rocks on the bottom for the water to drain out as you bathe from the bucket. When she came out the bathroom, the ring was gone. She asked who took it, and no one knew. She told me, "I bet you anything Mom took it." A few days later, our mother brought the ring and told Pasei that she found the ring. She told her to put it on, and Pasei said no. We took the ring back to the witch doctor who told us that our mother tampered with it.

He told my sister that her life was in grave danger. She and I went to this lady who was a prophet. The lady immediately took her in. She kept my sister in a room that no one was allowed to enter. Every morning, I went there to check on her. The prophet would show me footprints of a gigantic beast in the sand, and she would be sweeping the yard and praying with anger at the same time. I was shocked the first time I had seen these prints. They looked like dinosaurs prints. There isn't any known animal that size walking the earth. "What made those prints?" I asked.

"These prints are from your mother's dragon. They are here every morning when I wake up. Your mother's dragon comes here at night looking for your sister."

"How did she know where to find her?"

"The dragon followed you." Right away, I looked around me as if I was going to see it. She said, "You need spiritual eyes to see it, my dear."

"Oh if only I knew at the time that the one that is in me is greater than the one in the world. I wish I knew about the lost blood of God's mighty son Jesus Christ." This is not a physical attack that you take a gun and start shooting someone. People like my mother knew what would happen before it even did. The only way to stop people like her is through fasting and prayers. We did not know this at the time. Mom went to the prophet's house one day and told her that she would report her to the authorities for holding her daughter hostage. The prophet got scared and brought my sister out the room releasing her back to our mother. Mom haunted my sister down like a hound dog. She threatened everybody that tried to help us. My sister and I did not know what else to do. Our lives were in the hands of God, and we did not even know how powerful God was or how to tap into that power. With God, everything is prayers and fast.

Mom said she was going to help Pasei, but we knew that was lie. What else could we do? Everyone was afraid of her. And they wouldn't help us. She said she was taking her somewhere where she could get help. Around 4:00 a.m., Mom woke my sister up for them to go somewhere far where the person that could help her lived. I wanted to go to make sure, but Mom said no because the place was too far. They were gone all day. They came back at night. Mom said they washed my sister's eyes so she will not see a thing in the realms of the spirit anymore. The witches won't complain about her anymore. I asked Pasei what happened; she couldn't really talk. She could not remember a thing. She seemed zombiefied.

Even now, all these years later as I am writing this, I still get goose bumps and feel a deep sense of hurt for my sister. I wish I could have protected my sister from our mother. If Mom was not a witch, we wouldn't have to go through all of this pain and suffering. Our mother is a well-known witch in Africa. She was the child of the devil himself like I said earlier. She was nothing like an ordinary woman. She was a bully who knew she had special supernatural powers and was not afraid on using them on whoever stood in her way.

Pasadena could not have any more dreams. It was like she had amnesia. She completely changed. I felt really horrible about what happened, but like I said, there was not anything I could do. As the weeks went by, she started to come around. I was happy. She told me that she would be okay. We used to sneak to visit our older sister Cellia. Cellia was my stepmom's daughter. My stepmom was back in the States in New York at the time. Whenever we went to see Cellia, we never took our little sister Brittany with us because we thought she was going to tell Mom. Brittany was very young, and so Mom took her with her everywhere she went. One day, I visited Cellia, and Mom found out and slapped me straight across the face. It was shocking being that she did not put hands on me ever. She told me that Cellia and her family were evil and that Cellia's aunt was a witch. I didn't believe her for some reason. Every time I went around Cellia and her family, they were really nice to me. So I hid myself better and still visited Cellia. I have also been very stubborn. I believe in seeing the proof with my own two eyes, which is not always a good thing, but that's who I am. I did not sense any evil out of them.

One night, Mom was in the neighbor's yard visiting, and I wanted to bathe, so I put my own water in the pot and put it on the hot coal pot. I felt it with my fingertips to make sure it was not too hot. It was a big pot. I was not used to picking up anything like that. Pasei and Mom always prepared my bathwater. But this night, Pasei told me she was tired. I knew she was, but I couldn't do it myself. And I begged her, and she said no. So I proceeded in doing it myself. I have always hated on depending on anyone to do anything for me, so this was fine with me. I was determined to do it myself. I felt the water one last time with my fingers, and it was just right. Then Pasei came over to me and started to help me. I was happy, so I flanked the water that was dripping from my fingers on her, and then she started to scream loud and louder, and she dropped to the ground and started to roll all over the place. At first, I thought she was just joking. But she kept holding her chest. I got scared. I got on the ground and took a look at her chest. Her chest was badly burned. All the skin came off. The landlord came running over to see what was happening. I kept screaming for Mom to come from where ever she was. She came and started asking me what had happened. I didn't know what to say.

I told them that I flicked water on her with my fingers. So I started to look at my hands to see if they were burned too, not even a blister was on them. But the water came from my fingertips. So if anything, I should have gotten burned first. Nothing happened to me. The landlord went back into his house and brought back something that looked like fur and started to stick it all on Pasei's chest that night. This was the most hurtful thing ever would never hurt my baby sister; I loved her so much, and she was my heart. The landlord gave her something else to calm her down. The strange thing was that our mom didn't look surprised at all. She didn't do anything to help with Pasei. As time went by, Pasei recovered just fine. But she still has the scars up to this date. It was around that time Mom told me that a lot of men had been asking her if they could sleep with me. She said, "Your sister told me you were having sex with her husband. This is why she sent you here to me."

I said, "Mom, that's a lie."

She then told me, "You are a big girl now. It is time you started having sex." So I said no.

She said, "Your big sister is not here to support us. Do this for us so we can have food to eat." I started crying. She got on her knees. "Please, I am begging you to do this for us." I couldn't believe my ears. My mom was asking me to prostitute myself. She started crying. "I would never ask you to do this if we were in Liberia and everything was okay. Your father is not here to help me. I am too old to do what I am asking myself. Your sisters and I will not survive if you don't help us." I was feeling really bad. I didn't know what to think. I didn't know the town, so I could not run away. I couldn't even speak French. I had only been here six weeks. I don't know where the hell Hamilton is. What am I going to do? She had already made arrangements. I loved my mother, but I am starting to think otherwise. The next day, this old man came to the house to see her. My stomach started to turn. I knew this was one of the men she was talking about, although I had never seen him before. After they talked, he left; she came to me and said, "That is one of the men. He would be back tonight." I started to cry. I had never felt so helpless in my life.

I didn't know what to do. I couldn't run away to anyone because they will tell me to leave like they did Pasei. Like I said, "Everyone was afraid of her." She could do anything and get away with it. Later that night, she made me water, bathed me, and started to what she called preparation on me. I got dressed. She walked behind me every step of the way. Who showed up? It was the old man. And I was planning to tell him not to touch me when we got wherever we were going. To my surprise, my mom told my oldest cousin to go with me and make sure that I do what I was supposed to do. I couldn't stop sniffing. I tried not to cry, but I couldn't help it. She said we could leave. On our way to the man's house, I told my cousin that we should dish him and runaway since she knew the area. She said, "Hell no, you must be trying to get me killed?" And she refused to talk to me the rest of the way. She was there to ensure that I did the job. I knew I was about to pay for a sin I have not committed. When we got there, he said to follow him to the bedroom. My cousin grabbed my hand and pulled me in the room. She and the guy were talking, but I couldn't understand what they were talking about. They spoke French. She closed the door behind her and stood by it.

He started to take his clothes off. I was looking at her and pleading with my eyes. She didn't care. She asked me if I was going to take my clothes off. I said no. So she walked over to me and started taking my clothes off herself forcefully. She and I started fighting, but I was no match for her. The old man was already naked, and he was lying on the bed. She told me, "You better get on that bed right now!" She was not nice to me at all since I met her. She was always mad. So I sat on the bed. Then she pushed me to lie down and held me down by my thigh while the man held me down by the other thigh and did what he wanted to. I gave up and stopped fighting because it was no use. She lay down next to me to make sure I didn't get up. He climbed on top of me; he was heavy. He was looking in my face, smiling. I did not smile back. He could clearly see that I didn't want to have sex with him. I was holding my legs as tight as I could. He and my cousin were finally able to pry them open again. She held my leg on the bed while he went in and out of me holding the other leg down just to make sure I stay in that position. He ejaculated in me. "Yuck," I said to myself. He got off me and put his clothes back on. I went to the bathroom and started crying.

Anastasia started to look better right about now more than Mom. I wanted to be anywhere once again but here. I cleaned myself and put my clothes on. He gave her money, and we went on home. I refused to talk to her the entire time we were walking.

She told me, "If you are going to be doing this, you need a condom. There are a lot of diseases out here." I wanted to tell her to shut her stinking mouth. But she was older, bigger, and stronger than I was. I didn't want to her beating me up. When we got home, Mom came to my cousin and asked her about the money.

She gave it to her, and I heard her say, "Two dollars. That's it?" Then Mom asked me, "Is that all?" I looked at her and walked right past her without saying a word. I was very disturbed by what just happened. She turned to me and said, "Next time, I would find someone who pays better." I couldn't even talk to anyone about this. A few days later, she had found this other guy that paid her half, and when I would have sex with him, he would pay her the other half. Whatever half was, I did not care; it couldn't ever have been enough. He came to the house on a bicycle; on the back of it were eggs in a basket. He had a lot of missing teeth in his mouth, and the remaining ones were all dark brown. You could smell his breath from a mile away. This guy clearly did not know what a toothbrush was. *Where is she finding these people?* I thought. He looked really dirty and greasy.

"She said you have to go with him." I heard the voice calming me down, telling me not to worry. I did not know help was on the way.

I had to walk behind him, and everyone that saw us knew the only way we would be together was if we were going to have sex. So imagine what people were thinking of me. They were looking at me and probably thinking of me as a whore. Saying, "Isn't that the girl from America? Why is it everywhere we see her she is with a different guy?" I would see the same people come to visit my mom. I used to feel so bad, so embarrassed. Here it is these rumors already circulating about how I slept with my older sister's husband, and that's the reason I got sent back here. I was in a horrible situation. Every day she would find someone else. Then they started repeating themselves. The same guy would come back several times a week. I never saw any of the money they were giving her nor did she buy me anything. Once again, I found myself in another horrible situation. She seemed a little happier now.

I told her, "You know that I am not going to do this forever, right?" She got on her knees and started to cry once again, so I left her on her knees and walked away from her. I realized at this point she was using my love for her against me, and I had to put my big girl panties on and realized that I did not have a mother. Something in me died that moment, and I learned how to build a wall around my heart. That was the day ice started to grow on my heart and the flames started to go out slowly but surely. Thinking what to do and how to get out of this situation, I started to take little walks here and there. I needed to know my way around. I was plotting to escape from this whore house. I felt like since my sister were not as physically developed as I was, they would be safe for now without me. I knew I had to get out some way somehow.

One day, I took a walk on the road, and I met this guy. He told me his name was Mamudu. He seemed friendly. He spoke English fair enough. He took me out to eat. Then he took me to his place and did not try any nonsense, so I thought he was a nice guy, which at the end of the day he really was. We spent the whole day together, and he put me on his motorcycle and took me home. When we got in the yard, my little sisters ran to us. They were happy to see me again. Then they started to ask him for his name. He told them. He reached in his pocket and gave them money. They ran off to buy what they wanted. My mom was not too happy to see him there. She asked him questions, and then they talked. He gave her money. He said he had to go. So we said our good-byes, nothing sexually. She asked me after Mamudu had left if I had sex with him. I told her no.

"You should not have sex with any of these young boys because you are too beautiful to be with just one man. He will never have enough money to support you, and he will not allow you to work."

I said, "You mean prostitute for you?" I had no motherly feelings for her because of the life she wanted me to live. My feelings were numb. I went back up the road that same evening just to get away from her. I could not stand her. On the road, I met this guy sitting in the restaurant calling my attention. I stopped and looked, and he was telling me to come to him. So to let him know that is not how you talk to a girl, I walked away. And he did just what I expected him to do. He ran after me and stopped me and asked me if I could please sit and have tea with him. He told me his name was Lago Bi Tra Laurent, but everyone called him Laurent. He was about six feet five inches, and he was twenty-four years old. He asked me what I wanted to eat. I told him anything he thought was good for me. He said, "You are that girl from America? Everyone is talking about you. What is your name?" I said Evelyn. He repeated it after me, but it sounded different with the French accent. He went in the restaurant and made me something to eat. I was impressed with his cooking. He told me his family owned the restaurant. Then he took me to see where he lived. I told him that I had to go home.

I had to work. He said, "What do you do?" I just told him out front what my mother was making me do. At first, he thought I was making it up until I told him I was not. I told him that tonight I have to go sleep with this guy. Mom wanted these lappas (fabric African women wore) that he promised her in exchange for sex with me. So Laurent went to see her where I lived, and then he waited on the road while I was getting dressed. When I came out, I showed him the house that I was going to be in. So he hid himself in the bushes so the guy would not see him. I went into the guy's house, and he had sex with me. I came out with lappas in my hands. Laurent made himself visible so the guy could see him. We left and went back to my mom's house. Then he hid himself again and watched me give her the lappas. And I left. She didn't care where I was going as long as I was back when she had an appointment for me. This was a sick business she wanted us to stay in. This is Laurent's first day meeting me even though he had seen me walk by on the streets before. I can't believe he actually is listening to me and letting me prove all these things to him. After all he had seen, he asked me, "What are you going to do for this stop. Do you have a family member that you could stay with?"

I said, "No one would take me in. They are all afraid of Mom."

He said, "Then you can stay with me."

"She will be mad at you," I told him.

He said, "Is she doing all of this because of the money?"

"Yes," I told him.

He said, "Well, then I will give her money every day." I told him about my sick sister Cellia and how she was dying. I told him that my mother touched her when she was not supposed to and how my sister was already warned not to come into the yard where Mom lived. They told her about Mom's dragon that was going to attack and kill her. She had told me about the dream, but we just laughed about it. Now it's my fault that my sister is dying. Cellia lost a lot of weight, and her eyes where sunken, and her mouth was shut by what seemed to look like spider webs. She looked like a skeleton. She looked like there was no chance of survival, but where there is a will, there is always a hope. She could breathe even though she was in a comma. If I had not called her into the yard that night, Mom was not going to touch her and seek her serpent after her. I felt so rotten inside about all of this. Laurent told me that my sister was going to be okay. Then he showed me a shortcut to Cellia's house. He was so nice to me. I started spending my nights to his place. It to me was better than sleeping with random guys every night like Mom wanted.

Laurent gave me money every morning for my mother, so she won't think that he couldn't support us. However, that was not enough according to her. She wanted money from several sources. I started to think. *What kind of a woman is she? She is very greedy and cold-blooded.* If it was not because of my two younger sisters,

I was going to disappear from this money hungry woman, what the hell! Anyways, life goes on. Her excuse was the Ivory Coast was not Liberia. She said she was a refugee, and she needed to survive. She was good at looking a person in the eyes while lying to them all under one breath of air. In my culture, a youngster is not allowed to look into the eyes of an elder when they were talking. It is considered an insult. Since I was caught between the American culture and my native culture, it was hard to remember at times. So I did look her in the eyes at times while she lied to me.

One night, Laurent came home as I was getting ready to go take a bath in the outside bathroom. He noticed an owl in the tree right near the bathroom looking toward me. He asked me, "How long have this owl been here?"

I told him, "Oh, that owl is here every night when it's time for me to take bath.

"What a sweet owl," I told him.

He said, "Evelyn, get back in the house." And his tune of voice was very firm. I just went back in the house asking no questions. A few minutes later, he came to get me, and the owl was gone.

I said, "Where is my friend, the owl?"

He said, "Well, you will you never see that owl again."

"That was not an owl," he said. I was confused, and he distracted me from asking questions. All my clothes were at Laurent's house at this point. He washed them by hand when they got dirty because in the interior were no washers and dryers. Everything was done by hand. I never ate at Mom's house; Laurent made sure I had enough food at his house. Mom started to get really mad at him.

One day, she came over to Laurent's house; she had made me have an abortion, demanding I come home with her. I told her my home was with Laurent and that she needed to leave. She left. "Are you kidding me?" I asked myself. This bimbo is crazy, is she serious? After getting pregnant for the very first time with twins and having an abortion because she lied to me, she couldn't be trusted. Why would I want to live with her? When I got pregnant by Laurent, Mom told me that immigration was not going to allow me to come to America pregnant. I told her, "Well then, let me stay here with Laurent in the Ivory Coast."

She said, "No, if I stayed, then immigration was going to deny the rest of the family from going to America. Then she said, "Think of your two younger sisters, Brittany and Pasadena." She made me feel real guilty with that one. I have always been a sucker for family, and that was one thing that would almost get me killed. That was the only reason I agreed to have the abortion. I couldn't deny my sisters the privilege of living in America. That would have been really selfish of me. Mamie, the girl who would perform the abortion, came to Laurent's house with some weird-looking stick in her hand. She inserted it into my vagina, all the way up to my uterus. This stick was oozing out some sort of serum that burned through the flesh. It only took two hours for the babies to drop right out of my uterus and onto the ground. That's when I knew I was pregnant with twins. Luckily, Pasei came to see me, and it happened right in front of her. She picked up the babies and threw them away. Then she helped me get cleaned up. That was one of the most painful things to go through. The serum from the stick burned a hole into my uterus. And while that was healing, the pain was horrible. Life goes on. What I can say.

A few days later when I came from seeing my sister Cellia, I met a sad Laurent at home and not at work. "What happened?" I asked him.

He said, "Go and look in the house." I looked, and I noticed all my things were gone.

"Where is my stuff?" I asked him.

He said, "Your mother came and took your stuff. He asked me if we were going to break up. I told him nope, but I would be back shortly."

He told me, "Your Mom said she will not give your stuff back."

"We'll see about that," I told him as I walked away. When I got to my mother's house, there she was, with an uncle of mine. I told them to get another elder right now because I had something to say. They quickly got another elder. I told my mom in front of them all. "I don't want to know why you took my clothes, but I want you to return them immediately." My uncle started to talk, and I told him to shut up; this had nothing to do with him. At the time when I was angry, being polite was the last things on my mind. Mom's excuse for taking my clothes was that my father was coming to Africa for a visit. She said she did not want him to see that I was living with my boyfriend at the age of fifteen. I told her I did not care about all that, and Daddy needed to know the truth as to where I lived.

My uncle said, "Well, your clothes are hidden right now."

I told him, "I don't care where you have hidden them. I just want you here to bear witness to what I have to tell her." I told her by the time I got home tonight, my clothes better be back and arranged the way she found them. If this is not done before I get home, I will burn her whole house and everything in it down ground. I told her, "If you do not believe me, keep my clothes." I left and went to visit Cellia. By the time I got back to Laurent's house, my clothes were back and arranged like I had left them. She put everything back by herself, Laurent told me. The next day, I went to see Cellia. Not a day went by that I did not see her. *My poor sister how can I help her?* Our aunty Esther told me not to let anyone know where Cellia was because my mom was looking for her to finish her off. "I promise I won't, Aunty." They said my mother's dragon had swallowed Cellia, and it was left just her head for it to swallow her whole in African signs (witchcraft), and she would have died in reality.

My sister took a turn for the worse. Aunty asked me not to come because I was being followed by the shadow demons. I cried, and she assured me that Cellia was going to be okay. After a while, Cellia came out of the coma. But my mother did find Cellia; luckily for Cellia, she had the dream the night before that my mother would show up in the morning to finish her off. Just as she dreamed, it happened the next day. So Aunty Elizabeth, my stepmom's younger sister, yelled and insulted Mom really bad. She was up to no good. People like Mom you can't put anything past them. She went there to finish what she started, and if Aunty had left her see my sister, Cellia was going to die. Evil witches have no mercy. When I went to give her the food money, that morning, she told me Aunty cursed her out when she only went to say hi to Cellia. I was angry at Mom. "Why the hell are you going there? Have you not done enough damage to the poor girl?"

I told her, "If I hear that you went there again, I will kill you myself!"

She knew I did not make empty threats unfortunately for her. Back at Laurent's house, strange things started happening. He was always at work but would check on me several times a day. One day, I was taking afternoon nap since I couldn't visit Cellia anymore. I heard Laurent open the door. Then he said, while he was still standing at the door, "Evelyn, don't move, don't look around you, just keep your eyes on me." She was speaking in a very calm voice. Guess what? Yours truly decided with her dumb self to look around. Everything under this sun that was a creepy crawler was in there with me as I was sleeping. Maggots, millipedes, snakes, worms, centipedes, caterpillars were all over the walls, the floor, and the bed. You could not see an inch of the wall or floor. They had put me in a circle on the bed. The only spot they were not was the spot I was lying in. He said, "Stay right where you are, and don't move." That I did. As he was walking toward me, they started clearing his path. What in the world is happening to me? This is worse than *A Nightmare on Elm Street*. He picked me up and took me out of the house. He told me to wait outside. *Gladly*, I thought. He went back in and closed the door behind him. He was in there for about five minutes, and he came out. He told me to go back in and not to be afraid. I did, to my surprise, there wasn't anything there. As if it did not happen, I looked all under the bed, not one creepy crawler was left. Wow! Whatever he did, it worked, and that was when I knew that he too knew how African signs worked and what to do in the case of an attack.

A few days later, Laurent opened the room door, rushed toward me, and started making passionate love to me. Wow! He had a lot of energy; he must have been missing me. As Laurent was on top of me, the room door opened, and it was Laurent. The Laurent on top of me flew out the door screeching in a loud pitch noise. I started screaming. "Who was that if it was not you?"

"Your mother is mad at you, Evelyn," he said. "She is a more powerful witch than I thought." He really tried to calm me down. She changed herself to look just like Laurent. I did not know that she was a shape-changing demonic witch at this time. "Hell! I didn't know what I was up against." He looked at me and told me he had to travel far. There is an old man in my village that can help you. I started to cry because this meant that I had to stay with Mom. I had nowhere else to go. He told me that I would be ok. If my memory was not erased by my mother when I was a child because of my gift of sight, I would have remembered who Jesus Christ was and the power of the precious blood that had been hidden from us. This crap would not have been happening to me. I reluctantly went to Mom's house.

While I was asleep one night, I felt something ice-cold on the bed. I looked, but there was nothing there. She told me to go back to sleep. Oh, and guess what? I had to sleep on the same bed as her. The dark aura that surrounded her made me feel like I could not breathe. And she knew it. In the morning, I found several centipedes in my blanket dead. A few more days of this, I thought later that evening as I was lying in the hot room, and I will be out of here. She asked me where Laurent was. I told her he had to go to the cities.

I had a vision, and Laurent came to the room window to tell me he was back. Not even an hour later, he came to the room window and whispered my name. I heard him and ran out, yelling, "He's back!" It was finally time to get away from this woman. I used to wonder why did God looked at all the nice women on earth and decided to make my mother a mega witch. What is the meaning of that? Anyways, certain things you have to let go off. This was one of those things. I said 'bye, and we went home. He knew I would be in the room. I had no friends to visit; my sisters were my friends, and Pasadena was already home. He took me to the house where this old man was waiting. I said hi. He looked at me and smiled without saying a word. He had only one eye and several missing teeth. I did not know what to think of him. The old man pulled a long root out of his bag and tied it to the bed. After the old man left, then Laurent told me that none of those weird things would happen to me again. He was very protective of me. I didn't know that God always sends one person to protect me from my mother at all times.

It was September of 1993, and Laurent was so very nice to me, but it was time to go back to America. I did not want to go. I remembered how it was living with my sister in Minnesota. I was not happy there. To me, there wasn't anything to look forward to. Anastasia and my mother were both going to be with me in the same house. This was going to be bad, I though. The only positive thing was my father was going to be there too. I promised Laurent that I was not going to forget him. I had planned on marrying him when I became an adult. Unfortunately for me, I had forgotten about Anastasia's little snitch, Jasmine, that told her everything. Oh man, there go my plans again. I finally arrived in the states. Laurent wrote me. I received several letters from him, and then they just stopped. They intercepted all the letters Laurent wrote me, and I did not find out about it until years later.

All I thought was he moved on with his life and forgot about me. I did not have an address for him after he moved away to Guinea. How mean is that? I had lost touch with him forever because of those two. And he was a true friend to me. Anyways, life goes on, right? I can't even imagine what was going through their minds when they were doing that to me.

CHAPTER THREE

GETTING PREGNANT
WITH THE TWINS

It was September of 1993, and we had just arrived in America. Jasmine seemed happy to see me, but I knew it was not for long. I was sad leaving Laurent back in the Ivory Coast. I just had an abortion for him and was still bleeding. I told Anastasia that I was living with my boyfriend in the Ivory Coast and not Mom. I just had an abortion right before we left Sister. She didn't seem to care. It was clear that she still did not like me. She was still holding a grudge for what her stupid husband did to me. Anyways, I ignored her. I asked if she could please take me to the doctor so I would get checked; the abortion was not done in the hospital. I might need birth control too. I am not a virgin anymore. I told her how Mom prostituted me and how I ran away from home to live with Laurent. She looked at me like whatever. I have always felt alone in this world because of my siblings not caring about me. While we were living in Maple Grove, I got back in school and skipped the eighth grade. I started again in the ninth. I did great until the end of the school year. A classmate of mine told the principal I had brought a gun to school. Never have I physically seen a gun but on television. She thought she was a bully. And she was trying to get me kicked out of school. Little did she know she was about to get it real good from me.

The next day was the last day of school, so I beat her up really bad, and she had to get thirteen stitches. She lied on me, and I could have gotten expelled. The cops came looking for me that evening. They told Anastasia what happened. After they left, she beat the crap out of me. My mom sat there and did nothing. She hit me in the face with her stilettoes and left a hole under my eye. I never thought it was ever going to close up. Thank God it did. I was not allowed to get out of the house until it healed. My dad felt so bad, but he couldn't do anything. Hector, my brother's friend from Zwedru and the Ivory Coast started coming over when he heard I was in America. He used to like me in the Ivory Coast. He was shocked to see a hole right under my eye. He said, "She could have burst your eye!" He used to come over to my brother all the time because they were friends. Then he showed up to my job at McDonald's one day and took me out. Hector was about 15 or more years old than me. But he did not look his age and he was very handsome all the girls wanted to be with him. We had sex twice on two occasions and I got pregnant. That birth control could have come in handy right about now. I hid the fact that I was pregnant because I knew what would happen. I needed one hundred dollars to add to the four hundred I had for the abortion. I told my cousin that I was pregnant, and she told my mom and dad.

Anastasia came over the apartment we were living, and she and Mom started beating me until they were exhausted and ran out of breathe. I turned my back toward them so they won't hit me in the stomach. Anastasia looked me in the eye later and told me she should have never divorced her husband because of me. I thought to myself, *why would she want to be married to a child molester. If not me, it would be another child.* I just smiled at her, and that made her even angrier. The voice always told me not to listen to her; she was trying to break my spirit. About a month later, she told me that we had to have a meeting with Hector's parents, not knowing she had a hidden agenda. We went for the meeting, and they talked. When it was time to leave, I got up. Anastasia said to me. "Where do you think you're going? This is your home now."

I asked, "What about my clothes?"

"I will drop them off," she said. I went in the bathroom and started to cry. I didn't know these people and had never been at this house before. I had to suck it up.

"Can you ask why it seems like I am not that nice child that you remember anymore, Anastasia?" Hector did not live at this house. I found out that he had a serious girlfriend. I told him to take me to his apartment. There was no electricity or food in there. It did not matter. I could not stay in his parents' house where a hundred people visited a day. His parents were well known in the Liberian community. They were nice people; I just was not comfortable there. As a loner, being around all those people was not comfortable for me. Hector's girlfriend found out about me. She came to his apartment and got me. She said I should live in the house with them, which I did for a little while until I found out she was only being nice to me for a reason. She had planned that her best friend would adopt my twins. I aborted my first set of twins, because I felt like I had no choice in the Ivory Coast. Why would I carry these ones and birth them just to give them to someone else? That doesn't make any sense! I said no, the best friend got mad and told me she was going to kick me in the stomach so the babies could die. I told her if that happens, she should dig a hole and bury herself because she was also going to die. I was a no-nonsense gal. God had to train me himself. Now I am much calmer and a better person, no doubt because of all my life-changing experiences.

After some months, Jasmine called my parents and told them that I needed to come home because of my living condition not being suitable for me. They took me back. I could tell Daddy was happy to have me home. I was taking a shower one day when my water broke. I asked my mother what I should do now. She said it was no big deal and that I should go to bed. I heard the voice tell me to call my doctor. So I did. My doctor told me to get to the hospital right away. Jasmine took me to the hospital right away. She was really nice to me when she found out I was pregnant. She was there the whole time. My twins came in this world with lots of love from their mommy. Hector did not support me during my pregnancy at all. As a matter of fact, he disowned the pregnancy. His girlfriend told him that I was not lying on him and he was only saying it from shame. She was the one that brought him to the hospital to see the kids; he didn't want to come. The twins had to stay in the hospital for a month because they were premature. While they were in the hospital, this was when my younger sister Pasadena got sick. She lost forty pounds in a month. She could not stand, and she would faint. I had to always stand behind her so she would fall in my hands and not the floor.

Sixteen specialists worked on her, and they could not figure out why she was dying. My dad and I practically lived in the hospital changing shifts. My kids came home. While she was sick, my mother said it was because she had sex and was deflowered. My mother stuck her finger up into my sister's vagina to see if she was a virgin or not. I was downstairs, and this took place upstairs. I couldn't climb the stairs because I was in a lot of pain from the C-section. I believe this was why Mom took Pasei upstairs. I did not hear anything. When they came downstairs, I asked Pasei what happened upstairs between Mom and her. She said Mom stuck her fingers in her vagina to see whether or not she was a virgin. Before I could respond, yours truly was already entering through the front door. Anastasia!

This in my opinion is when Mom put another demon into my sister besides the incident in the Ivory Coast when she took her to get her faced washed and came back a zombie. Mom told Anastasia what she suspected about Pasei. "Your sister had sex," she said, so Anastasia grabbed my sick sister and started to choke her in the laundry room, which was right next to the living room where I was sitting. I just had a C-section a few days ago. I still had the stitches in me. While Anastasia was in the Laundry room with Pasadena, I could not hear anything. So I got off the chair in pain and walked toward the laundry room, and she was choking the life out of Pasei. I could barely move, but I did my best because I had to. I tried to take her hands off, but she had a tight grip around Pasei's neck.

So what I did was choke Anastasia as she was choking Pasadena. She was going to choke her until she passed out and died, and they were going to blame it on the illness. How wicked is this woman; she is her mother's daughter, and this apple surely did not fall off the tree at all. She let go of Pasei's neck and got mad at me. At that moment I told my mother to stop her stupidity and to put her dog on the leash before I kill the both of them. My mom looked at Anastasia who decided to leave without saying a word. I did not care what the heck she thought of me. Mom, I believe, did something to all her children at birth that made them do evil things without thinking twice, and whoever did not fight hard enough to get rid of that demon still have it. I believe it had to do with their umbilical cords. She never had access to mine because she fainted and the nurses took me. They always come to her aid, do whatever she asked of them blindly as if they are all in a trance and asleep spiritually. Just like I was before, I woke up out of it. It took the act of God getting me to this point of being remorseful. But as for the rest of my siblings, I am not so sure; they knew more about Mom than I did, yet even if they knew Mom was a witch, they were still going around her and treating her nice.

After our duo, Anastasia told my parents that she will only visit them when I was not home. How sad; she acted as if I was her worse enemy or something. My sister just had her head filled with all these negative things about me, and I was not going to stand by and watch her treat Pasei and Brittany the way she treated me. Not in my presence. She was stuck on herself and needed someone who could stand up to her. I was that someone and she hated me for not doing things the way she wanted them done. What I said about that was too bad. I only have one life to live, and if I spend it doing what other people wanted instead of what I believed in, I will die and leave this world with too many regrets. I can't have that. I want and will take responsibility for my own actions. When I stand in front of God on judgment day I don't want to say so so and so made me do it my LORD. No way Jose!

When I got better, Anastasia and I got in a fight. She had it coming with her nasty attitude always walking around like she smelled something. This woman was old enough to be my mother by twenty plus years. But she had no self-respect because of her temper. She always let her anger get the best of her. As we were fighting, I accidently punched my mother in the face trying to punch Anastasia, oops. Mom fell down, landed on her butt, and started crying. I told her, "See what you made me do?" She got mad and left. I told Mom, "Please don't cry. You know I did not mean to hurt you." Before I did anything vicious to anyone, I always warned them by telling them exactly what I was going to do, giving them enough time to clean up their act before I strike. She knew I was no liar, so she stretched out her hand for me to help her get up. I helped her up, and she begged me to please forgive my sister. I told her that I had no problem with her as long as she kept her hands to herself. I told my mom, "Your daughter is very close to having her throat sliced opened any day now." I could barely move because of the stitches, and this happened upstairs while I was downstairs.

Pasei was in and out of the hospital all the time. One day while Pasadena was home from the hospital, she and I decided to take an afternoon nap. My son Elijah slept in the middle of us while Cody was awake with his grandparents downstairs. They were both asleep, but I was awake. I had seen three shadows demons come in right through the door. One got on top of me and held me down, and it started fighting me. As we were fighting, the other two started pulling the breath out of my son and my sister. I was helpless and couldn't move. They did that for a while, and then they left. I was able to move, so I woke my sister up and told her what had happened. I had scratched marks all on my arms. She was scared. We opened my room door to get out. In front of the door was red and black thread wrapped up in a ball. I leaned over to touch it, and Pasadena slapped my hand and told me that was a sign of a dragon. "Mom," she said.

"Mom? I thought once you cross the ocean you lose all your powers?"

She said, "Me too." There were scratches all over me from fighting the demon. If I had known about the blood of Jesus that was kept such a secret from me, all this was not going to take place. I would have pleaded the blood of Jesus over us that day. What you don't know can surely hurt you.

One week later as I was taking my son Elijah upstairs, I heard the voice saying, "The child you are caring in your arms is going to die before the week is over."

I asked, "Why?"

"You will find out ten years from now." Ten years later was when that witch doctor told me who killed my son and how he died. My mother had my son Cody sleeps in the room with her since he was born but not Elijah. Every time she held Elijah, he would scream his lungs off. He hated her with a passion and won't let her change his diapers or feed him. He would refuse to eat if she was the one feeding him. And if he ate, he would vomit everything on her every time. So my dad had to feed him if I was not home. I now know why. The child could see right through her. I would come home from school, and his diaper would be soaking wet because he refused to let her touch him. I feel like I disappointed my son by leaving him in the hands of a witch that killed him in the end. I had to live with this guilt for years, but I did not know she was a witch. Remember she had erased my memories of the supernatural things I knew. I had to find a way of forgiving myself over the years. Because I knew if I did, I was going to self-destruct. I made a vow not to let her kill anyone else as long as I was breathing. I was going to find my mother's antidote and stop her once and for all. The voice always told me that if he had not allowed it, I would not see my mother for who she was. He said that was the reason he gave me two. And he would always allow me to see glimpse of Elijah in heaven.

I am so thankful that God had a way of soothing my heart in my times of deep trouble. My son was not sick when he died. I heard Cody crying in my parents' room, and his voice woke me up. On May 11, 1995, my son Elijah did not wake me up in the middle of the night like he always did, so I checked on him. We slept in the same bed. I felt him sleeping on my chest, which he always did, but this time, something was different. I called his name, and he did not make a sound. I felt him and he was as hard as a rock and his legs were very cold. I yelled to my sister Brittany who was sleeping next to me on the floor to put the lights on. By the time she did, I had him in my arms. When I looked at my son, he was clearly dead. His legs were blue. I dropped him on the bed, and my heart literally fell out of my chest.

I started screaming and asking what is the number to 911. My sister said it was 911, and I realized that. I dialed the number. My dad came running to me and went in the room to the child. My mom came out and met me in the hallway. She asked what happened. I told her Elijah was dead. She said, "Is that why you are crying? Don't you know twins cannot survive in my house? Would you rather your sister that you love so much die than a six-month-old baby that you don't even know? Or your father whom you love so dearly?" My dad was very sick also during that time. And she walked back to her room like nothing happened. She was simply telling me that the powers she had would not allowed both my boys to live because they were twins and I was her daughter. Witches believed that twins possessed natural powers, and she had to sacrifice one to capture his powers. I could tell my father was very annoyed, upset, and hurt all at the same time. From the expression on his face, he knew exactly what she meant, but he did not say anything.

EMT tried to revive my son, but they couldn't. This was around 3:00 a.m. I had just told him four hours early, "Tomorrow will be Mommy's birthday." My son died on my birthday, on my chest, while I was sleeping, and it was the first thing I have seen on my birthday. I have not celebrated my birthday since then. As the years went by, I realized that his other grandma called and requested to see only him and not his brother, and Elijah spent the day with her. He died that same week. My mother was the one that told me he should go. It did not click to me at that time that it was something the both of them had planned. I accused her openly of being part of my son's death. Why else would she only request the one and not the other when they were twins? That was the mistake she made that have me still suspecting her. But God in heaven said vengeance is his, and now that I know his word, I am not going to take anything in my own hands anymore. Deut. 32:35 Vengeance is Mine, and recompense; Their foot shall slip in due time; For the day of their calamity is at hand, And the things to come hasten upon them. I will be of good courage and wait on the Lord. Ps. 27:14 Jesus, where was the Holy Bible when I needed one? Anyways, God knows best! Ecclesiastes 3 To everything there is a season, A time for every purpose under the heaven.

After my son died, it cost five thousand dollars to cover the funeral expenses. The both grandmas had a meeting at the house, and my mother asked Hector's mother to pay half the price. She got mad and said she was not going to spend that amount of money for a bastard child. My son was at the morgue in a freezer, and this was what she had to say about him? I heard her saying this while I was upstairs in my room. *Okay, this is some of the reasons why people say I am disrespectful. Guess what I did to the bimbo?* I calmly went downstairs, walked past her, and opened the front door. I grabbed her by the hand and shoved her out the door. I dropped kicked her in the stomach so she could go farther from the house. She almost fell. Then I closed the door behind me and sat on the chair next to my father without saying a word neither did he. My mother tried to get up to open the door. I told her, if she touched the door, I would go in the kitchen, grab a knife, and butcher both of them since she loved her friend so much. She sat back down. Hector's mother told everyone what I did to her. And she kept calling out to my mother to let her back in. Mom knew better than to get off that couch. I sat next to my dad and watched TV as if nothing happened. My parents knew me very well and knew not to ever counteract my actions or all hell would break loose. I never did anything horrible unless it had to do with someone being unfair in a horrible way. Hector's mom was outside the door screaming and cursing until she got tired, got in her car, and left.

I could care less of what anyone thought of my actions then or even now. Who would sit there and not do anything when your child is still in the morgue and some idiot is there insulting the innocent baby? The bimbo had it coming. At the funeral, she was the only one wearing purple. I wanted to kick her out of there too, but my parents begged me not to. Anastasia came through as a big sister; I didn't know how she took care of all the expenses for my son to have a decent burial, but she did. I was very proud of her. After he was buried, my son kept showing up in my visions and dreams as a giant baby guarding me. He was urging me to move out and do it quickly. He told me that mom was planning on killing me next. He showed me how my mother killed him. In the realms of the spirit, she ate his eyes, his stomach, his brains, and all his vital organs. He said she was about to do the same to me. Within that time, my mother's dragon started appearing to me more and more, attacking me night and day. My father was a very quiet man, but one night after the dragon attacked me, I ran out of my room and into my sisters' room screaming. My parents came to find out what happened, and I explained. I knew I had to move away from my mother once again, except this time it was for a different reason. How was I going to do this? I had no job, money, or car. God was watching.

My mother said, "You need to go back to your room.

My father yelled at her and told her, "Leave her alone. Don't you think she's had enough?" Writing this book and exposing my mother as a witch was not easy for me on so many levels, but God wanted me to tell the whole world what he has done in my life and how people like her exits. He wants everyone to know that he is alive and real and so is his son Jesus Christ who will be coming soon. When, no man knows, not even the angels in heaven, says the Holy Bible. Mark 13:32

On June 11, exactly one month after Elijah's death, I met this guy name Jeff the following month at my buddy's graduation party. He introduced himself to my parents and we started dating. A few months later being depressed over losing my son I tried to commit suicide. Luckily he found me and seen all the empty pills packs next to me and rushed me to the ER. The hospital put me on a medical hold in a lock unit so I couldn't escape. That made me feel even worse because I would be there by myself until he came from work and came to visit me. I asked him not to tell anyone especially my parents because they were going to freak out. He pleaded to the doctors on my behalf until they released me. To make me feel better he bought me a car not brand new or anything but very decent. He thought me how to drive and I got my license. He bought me a descent used Honda prelude which I loved. Shortly afterwards I moved in with him. He gave my mom lots of things including huge sums of money. My parents loved him because he was very kind to them and respectful also. My father and Jeff loved talking about politics every time they met. I moved in with him, and he was just the sweetest person at first. But his sister was another story. She came one day in his room and attacked me on the bed biting my finger almost off because of something she accused me of saying to their dad. She never even gave me a chance to explain anything before leaping on me. I left and went home to my parents, and he came there to get me. When my parents asked me what I did to her, they were surprised to hear me say nothing. They looked at each other in shock. Then Jeff told me, "Next time she jumps on you to fight, fight her, and if you can beat her up, then do it." My parents again looked at each other in silence. I did not do anything to her at that time because I needed to talk to her brother about her behavior first. I will just say after that it was on and popping, and she never got froggish with me ever again. Sometimes it's best not to waken the lioness when she is asleep and just let her be.

I attended the nursing assistant program and the day I was supposed to finish May 11 was when Elijah died. So I went back to test out and I passed. They gave me my certificate and I was good to work. Not too long after I moved in with Jeff, I got approved for my affordable housing. It was a two-bedroom townhouse, and my rent was only $27 because I was not employed. Section 8 was the name of the affordable housing program, and they based your rent by your income. Jeff was much older than I, ten years plus. So after a while, we really did not get along. He stopped talking to me completing unless he wanted something. We really did not have bills to pay and since his name was not on my least there wasn't anything in his name. I used to have to take sleeping pills to fall asleep every night. He hated to be seen in public with me because he said I dressed too fancy and I was too flamboyant. Hush boy I got me one life to live why should I walk around with my head bow down? He used to pack up all his things and move out almost every other week. No one knew the details of our relationship because those were not the kind of things I discussed at all. I was very friendly and knew a lot of people but an extremely private person. I guess I had been through so much by the age of eighteen already that I was numb. And I was still mourning the death of my son.

People thought Jeff was the nicest person, but what they did not know was he was a selfish bastard behind closed doors. He did not want anyone in the house at all. He did not even like his own cousin coming over to eat. And I was the opposite. I was nice and very welcoming to everyone unless they were evil. I had three friends, and they were all related. Whenever they came over, he would be super nice to them until that door closed behind them. That's when he would tell me all these horrible things about them. I never told them, so they never knew. I have never seen my mom ever talk about my father in any negative way, and I surely did not see them argue like that.

Whenever people were around, Jeff and I would pretend everything was perfect, and we were very good at that. I started to get tired of his behavior. I was not free to be myself around him. He was very uptight and I was a live in the moment kind off girl. He was never home. I saw him for like two hours each day. I saw him in the morning for an hour, and then he said he was off to school then work. And then I would see him for an hour at night before bed, not knowing the sucker was lying to me for years about being a student. One day, I happened to call his job just to leave a message when the girl told me he would be right back, he ran an errand. I asked her what time does he start work, and she told me he was there on time every morning. He was so mad why I had to find out that information that he fired the girl. Then there was the issue of this chick that always called me to curse me out on the regular. She said she and Jeff were in a relationship and had been for a long time now. Almost as long as he and I were dating. According to her, they were dating before he met me. Every time I asked him, he would deny it. At that time, I was faithful until I spoke to my mom about it. She said all men cheated and that I should do the same just make sure that I did not get caught. When I spoke to Hector's wife, she told me the same thing. I always had a thing about confiding in elders. I felt closer to them than my peers. Sometimes peers don't keep each other's secrets because of the whole competitive attitude. I got to be better than you all the time type of stuff. It was very hard for me to learn anything knowledgeable from my peers, so I never bothered asking them about anything. They always had more to learn from me than I could from them. That's just how life was for me.

So anyways after gathering this information, I started to cheat on Jeff. I knew the girl was not lying about being his girlfriend because she knew things that she could not possibly have. So every time she called me to curse me out, he got an ass whooping. I was not having that. But when I cheated on him, stupid me I told my friend, and she left a detailed message on the phone saying everything I did, and he heard it of course. I made sure when I cheated, it was with someone better looking who had more money. *Hello.* That's what I'm talking about. We two can play that game, brother man. I did it bigger and better, and I was not nice anymore. Come on now! I never felt bad the way I treated him because like I said the man was an a—hole. I really should not have dated anyone because of the trauma I suffered over the years, but I never did stop to think anything through. Thinking things through for me at this time was not the right thing for me. When you sit to think things through then your conscious mind starts to play on you and you start thinking of cause and effect morals and all that. No thank you just doing me was all I wanted to do.

As embarrassing as my past may be, I have to tell the truth. This is a tell-all book about my life, the good and the bad. Like I said, when you don't know God, you can treat anyone the way you want because you don't even know better yourself. I had no morals at the time. I felt because I was getting money and gifts from these guys I was sleeping with, I was the bomb. After that whole phone message incident, that's when I remembered what Mom said about friends. I made sure that never happened again, that's for sure. I thought I had been a nice person. Whenever someone needed anything, they could count on me to give it to them no matter how valuable it was. There is no use for material things once you are dead and gone in my opinion. My mom always used to ask me, "Why don't you have a jealous bone in you? Why don't you keep your valuables for yourself? Don't you know you will be poor if you keep giving all you have away?" I didn't care. That was how I got my high. I was not smoking or drinking at this time. Even though I cheated on Jeff, it was with four guys, and that was it. But sometimes I slept with all five of them in the same day. How gross now when I think of it? These men had girlfriends; I don't remember ever sleeping with a married man. There are women out there that I cannot remember that don't like me, I am sure.

Jeff broke up with me because of pressure from his family. See, after the 1990 civil war in Liberia, there were two main tribes that really don't like each other, and one blames the next for all kinds of political reasons. The Krahn and the Gio and Mano people don't get along very well, and Jeff was Mano, and I was Krahn. It would have made a nice Romeo and Juliet story. I was only in the relationship because of what he could do for me toward the ends. He took good care of my parents financially. This relationship was doomed before it even started. I was used to having the best things in life from when I was a little girl living with my parents in Liberia. So that's all I knew now as an adult. I would spend several thousand dollars a week buying clothes and other things for myself and people I cared about. Yes, I guess I was a bad girl, good girl. I used to always feel like night and day were both dwelling within me, and it was a constant battle of good and evil. Being good came naturally, and it healed the heart, but being bad, when I took revenge into my own hands, was a temptation that I didn't know how to resist. I did not have any remorse for my actions at this point. I made people aware of what a pain in a horse's patoot I could be when provoked. I didn't know that the word of God said, "Don't take vengeance into your own hands." Heck, I still had not gotten the introduction from God yet. I must tell you that I now know better.

Anyways, my relationship with Jeff was very boring and awkward. People would ask me in his presence, "Why are you with him? He is not your type." So I bought a new wardrobe for him and thought it would make him want to be seen with me in public if he also dressed nicely. Yeah, I was wrong. Menni, my best friend at the time, and I spent all day preparing a romantic evening for Jeff. When he got home and saw all his new clothes on the bed (over thirty outfits) surrounded by roses, a warm bath waiting with rose petals, I really thought he was going to be excited. Okay, I was wrong. The first question he asked me was, "Did you prostitute yourself to get the money to buy all this?" He was not happy, at all. I had to drain the bathtub out. I was so turned off by him, and at that moment, I knew I was wasting my time being with him. That made me turn off any feelings I had for him completely. There are so many fish in the ocean. Why eat only one. Jeff's cousins confirmed the relationship between him and the girl; Jeff had been seeing her for many years. I knew he wasn't as perfect as he seemed. I could never understand why people always felt they had to live by society's standards and deprive themselves from true happiness. Jeff loved the girl very much, but because she was ugly, they said he did not want to claim her publically. That is stupid. So what the hell did he do when they were together in their intimate moments? Put a paper bag over her head or doggy style only? I'm just saying. He was a brownnoser and a pushover, all the things I despised. He would tell everyone all these negative things about me behind my back, which I thought was a cowardly behavior. It made me not have much respect for him.

So I broke up with him. After we broke up, he told his next girlfriend that the only reason he was with me was because my son Cody had epilepsy. This was a blinking lie, by the way. When I found out, I went to his house and punched him in the face; drop kicked him, scratching his face. That's how I rolled back then. He called the cops. After they arrived, I told them officers I already did what I came to do, and I was just leaving. They let me leave, and that was that. I got my message across. I didn't think he was going to spread rumors about me anymore. I wanted to find someone to put a bullet in his head, but I had to think about my future and that of Cody, so I had to let it go. That one time I had to stop and think because of my son. Not too long after that, I found another fish. This fish proved to be more dangerous than the barracuda, just my luck. Come on, really? Not again. Anyways, keep reading on.

CHAPTER FOUR

MY DARK DAYS

I met Persevu Williams a.k.a. "Pevu" at the end of 1998. Boy this guy was quite the character. He was a complete nightmare. Don't get me wrong, he was nice most of the time, and people loved him. He had a lot of friends because he was a soccer player. Pevu was the one that introduced me to marijuana. I met him through my best friend's boyfriend. When she told me to come over to her house and see him, she said, "I don't think you will like him because he smokes weed."

I said, "So? I'm coming over." I decided not to wear my regular clothes and wore Jeff's overalls instead that he left at the house after moving. If this guy was going to like me, he would do so because of me. I didn't want him to like me because of my looks, like all the others from my past. That had never worked in my book if you ask me. We met and started dating. He was staying with his friend. I used to visit him all the time; it wasn't far from my house. He would spend the nights with me. I was happy to find someone that I thought was cool after Jeff and I broke up. "Yeah right!"

One week into our relationship, Jeff came over to my house around 5:00 a.m. He was so jealous when he realized that Pevu was in the house, and he, Jeff, had just woke us up. Pevu opened the door for him in his underwear. When I had seen who it was, I quickly got up. "What are you doing here?" I asked him. "We aren't going out anymore." I told him. All my exes always go nuts whenever we broke up. I think that is when they love me the most. This is stupid. They always take me for granted when we are together, even though I was not the nicest. But I was a very good woman. I was not nice if they cheated or did something really stupid. I don't think I am alone on that one, am I, ladies? Pevu had some big-name soccer player friends who would give me the looks. (Let's hook up, girl.) I thought that was funny when they did that behind his back. One day shortly after meeting, I decided to smoke weed for the first time when Pevu moved in with me. He brought home some marijuana. I told him I wanted to smoke some.

"Are you sure?" he asked me.

"Hey this is my house, and I am an adult. I can smoke if I want to. Absolutely, am I right?" I don't know if smoking was right or wrong. What would you have done if you knew beforehand what was to happen would change your life forever, would you still do it? I did not know what was to come. I went into this one blind, without a hint from God whose name is still meant for me to know. That's only because he wanted me to learn a lesson. He was about to prepare me for something far greater a problem than the one that I was about to learn right now with Pevu. Somebody help me please! Get me out of here! God is coming, take this from me, please. If nothing else, whenever God shows up, everything shakes, and nothing is ever the same again. Moving on, let's go. We smoked and got high.

I got addicted for years to come by the way. He never smoked in this house before. This was my first time to see or smoke marijuana. That night, we smoked in my bedroom. "Oh my gosh, I felt a rush like no other." Everything seemed so funny, very funny. I remembered my sister Pasei coming in the room that night because she needed some change. She knocked on the door and I told her to come in. She came in. She asked if we had any change. He said yes. He told her to close the door so he could get the change out of his pants pocket. So she closed the door. I, being so high that night, had no idea what the heck I was doing.

While bending down looking in his pants pocket for change, I told Pasei, "Oh, Pasei, look!" I total forgot he was naked.

So she opened the door, and she saw Pevu bent over, looking in his pants pockets naked. She immediately closed the door and said to me, "Eve, why did you tell me to come in?"

"Sorry I forgot." I was high. It was so funny. Pevu jumped ran to the bed and covered himself. He started laughing. Everything was so funny. That was unfortunately the night my psychic doors reopened since mom closed them in Africa before I came to America. It was as if this was the antidote to whatever my mother did to my eyes as a child so I won't see all that paranormal activity anymore.

Pevu and I were in each other's arms when all of a sudden a vision appeared before me of my late son Elijah, my late grandmother from my mom's side, and my mom whom was alive. My mom was making a high-pitched noise. This note is the same as that really high note Mariah Carey hits and then times that by one thousand. They were all suspended in midair. My grandmother was very angry, and she said in a loud voice, "Why did you open her eyes to this? Now she is going to be in grave danger." While this was happening, I was screaming as loud as I could. I was freaking out. When Pevu touched me, I freaked out even more because I could see all the blood running through his veins. I could see his whole muscular and skeletal system. It was so scary. I could see his heart beating in his chest. Everything was transparent. During the vision, Pevu told me that my face was white and had red polka dots on it. This, ladies and gentlemen, was only the beginning of the creepy, crazy stuff that was going to happen to me.

Pevu felt like he had to tell me exactly who he was that night. He told me how before coming to Minnesota, he enlisted the help of a witch doctor to tell him what his journey was going to be like. She told him he was going to fall in love with a beautiful girl. "But be aware. Her mother is a dangerous witch." He told me about some of the things he noticed around me, pointing things out to me one at a time. He told me my house, my very room was the meeting ground for the witches. It was where they held their secret meetings. I believed that because I used to hear a lot of noises in my room all the time. Whenever I went upstairs to look, no one would be there. And yet there were always voices that I couldn't make out coming from that room. That made me to stay in the living room when I was home alone. This was happening when Jeff and I moved in. The next day, I didn't freak out. Everything was forgotten optionally as usual. I didn't want to acknowledge what I had seen.

Weird things had always surrounded you, Evelyn, since you were a child. "Forget about this," I said to myself. Pevu wouldn't let me. He said he was sent in my life to teach me about witchcraft. He told me not to take him for granted. Pevu hated my mother even though he had not met her yet. How did someone else who does not know my mother could excuse her of witchcraft? What is going on? This cannot be ignored anymore. It's kind of hard when the devil, that old serpent, was residing in the same house as you. Pevu also told me that my mother had a great serpent that was thousands of years old. Prior to him telling me that, I already knew, but I wondered, *how did he know?* I never told him anything about my parents.

It killed my son. And then it haunted me in my mother's house. Then I used to see it crawling in the walls of our house in Africa. Do you remember me saying this in the beginning of the story? How could he have known what I had seen? This was what made me to move out of my mother's house to begin with. I haven't told anyone yet in fear they will think that I was crazy. Pevu was adamant to let me know the truth about my mother. So while he was pressuring me to open my eyes, I decided to seek another opinion. It is always a good thing to seek a second and third opinion. That way, you have more information to work with. I knew that in order to get the right answer, I must ask an old wise one. While working on the night shift, I decided to tell this old lady my concerns. You could tell she was wise just by looking at her. Grandma DG was her name. On our break, I explained some of the strange phenomena that happened to me. She said, "My daughter, when our shift is over, I want you to drive behind me to my house. I want to give you something." I followed her home in the morning. She gave me a feather and some oil in an old prescription bottle. She told me the feather was the feather of a dodo bird. If someone is a witch and they came in contact with this bird or its feathers, that witch would get a horrible spiritual whipping.

She told me to hide the feather out of sight and not to let anyone see it. "If your mom is a witch, you would know without a doubt. She told me to rub the palm kernel oil every night to make sure the witches that pulled on me at night won't be able touch me. The palm oil was like mosquito repellent. Except it was a witch repellent. These witches came as naked shadow figures and did stuff to me while I was trying to sleep. She was right. They used to play with my body and have sex with me all the time. They were afraid to touch me after I rubbed the oil. So they all just stood around all night watching me. I could see them. They used to be so mad. But the palm kernel oil was almost finished. Then I had seen my mother in my dream, and she told me, "Your oil is almost finished. We will see what you will depend on now." She looked happy that the oil was finishing. My mom is very evil, and I was about to find out just how evil she was. The incident in the Ivory Coast would be a walk in the park. Even though she did protect me from other witches, it was only for her to sacrifice me when the time was right. I guess she looked at me like a thanksgiving turkey now or a roasted pig on a silver platter with an apple in its mouth.

One night, Pevu, Pasei, and myself decided to go over to Mom's house to find out if she was a witch. Pasei put the dodo feather in her hair and hid it. When we knocked on her door, it seemed like she was expecting us. We were rubbed in palm kernel oil from head to toe. When we got there, it seemed kind of calm. So I asked her, "Where is Daddy?"

She said, "Daddy was in the bathroom taking a shower."

So I said, "It's almost 1:00 in the morning. Why is he bathing so late?"

"Oh you know your dad," she said. But I didn't know him to take late showers, ever. She seemed a little too comfortable.

My son kept asking me, "Mommy, what is that smell?"

I asked him, "What smell, baby?" I asked his grandma, "Do you smell anything?"

She said, "Like what?" It was not working. There was no obvious sign that this woman was a witch. So we decided to leave after it seemed like Daddy was not getting out of the shower any time soon. Pasei and I went back to the car and told Pevu what had happened.

He said, "She was expecting you guys. She is the one hiding in the bathroom, not your father. We should turn around and go back." I didn't know at the time that one of my mother's powers was shape-changing. She was also a shape-changer. She could take the shape of anyone or animal. I am not sure about objects because I don't recall observing that.

She thought she fooled us; she thought we went home. So we went right back to the house. When we got there, Pasei used her key and opened the door. Mom looked frightened and worried. She knew we were on to her. She went in the room and lay down on the bed as if she was prepared for what was about to happen to her. We followed her. She started swelling up rapidly. She got so huge like an inflatable balloon with whipping marks on her. She was getting bigger and bigger by the second. She couldn't talk anymore. I started to clearly see that she was going to die right there and then if we didn't leave. I knew for a fact now that my mother was a witch. She failed the test, and I had seen it with my own two eyes. But I didn't want her dead, not yet, so we left. Pasei wanted us to stay there until we saw what happened in the end. I couldn't see her go from 150 pounds to about 800 pounds within minutes. It was horrible, and I thought to myself, *I am not a murderer or a witch like her. I won't allow her to die by my hands.*

That was what the dodo bird feather did to her. Pevu's cousin was moving to Minnesota to live with us for a while. When JJ finally moved, we kept our mouths shut. Maybe he wouldn't notice that we had some guests from the underworld living with us. Neither one of us said anything about the paranormal activities that were taking place in the house. I found out these things are kept as big secrets from those that know about them. I think it is in fear for some and to maintain their powers for some. One day, JJ said, "I have noticed that my clothes keep disappearing and reappearing all nicely pressed and folded." Then he looked at me, expecting me to say I did it. I told him it was not me; Pasei told him it was not her. So he said that it was very strange. He touched the cross necklace around his neck and said he was well protected from witchcraft, out of the blues. One day that chain mysteriously disappeared. I was like, uh-oh! Now someone else is here, it's not just me, Pevu, and Pasei anymore. Pevu finally told his cousin the truth about my mom.

He said, "Okay, well now I know what I am dealing with."

He didn't act like it was a big deal at all. My things always disappeared too. I thought it was Pasei and Brittany. Pasei was over at my house all the time she practically lived there. But the funny thing was even though Pevu was there for me through this tough time, there was a sinister side to him. Don't get me wrong; he was super nice most of the time. We had a lot of fun together and I used to enjoy his company. But Pevu was very abusive. The first three months we were together, he beat the crap out of me. I remember thinking that it was too early in the relationship to start showing your ugly side. That's when I knew that he was going to repeat this behavior. There were people downstairs visiting us one night when he beat me for the first time. Something he said I did. It must have been something stupid because I can't even remember it to tell you exactly what it was. All of a sudden, he started to raise his voice at me.

Before I knew it, he kicked me in the stomach with his steal toes boots on. I dropped down to my knees and started to hold my stomach. While I was doing that, he took both his hands and banged them on each ear together. All I heard was a gong-like noise vibrating in my head, and then puff, nothing. I couldn't hear anything. Right when he was hitting my ears, Pasei came upstairs and saw me on my knees. She had seen him hit me. She was so angry that she went off on him and started to hold and console me. He didn't touch me again. It seemed like he went into a calm mode after that. Pevu's violent rages toward me only got worse. He came at me with a knife before to stab me, and I urinated on myself because I felt so sure he was going to stab me. He had seen that I was afraid, and it made him stop. I was trembling; I thought he was going to kill me. One day, he went out to hang with his friends and came home at night. I couldn't sleep, and the shadow demons in the house were making a lot of noise and bothering me. They kept bumping into me upstairs. So I decided to leave the house and go to the twenty-four-hour Walgreens. I picked up our photos and came home. He thought I went to sleep with someone else. I never cheated on any guy I dated before until after they cheated.

When I got home, he asked me, "Where did you come from?"

"Walgreens," I said. He slapped me across the face and told me that I was lying. Then he started to punch me like a punching bag. I had my earring punched right through my ear, and my ear started bleeding. He started to tell me the same things he always told me.

"Apologize to me." He plugged the pressing iron and was waiting for it to get hot so he could brand me with it. I was crying really loud, and the neighbor heard me, so she called the cops. He was also screaming at me really loud. They saved me that night. And he was arrested again. He always wanted me to bow down to him when he was like this. I always told him no. He would beat me to the point of me passing out. Passing out in Pevu's hands during his beating and sex was common. He stilled had sex with me even though I was knocked out cold. I remember coming out of a fainting spell one time, and he was on top of me screwing me, as if it wasn't anything. He said, "I wasn't going to stop fucking you just because you passed out." Excuse my language, but I have to write it like it was said.

Those days were my dark days. How can I leave this man who has been protecting me from my mother all these months? I didn't even know how to protect myself from her. I really did not know how to pray during this time. The devil made my life in a way that I was always in one bad situation while running from an even worse situation. What Pevu did not know was I was building a tolerance for him every time he beat me. One day I was home by myself cooking some pepper soup for us. From the corners of my eyes, I noticed a moving figure. I was the only one home. Right away, I turned and looked. "What did I see?" I had seen my mother floating down my stairs.

She had astral-projected herself into my house. She was staring directly at me. This was another one of her powers. "Holy cow!" I looked at her, then the front door. I knew that if I waited any longer to run to the door, we were going to reach there at the same time. And I would have been trapped in the house with her. I couldn't take that chance. This is the time we Liberians would say, "Foot, help the body." That means "Legs help me run as fast as you can." So I made sure I got to the door before she did. I jumped out in the middle of winter with no shoes or socks on. I had my sports bra and my boy shorts on. I ran down the streets to my friend's house. I ran so fast, I didn't even notice that I was on bare feet. I banged on my friend's door so hard. Her boyfriend opened it. She was upstairs in her room. I headed right up there. She said, "What is wrong?"

"I had seen my mom floating down my stairs!"

"She looked like she was about to do something to me!" I was home by myself.

My friend asked me, "Have you been smoking weed?" I told her I would think that I lost it too if only I had been smoking. I only smoked that one time with Pevu months ago. While my friend was being concern about me, I started to notice something weird. I could see the veins in her and her boyfriend's body carrying the blood back and forth. I could again see their whole system; they were transparent. My heart started to beat even faster. I couldn't look at them anymore. It looked so weird when she tried to reach for me, trying to console me. I could see everything but skin. I didn't tell her. I knew she was going to think that I was crazy. I was so scared. People, let me tell you, when you have been scared shitless so many times, you build a tolerance for it, and nothing scares you anymore. "Can I stay here until Persevu get home please?"

"Sure," she said. Not too long after that, Pevu was knocking on her door.

She said, "Your woman is here deathly afraid of seeing her mom floating down her stairs."

He said, "I knew her mom was going to attack her while I was out. That's why I came back. When I didn't see her, I knew something happened. She left the stove on."

She asked him, "What in the world is going on in that house? He told her that your friend is going through a spiritual battle. Everything she is telling you is true. Her mom is a witch. But I will protect her and show her what she needs to know. When we got back to the house, I was scared. I didn't feel right; I was still in shock. After my mother astral-projected herself into my home like that and seeing transparent people was a lot to swallow and enough to put you in a mental institute. But I swallowed it because of the voice; it kept me calm and assured me that everything was going to be okay. I wish I knew the name of this voice during this time. You're probably wondering, why did I not ask for a name. Well, it never clicked to me to ask, I guess. I didn't want to admit that I was hearing voices and seeing things. This is one of the things that my mother made me to believe after time. That I was hearing voices and it was not real. Even as a child, she believed me then like she believe now but by telling me I was hearing voices would make me wonder allowing the spirit of fear and doubt come into to me and dwell. For those reasons since I was a child, I did not tell anyone of this voice until now, in this book. It has been one of the many secrets I kept for my father in heaven, not even knowing it at this time. The voice told me who everyone was, good or bad. He would always tell me their purpose in my life. But again, I kept everything to myself. The reason I am revealing all these things now is because the time has come for the book of revelations to be opened. If you believe what's going on in the world is horrible now, then you are in for a shocker. But anyways, let's move on.

My half-sister from my father's side, Cellia from New York called. She was coming down to live in Minnesota. I was so happy. But I did not tell her there was an ancient serpent in the house that pretty much sucked on the air you breath out. The very dragon that almost took her life, when we were in the Ivory Coast. I didn't tell her of the people that would sit on you making it impossible for you to get up in the night nor did I tell her that my mother grew a penis and would hold you down and screw you through the night. It was really disgusting to see that happening in my dreams. Which were so vivid, they seemed real. Like *A Nightmare on Elm Street*, the dreams were my reality. Being under a sleep spell, they seemed to take the form of a dream. Witches have spells to put you sound to sleep, in other words, yes, the sandman is real. *Supernatural* and *Charmed*, the TV shows, those things they went through in all those episodes are not someone's crazy imagination; they are real. I happened to watch these shows years later after the facts. Sadly, I did not tell Pevu about these dreams with mom because of his issues of insane jealousy.

And now how can I tell Cellia that the very dragon that almost took her life is in this house day and night. It fed on our breath whenever we exhaled, it inhaled, which is our lifeline. Sometimes longer than it's supposed to, and then you wake up choking. I thought maybe Cellia would know what to do since it swallowed her before and she survived. Cellia also has the gift of sight. The witches made it hard for anyone to hear you when you are screaming; your voice would fade in and out. I didn't think she was going to come visit me if she knew all of that. Hoping, since she had knowledge of these things, she would help me deal with them. If she was here, I could leave Persevu and not have to put up with his abusive behavior anymore. It was a selfish thing to do saying okay for her to come to Minnesota, but I did not see it that way then.

I didn't know how to battle what I was going through at the time. Things started to get worse. When Cellia came, there were no words for how bad things got. My mother found out that Cellia was in town. She was absolutely furious. One night, Cellia saw her in her dream; she wanted Cellia to do her hair. So in Cellia's dream, she did some witchcraft, and Cellia's fingers became crippled and stiff. Cellia told me the dream right away when she woke up. I told Cellia that Mom had Jeri curls, that she never braided her hair. Right after Cellia explained the dream to me, Mom called. She asked to speak to Cellia. She asked Cellia if she could please do her hair. Cellia told her not today maybe another time, and she kept insisting. I pulled the phone out of Cellia's hand and told her, "Look here, Cellia is not going to do your hair, not today, not any day for that matter, okay!" Luckily for us, we were already dressed and were ready to leave the house when she and Brittany's friend pulled up to my house. At the time, Mom lived a few minutes down the road. She started saying, "Cellia, please do my hair."

So we said, "This is an act of witchcraft and desperation. We need to get out of here right now!" We drove off.

They started chasing us, turning everywhere we turned. That was funny now thinking about it. The last time Mom came in contact with Cellia, she almost killed the poor girl. "You almost died once because of me. That is not going to happen again," I told her. "Not on my watch." They chased us until they got exhausted. Brittany's friend who was driving was probably confused of what was going on. When Mom got ready to bewitch someone, she would stop at nothing. The person will either end up severely sick to the point of death or death itself would take them. Unfortunately for some, they did not live to tell a story of a severe attack from her. One time my mom made my aunt's breast bleed blood, for days, when my aunt made her mad. Cellia told me this because she was there; I was not. She had to beg my mom to please stop, and then she apologized to my mom. My mom was no woman to mess with if you are not a Godly person. She would deebbie diced (kill) you. She could kill you twice, first your physical body and then your spirit and keep it captive. This is also another power of hers. Holding captive the spirits the people she killed so they won't hunt her like Josephine did. Josephine's spirit is still in prison every now and then I hear her calling out for help. She told me mom was holding her spirit in captive. I don't know what how to help her be free but I know when the time is right I will find out. Everybody was gone one night. I decided to kill some time by hanging out with Jeff. Later, that night, he brought me home. The house was really creepy, and I did not want to be there at all by myself. From the parking lot I could see a big black panther standing right by the front door. He turned his headlights off. I told him turn your lights back on. He did. The panther walked around to the back of the house. I asked him, "Did you see that?"

"See what?" he said. Did you see a big black panther just now?

He said no. I hurried and went into the house before Persevu caught me in the car with my ex because I knew what was going to happen if he did. I would surely be dead meat then. I watched

Jeff leave through the window, and I made sure the sliding door was locked, with the stick behind it. It didn't click to me that it was a supernatural panther until Jeff said he couldn't see it.

Not long after that, Pevu came home. I did not tell him what I had seen. That night when we went to bed Pevu quietly woke me up. He said, "Do you see that?"

"See what?" I said.

"Look, by the door."

"Do you not see that big black panther?" The house was pitched black; how can you see anything? Then he said, "*She*, it's looking for us." We were very quiet. He said to me, "It's leaving." We did not sleep in our usual spot that night so it couldn't find us he said. The next day, my sister Pasei came to the house and said she came to spend the night, but there was a big black panther that kept patrolling around the house so she was afraid to knock on the door. Right/ away I knew that I was not crazy. Someone wants me to go insane. Somebody is trying to make me go crazy.

"That someone was my dearest mother. What the heck?" We went and checked around the house; there were huge paw prints all in the snow. I lived in a townhouse; it went around to the back, passing all the other houses and to my back door. The prints disappeared right at my back door. I asked, "Persevu, where did it go? Did it go in the house"? He said, "If the prints disappeared, that means it flew away." What in the world is this? This is an emergency! I need to be rescued from earth immediately, anywhere but here, Scotty! Please…beam me up!

Other mothers protect their children. But this mother is all for eating hers and others alive. There isn't anything average about Mommy (laughing). People always ask me how come you laugh all the time when you have gone through so much. Because I know that everything under this sun is vanity and death is not the worst thing that can happen to me. The worse thing that can happen to me is God turning his back on me. At this point, I had enough. The house was too spooky to stay in. I thought if I moved out, things would change and everything was going to stop. So I decided to give the rental office my notice, to tell them I was moving. In June of 1999, I gave my rental housing my three months' notice. I thought that was enough time for everyone in the house to find a place to live. I didn't tell anyone because they were not going to agree with me. On my way back from the rental office, my feet got stuck on the pavement as if someone crazy glued them down.

Then I heard a loud thunder voice that said, "My darling Eve, you are about to suffer a great deal. I want you to see, the people around you are not who they say they are. When you see 777 know that I am God, and I will give you all your heart's desires. In the end there would be only one left, and that is the one that would be with you forever. I am ready to bless you, but the people around you are not who you think they are."

And when he said that, my spirit asked him, "Even my sister Pasei?" looking toward my house where she was.

"Not even her," he said. My heart went *bang* within my chest, and I felt a deep sorrow. I almost did not want to believe what I was hearing. I loved Pasei way too much and felt she loved me the same if not even more. What about my best friend Mennei? All these people are fake towards me? *That is impossible*, I said to myself. But the voice has never lied to me before. I wanted to break down and cry, but there was divine love in my heart from the presence all at the same time, and I couldn't cry. Then he showed me a vision, and I saw a man standing in front of the throne where God sat. I was told this was Satan pleading his case to God saying that the only reason I was pure hearted was because he, God, spoiled me and gave me everything I wanted already.

I've seen God said, "This is not true. She is truly pure at heart and loves me. Than Satan asked God to take everything away from me to see if I will still love him. God agreed and said you can do what you will, but you are not allowed to kill her. She will not change her heart toward me in the end." This is what God told Satan. God looked at me and told me to give away all my possessions, everything of value that I had, and to live a life of that of a homeless street person. They just made a bet on my life, and I was allowed to see it.

I said, "Who did you say you are again?"

And the voice said, "Jehovah God." I wanted to run. But I couldn't. Like I said, my feet were stuck to the ground. I couldn't believe this was happening to me. I was at peace the whole time this voice was talking. Scared? Yes. I was. This is the first time I got his name as I can remember. All this happened on a perfectly sunny afternoon. I wondered why his voice sounded like extremely loud thunder, come to find out that is the voice he used when he was fed up about something. He was talking to me, and I couldn't see him. I looked around while he was talking. I noticed that the sound was coming from up above.

I didn't know who God was at this time, only heard the name here and there. It was like someone saying Elvis Presley was a musician and not knowing anything about him or his music. I thought it was just a name people said. This was the first time I can remember him saying his name, but I knew his son, Jesus. I just did not know his story nor did I know God was his father. You know about him dying on the cross and shedding his blood for our sins. I did not know any of that. So what I wondered is Jesus also the Holy Ghost? He always talked like he was teaching; he was stern, firm, yet gentle and never smiled. He got my attention every time.

He truly is the son of God, that Jesus Christ. And if you doubt that, there is no rock that you can crawl under to escape the wrath that lies ahead, now that the last book is open, the Book of Revelations. He is going to clear the unrighteous ones from among the righteous. I told everybody what happened, and no one knew what 777 meant. "Oh, okay?" Some people would get mad at me and say God has not talked to anyone since the days of Moses. I know what I heard, and that voice is like no other. It did not bother me what some people thought or said. I continued to ask questions about 777.

Little did I know that I was not going to get an answer to my question for many years to come. Some days later, I heard the voice saying, "Remember to give away all your possessions and do not keep anything for yourself." I had a lot of expensive things during this time. All of my dresses were over five hundred dollars apiece, and there were many of them. I never wore the same thing twice to any gathering. I did not argue and neither did I question the voice. I had an open house and told everyone, friends, family, and neighbors to come and take anything in my home they wanted. People thought I had lost my mind. But the voice told me to live a life of a homeless person, to see who cared about me or who cared about me for what I had. Wow, this is what God meant when he said the people around me were not real. Now the Holy Spirit is leading me toward the path of truth. Ooh yes, I did find out. You would be surprised to see who loves you only because of what you have or who you are. What have the world come to? People are so greedy. Indeed, the off springs of Cain still live today.

Jealousy, envy, pride, greed, lust, malice, gluttony, etcetera— these are all spirits that manipulate us human beings. If you think these spirits and witchcraft is only an African thing, then you need to start doing more research. My people are destroyed for lack of knowledge. Hos. 4:6. And by the way, whoever came up with the phrase "What you don't know won't hurt you"? That person has already hurt us, by that lie alone! What you don't know can really harm you. If I had known how to fast and pray and most of all about the blood of Jesus, I was not going to suffer like I am about. Ignorance is a disgrace, and no man likes to be disgraced.

One day, Mom called me and told me to kick Cellia out of my house, or she was not going to keep who and what she really was a secret from me anymore. She was threatening me. *Say what? Oh no she didn't*, I thought. I told her to "Bring it on!" She told me that she was going to make my life a living hell. She did a mighty good job at that, I tell you. After that, all hell did break loose. I called all her children and complained to them. Anastasia said, "So if Mom wants to kill you, she was the one who gave you your life anyways."

I told her, "Thanks for feeling that way about me, but I don't feel like dying, so I would fight." Mom wants me dead, and for Anastasia to say that once again, reminded me of her strong hatred for me. *Hello*, what the hell? Thank you for your concern!

My brother Hamilton said, "She almost killed me [referring to his leg], so since her attention is off me and on you, I would like to keep it that way. Sorry I can't help you!"

"Oh, okay, it's like that, huh? I didn't think you would help me, but I thought you needed to know that Mom and me are about to have a nasty spiritual war."

After that, I called Jasmine. Jasmine said, "Well, I don't know what to say."

"Yeah, you never know what to say when it comes to me." I remember she too didn't like me.

"Well, I am calling all of my mother's children to let them know that Mom has threatened me, and now she wants war." I was on my own once again. I knew they couldn't help me, but I wanted them to know that I was at war with our mother. And a war in which I did not plan to lose because of who was backing me. This God person I thought. "Silly girl." God is not a person! He is the creator of us all, good and evil. Now I know. Why didn't anyone tell me all this before? I believed this was the appointed time that he wanted me to know his name and see his wonderful working powers.

My siblings were all punking out and leaving me in the arms of our mother to die, at least, so they thought. I remembered my father had a big black book. On this book were written the words "Holy Bible." It was hidden away among his things in their room in a locked box. Every time I went to visit him before all this happened, he would briefly bring it out from hiding and tell me that I would need this book one day. It will be extremely important to my very existence, he would say. I did not know what he was talking about then. My mother would always bang on the door and demanded he unlocked it so she could come in. Then she would always ask, "What were you guys talking about?" He would say something totally different from what he was trying to tell me. He was my best friend, so even when she would ask me behind his back I would tell her the same thing he told her. He wanted to talk to me about this book desperately.

He would ask her if she needed anything from the room first before we went in. She would say no. But the minute we got in the room and he pulled this Bible from hiding, she would bang and bang on the door, and he would hide it again before opening the door. I used to laugh. I thought it was funny. Not knowing my poor daddy had been living in fear for years. All he could ever say was "Make sure you read this book." Now I see why. You would think that I have learned the Bible, word for word, but I haven't, not yet, anyways. Many things that take place in my life and things I tell people, they always tell me it is written in the Bible. Whenever I open a Bible, I will read things in it that I have seen in my visions or in my dreams. That scared me for a while, because I didn't understand what was happening to me.

My very salvation was in this book. All the answers to my questions were in this book. The very God that had been talking to me was in this book. This book, I come to find out is alive every single word can come to pass. Anyways, let's move on with this story. We will come back to this later. Wait, if you think this is bad, keep reading. I was not born in America, but I came here as a child, so comprehending all these things that were happening was hard for me. Like one day when Pevu tried to reach for a glass of Kool-Aid. All of a sudden as he was reaching for the glass to get his drink, the glass broke in many pieces. But it was in a very odd way. Every piece that broke off was identical to the other. We were looking at him talking before the glass broke. I saw his hands; he did not even touch the glass when it broke. Pasei and Cellia were right there when it happened. Of course, we took pictures of this incident.

Later on, all the pictures mysteriously disappeared. There was someone among us who was working for the underworld with my mother. But at this time, there were no speculations in my mind that this might even be occurring. Pevu said my mom was trying to poison him. That's why the glass broke, he said. He said that he have protection from poison in African signs, when someone was trying to poison him, he would know. The food would either fall from his hands or the plate or bowl the food was in would break. I had that same protection. Mom had this old man come from far away to the house when I was a little girl in Zwedru. He sliced open our wrists and put something in there, and Mom said it was for poison protection. I don't know if it works or not, but one of my sisters almost got poisoned in African sign when her ex-boyfriend decided to put his pubic hair in her sandwich so she could love him forever. It dropped out of her hands, and he was busted. He confessed to what he had done. The pubic hair was used as a point of contact, something witches and warlocks need in order for what they are doing to be effective. It can ranch from anything hair from your scalp, your underwear, clothes, nail clipping etcetera, something that is associated with you. Mostly something that has your DNA. Now, the saddest part that I had not realized during this time was, we had a traitor among us.

Cellia started to complain of someone sitting on her at night and how she couldn't get up to use the restroom. She noticed that whenever she took her clothes off in the room, someone or something would push her onto the bed and make her extremely weak to the point where she couldn't get out of bed. How would she know what has been happening to me here to me lest she had experienced it? I didn't tell anyone. It was now happening to her. I noticed when they throw you on the bed like that, you get this strong orgasm feeling that happens over and over softly until you fall asleep; and then something or someone would make love to you. You would know they are there. But it would feel so good; you wouldn't want them to stop. But it was not right, so knowing that by it was nasty. But you would be too weak to stop them. Like I said earlier, sometimes I would see my mother making love to me with a penis in my dreams, but I would be too weak to stop her. I was not a praying person. I did not even know what prayer was anyways. Then I told her that it had been happening for a while, and I couldn't tell her before she came. I really needed her help. I knew she could help. And I missed her and couldn't wait to see her. I told her for the first time what I had seen before Elijah died. The shadow demon that looked like a blob. She knew that I was telling her the truth. She used to see it too. She was not mad with me.

She knew that I would never ever harm anyone deliberately. She was the brave one. She never really bothers anyone. That means she's easygoing. She was always calm, cool, and collected. I started to notice that Pasei was not happy about the fact that Cellia was there. She used to ask me all the time, "Why is she here? She needs to go back to New York. She was not too happy with me." At that time, I just thought Pasei was being jealous. I thought she felt like I was going to spend more time with Cellia than her. One day my big brother called me and said, "I heard Cellia is in town?"

I said, "Yes, but I don't want Mom to know. You know she doesn't like Cellia." This was before Mom threatened me.

He said, "Oh well, I already told her."

"Oh my goodness." I lost it at that moment. I started to go off on him. Hamilton is not mild temper either. So we went at it. I told him that he wanted Cellia dead. How he was such a big idiot. "I'm coming over to your house to stab you in the stomach." I grabbed the knife and started to go over there; someone had called the cops, and they came to my house. I hid the knife in the flower bushes next to my house. Hamilton lived right across the street from me. Cellia had called him to talk about the situation, and he told her that he was just joking. He never told Mom that she was in town. He really didn't know how Mom knew.

There was a snitch around us, and we still haven't put it together yet. So I apologized to him. But things continued to be bad in the house. Everyone that was living in the house didn't have anywhere else to live. Except Pasei, she could always go home. But she said she didn't want to live with the witch. So we all went about our normal business like nothing happened. We had friends that would stop by and visit us every day. Sometime there were fifteen to twenty people in the house at once. Persevu said that the witches didn't like that. "The time would come where no one would visit us," he would say. They just needed time to work out the details so they could rule the house. I thought to myself this was the right time for Pevu to move out into his own place. I wanted for us to break up. He gave me the sad story; I was so naive back then. I believed him when he said he would move out. He didn't. Cellia told me she was moving out to live with her longtime boyfriend who was now residing in Minnesota. This scared me a little, but I knew how much she loved her boyfriend. So I had to think of something, and fast. From the time Cellia told me to the time she was actually moving was only a few days. He didn't lay a hand on me the whole time Cellia was there. I knew if he didn't move out before Cellia left, he was going to use me as a punching bag again.

I kept hearing the voice saying, "You were very abusive to Jeff. Everything Pevu is doing to you now, you had done to Jeff. You have to learn from him how witchcraft works. Until then, you are not allowed to leave. I will be sending a man in your life that will be against abuse. You will not be able to keep him if your behavior does not change and you will need him. You have to know how it feels, in order for you to change." This was when I learned that some people only changed a habitual behavior only if it is done to them. They have to understand how it feels when the tables turn. And I was one of those people. My best friend at the time used to say that I was being punished for the way I used to treat Jeff. Jeff was the only guy I was like that with. Because I had no patience or respect for anyone who made me mad. So the first response I had to unfavorable situation was exhibiting violence. That voice kept replaying in my head whenever Persevu beat me, and I wanted to just kill him. I would calm down after remembering what the voice said.

Mom's behavior toward me started to get worse. She told me to get rid of Persevu; she said he was not good for me. She never met him. She said it was because of his tribe. So I said no. She made my father come to the house to tell me, if I didn't get rid of the young man he was going to take away his television that I was using. So I told him, "Go ahead." His old self, he struggle with the TV until he got it in the car. Pevu tried helping him, but his pride wouldn't let him accept the help. It was all too funny. I asked him, "Daddy, where do you think I get my stubbornness from?" I told daddy that Pevu could see Mom in all her witch forms, and he knows how to slow her down, that he was teaching me the signs to look for. That was the reason she hated him. Daddy just looked at me and knew what I was telling him was true. He didn't say anything again, and he left. Now thinking about it, was it really my dad that day? Or was it my mom, the shape-shifter?

One of Persevu's friends that had a crush on my sister Cellia told him that Mom went to his house taking the form of Cellia and tried to and have sex with him. Luckily for him, he had the gift of sight also. So he rebuked her and told her to leave. She was really good at shape-shifting, which was one of her many specialties. But now I was faced with another dilemma. Pevu woke me up while crying one night to tell me that he slept with my sister Cellia. I asked him what happened and where was I. He told me that I was out and about that evening. He really wanted me to believe him. I did, but I did not want him to know that.

He went on with all these details of what they did and didn't do. "Cellia wouldn't do anything like that to me," I told him. He never wanted me to ask her. But he wanted me to tell her to leave. He and Pasei really pressured me for me to kick her out, but I refused. Whether or not it happened, there was no way I was kicking my sister out before she was ready to move on her own, no matter what. I just told them Cellia was my guest, and she could stay for as long as she wanted. I was not going to ask her to leave. Cellia moved out with her boyfriend soon after that anyways. I never told her what took place until years later.

Now I'm back to square one. Persevu says my mother knows he has a temper and that was what she was using to get him aggravated. So when he gets mad, I should just beg him, and we would be okay. "Hell no, I don't think so." I am not too big to apologize if I have not done something wrong. But I will not apologize for stupidity, especially on someone else's behalf. There was this incident at Jeff's house when Pevu jacked me for dancing with his cousin who lived in the house with us. Someone told Jeff, and he came running to the scene. He grabbed Persevu by the neck with one hand and started choking him.

"Ha ha, get him, Jeff."

He told Persevu, "If you want to fight, fight a man!" He was really angry; I had never seen him hurt a fly before physically. By then someone I knew pulled up and told me to get in the car. I did, and we pulled off. I looked back, and Jeff was still holding him by the neck. I didn't go home that night. When I came home the next day, he wanted to know whom I spent the night with. He locked me in the house with him for one week. No one could come in or go out. He cut the phone cords with scissors. Every time someone knocked on the door, he would give me a threatening look like "I dare you get up. I would tear you to pieces." So I didn't even bother seeing who it was. This fool, he did not know it was not him I was being obedient to. It was the voice that I was obeying. I would have torn him to pieces by now if it was not for the voice. God was building in me a sense of remorse, something I absolutely didn't have at that time. He thought I was some trophy that he should only have to himself. He didn't want me to have friends. No one came to the house for me nor was I allowed to visit anyone. He gave me a black eye every week with blood spots in them. He told me that my best friend Mennei was not a real friend to me; all she wanted from me was to use me. He said she always wanting something. Then he said she wanted to sleep with him. Everybody wants to sleep with Persevu according to him. I had to slow down my friendship with my Mennei for several reasons. I did not want her to get in my mom's way before Mom attacked her.

It would have been easy because my friend knew nothing of these things of the underworld. Another reason was she loved putting me down to make herself feel good when I was in her presence. She said really hurtful stuff to me all the time. She would tell me I was too fat to wear a skirt. I did not have a pretty shape. I did a lot for her but I cannot remember her do things for me. I knew at this point she was one of the people God spoke of who were fake to me. It took me awhile to accept this. She would put me down in front of her boyfriend, whoever she was dating at the time. One time she said if they put ten outfits on the bed and told she and I to try them on only one will look good on me, and she would look good in nine. She said the one outfit would only look good on me because it would be made for fat people.

One time we were out, and the mosquitoes where biting her legs and not mine. She said they were only biting her because she had the sexiest legs. But the funny thing was whenever we went out; men would always come on to me and not her. I never got turned on by men who drooled over me. But whenever someone had negative things to say behind my back, she would jump at my defense or that's what she told me. That was never a proven fact by the way. When things started going wrong for me and I was going through the wilderness, that's when she would always ask the question as to why she even bothered talking to me anymore. I had nothing to offer her, she would say. *Yeah, I guess not anymore,* I thought to myself, remembering what the voice told me.

This girl, at one point in her life, I bought for her everything she owned. I would never say anything about such things, but I am writing a tell-all book, so let me tell you in order for you to understand. I let her and her husband stay in my house for one month before they could find a place to move. I let her use my car whenever she needed to. Hell, I taught her how to drive. I always babysat for her. She never needed to hire a babysitter. My parents used to be upset with me about that all the time. It came a point the baby knew me more than he knew her. He and I had all these special routines. I could understand what a baby was saying as if it was an adult talking to me. But I never told anyone about that gift until now. So her baby and I got along just great.

But Mennei couldn't control herself in the end when I lost everything I ever had. Her true colors started to show, and she did not want to hang out with me anymore. I tried over and over to explain to her what God told me. I did not want her to fall in that category of not being a true friend to me. If she could comprehend what I was saying at the time, she was not going to be one of those that criticized me when I give away all my stuff. She really meant no harm. Actually, I do remember her helping do my laundry because I could never get it right. I had so many clothes I only did laundry twice a year. But imagine it was an all day ordeal when we did it. That was just who she was. People however can change and grow up. She always used to tell me that none of the guys she dated would find me attractive because I was fat.

She said the only guys that would find me attractive were guys who loved fat girls. I chose three of them and slept with them at different stages in my life. I wanted to prove to myself that it was not the case. They were very much attracted to me and wanted to take things further. They came after me. I never went after them. I couldn't because they were just my test objects. I told her what I did thirteen years later when God wanted me to come clean to everyone I ever did anything wrong to. I had even forgotten that I did that. But the voice brought it back to my memory. She was upset, but she called me one day to tell me that she forgave me. Like I said, I was a sweet and sour onion. Thank God for the Holy Spirit.

I remember during my time of struggle, Mennei bought a brand-new car that she drove me off to my parents' house with one day. While Mom and I were standing as she was pulling off, Mom asked, "Is that your best friend in that new car?"

I said, "Yes."

She said, "How come you don't have a new car?" I said because I did not work hard to get a new car. And I don't want a brand-new car right now. She said, "Well, if you want, I can help you kill her so you can get a new car." She was serious.

I looked at her and said, "Mom, if I really wanted a new car, I know how to get one, okay?"

She once again asked me, "Why don't you have a jealous bone in your body? How come I am your mother, but your heart is nothing like mine?" Even though she was my mom and my dad was my dad, it always felt like I came from somewhere else, and I could never explain that. There is no need to be jealous when you know who your Father in heaven is. And everything under the sun and in heaven is for your Father, and you are entitled to it all. Why be jealous?

His word, I came to find out, says, "Ask, and it shall be given to you." Even though you have travelled far as a child and don't know his name, he is still there for you. He will make himself known to you when the time is right. So those kinds of things really don't bother me. I am not materialistic. I can give anything of mine to anybody. All the supernatural things that were happening to me were going to affect Mennei. I did not want her harmed. One day, Persevu bit me so hard on my arm several times on the same spot until it turned black and blue. He would look at me and bite down as hard as he could, and then he would look me in the eyes as he was doing this to see if I would cry. I refused to cry and sucked it up. He did this over and over until he gave up. I just politely walked away from him, went upstairs, and took a shower.

When my friend Mennei came from Texas and saw the mark on my arm. She was disgusted with me. I tried to explain to her how the voice told me that I needed Pevu to teach me things about witchcraft that were going to help me in the future, she said it was my excuse for being in a relationship like that. She told me that he must be good in bed. That's when she told me, "While I was in Texas, I started to think and wonder why we were friends. You don't have a job. Since Jeff left you, you don't have anything going for yourself." She did not understand what I was going through or she didn't want to. I couldn't blame her. Unless you have had personal experience with the supernatural, it is really hard to understand. You can sit there all day trying to explain it and to some it just doesn't add up.

"It sounded as if you were making excuses for why your life was the way it is. No situation stays the same forever," I told her. "Jeff took care of me, but I was the one that broke up with him, remember?" I asked her. "Right now, I am going through something supernatural, and it is for a reason. My life is not always going to be this way forever, you know." I wanted to tell her that I am going to be well known one day. I wanted to tell her all the things God promised me he would do for me. But if she could not even be there for me at this time, would she hang in there with me throughout the horrible struggle God revealed to me that I was about to go through? You cannot keep beating a dead horse, you know. The bottom line was she did not want to be my friend anymore because I had nothing to offer her. I think what she was really struggling with was how do you let some go after all they have done for you? I think that was her battle. But she finally made that decision, and I had to except it. I was so hurt for many years I just couldn't believe that people would care about material things in life more than life itself.

One day my times of trials and tribulations will be over, and I will live the life God has intended for me. I love Mennei very much; she is a sweetheart who just had a mouth she couldn't control, that's all. That's what made her who she is. She says whatever came to her mind. I can respect that. Actually, I like that. Tell me like you see it; don't sugarcoat anything. She was the only one that told people just like she saw it. To me, sugarcoating things to people is like insulting their intelligence. It's like I really don't like you and I can't stand the sight of you, but I am going to tell you all these great things that I think you want to hear because of what you can do for me. That is a bunch of BS. What is wrong with honesty these days? Has it gone extinct?

Mennei was very fun to hang out with. But I know her mouth still get her in trouble every now and then. But I have to remember in the back of my mind that she said she was going to seek revenge on me about those boyfriends of hers that I slept with. She is just going to have to pick a number and wait in line. The word of God said that he was going to lead me in path of the righteous for his namesake. In order to get to that path of the righteous, you must first cut the bushes and thorns out the way. God will do that for you. Christianity is not a bed of roses, and there is no easy way or shortcuts to the kingdom of God. And God cannot even be bribed, so no matter how much money you have, that too won't help. Just plainly accepting Jesus Christ, as our Lord and Savior, will give us salvation. But that does not mean you will have access to the throne. If that was the case, everyone that voted for President Barack Obama would be having dinner with him every evening. No, you must put in the work of righteousness. You must walk the walk and talk the talk. Because faith without works, is dead. I am going to stop preaching now and get back to the story. I still have so much more to share with you, so let's go!

One night Persevu pulled me off the toilet and started beating the crap out of me. We were about to have sex, and I got some sick news of my son, so right away; I grew butterflies in my stomach and felt sick. After one of my twins died, I used to freak out any time the other one was sick. He didn't care. After beating me, he told me to get on the bed and open my legs. I didn't, so he pushed me and climbed on top of me. What a jerk. He started having sex with me, and I laid there like a sock of potatoes. He told me, "You don't have to move. All I need is the hole. I'm in anyways." He told me to take a shower. When I put the hot water on, he said no; he turned the cold water on. And he sat there and watched me take a cold shower.

I never did tell him what I went through as a child with Anastasia. All these things were bringing back horrible memories. I can understand why some people snap. Imagine if the voice had not been there for me all this time what would have become of me? Who really loved me besides my dad in this world? I mean, a human being not the divine ones. Okay, how much longer do I have to go through with this? He beat me so badly that I could barely talk because my neck was so swollen, and I was in a lot of pain. Someone called the cops again, and they came. When he opened the door for the cops, he had his hands ready to be cuffed. He went to jail, and I went to the hospital.

Mennei went with me to the hospital. The doctor was so angry with me and said, "Women like you make me sick because you always go back." She was not nice to me at all. But then again, she didn't know why I was in the relationship. And this would be the time Satan sees to tempt me. He said, "Just wish your life on her so she can feel what you are going through. Then you won't have to go through this, and it will all stop." I never even gave it any thought, and I told him he needed to be gone.

That is a satanic act, to wish your horrible life and experiences on other people. No, sorry, dude, I'm good. I went home that night. No one knew the real reason that I was with him. Some people thought it was for the sex; he was not the kind of person that I would date, not even sleep with for the fun of it. He did not have money. I have no idea why I even dated him at the time honestly. But he was there to slow my mother down from killing me. Like I said, God always placed someone in my path that would help protect me right before she launched an attack on me.

This time, it just happened to be someone who had the same violent attitude as me. Then and only then was I going to change my ways. It made me change forever. Persevu's baby mom told me one time that he hit her head against the dashboard and split her eye brow opened and she had to get stitches. He broke his last girlfriend's ribs, and she had to be hospitalized. When he got out of jail, I was scared to get out of my house or answer my phone, not because I was afraid of him but rather what I would do to him if he pushed me too far. And I knew he was going to hold me hostage in my own house again. Everyone who lived in my house had moved out. I was here by myself. One day, I told the shadow demons in the house, "I'm not afraid of you." I put my outfit on the chair, and it went flying across the room. I just politely picked it up and wore it. I decided to spend the night at Jeff's house.

Right away, I had a vision when I laid down. I had seen the dragon looking for me. It went to my house, and I was not there. Then it went to my friend Mennei's house, and I was not there either. It got mad and started to scream. It turned and started flying toward Jeff's house. I started to panic. I told him that my mom's dragon is flying over here. "It would be here any minute. I have to go."

He said, "No, don't go." Right away all the windows flew open and this great wind came in. "Whoa," he said. "This is not a joke, is it?"

"No, it is not a joke, and I have to leave before it does something to you."

"Okay, I'm going back home." I went home and lay down; it came and corded itself around me all night until morning, and I could not move. I was home alone. I felt so helpless. Tears dropped from my eyes as I lay there with this gigantic snake wrapped around me. I have never felt so alone in this world. I could not move. It was feeding on my energy. This was the great serpent my mother sacrificed my son Elijah to. Every now and then, it would come at night and cord itself around me. As I was lying there, I could hear the shadow demons upstairs. What have I done to go through all these things? Things more than enough to drive a sane person into the mental institute.

One night, I was leaving the house. Persevu was hiding in the flower bushes. He grabbed me and took me back in the house. He said, "I don't want to hurt you, but I have nowhere to stay." I didn't want to take him back, but my lights were shut off. There were witches and shadow demons in my house, a thousand-year-old serpent that fed off my spiritual strength at night trying to shorten my life line.

"Okay" was the only answer I could give him, looking at my situation. What would you do if you were in my shoes and the only other people you could turn to are the very ones the problems coming from? Most people would run home to Mom and Dad. In my case, where do I run to? None of my family member houses would be safe for me. It was almost time to move out of here anyways. So Persevu started to do his spiritual stuff, and some of the things calmed down a little bit. He said that my mom planted something physically in the house.

He said, "Your mother has been in this house physically before." He turned the house upside down and didn't find anything. Then he asked me, "Has she ever physically entered into this house before?"

I said "Yes, Jeff had brought her here before, but I was not home. I did not know anything about it. So I don't know what she did. I knew there was something awful about my mother, but since I did not have my family's support, I did not want to scrutinize her, and it was time to move anyways. I told my parents I was moving. Mom said that she needed stuff. So she said she was coming over to get some stuff. I told her I gave everything away already. She insisted she would check herself. She and Pasei came over. Then she said she had to use the bathroom. When she got done, she stood on the top of the stairs, and she rolled her eyes into the back of her head. Only the white of her eyes were showing. She started to chant something. So I called Pasei to come and see what she was doing. Pasei asked, 'What the hell are you doing on those stairs, Mom? Get down here right now! You are a witch and just get what you came to get, and let's go. Let me take you home.' She said she didn't want anything, so Pasei took her home."

As I am now writing this story, the Holy Spirit (the voice) had just revealed to me that she came to get what she physically put in the house the day Jeff let her come over. Jeff was blinded by my mother and could not see her for who she really was. But there was this one time he told me when he first met my mother, he said when he shook her hand his hand got super-hot. He said that was how he knew she was a witch, but he did not want to tell me before I got angry with him for such an accusation. Later on that day when Pevu came home right from the door, he said, "Your mom was in this house today, wasn't she?" He started shaking. He said his feet were getting cold. I felt so bad.

"I let her in the house. I am sorry."

He said, "Take me upstairs so I can sleep." While he was upstairs sleeping, the serpent came hovering over him sucking the air out of him. I woke him up and told him what I seen. He told me, "Thanks for waking him up." We finally moved out. But we didn't have anywhere to stay. That was the beginning of my struggle. Would you live in a house like that if you were me?

One of my friend's parents took me and Pasei in. This friend used to practically stay with me, which I did not mind. A lot of people lived in my house from one point or another. I didn't live with her parents long. Her dad, Uncle Murdock, I called him out of respect, used to ask me out all the time. I told him I could not do such a thing to his wife, the woman whose house I was staying in. So he told me, "Well, I am going to ask Pasei out, and I told him she wouldn't agree. I was very wrong. They started to have an affair, and that made me so uncomfortable. The wife knew something was going on, but she thought he was sleeping with me, and she was plotting evil things in her head that she could do to me, and I could have just felt this chill come over my body whenever she came home. I got the same feeling goose bumps I got from my mom. I felt the wife was not happy with me being there at all. So I told Uncle Murdock that I was leaving.

Pasei wanted me to stay there, but I told her no because she was putting my life in danger by her actions. She had contacted this witch doctor, the same one Pevu saw before moving to Minnesota. I spoke to the lady, but my spirit was not comfortable with her. So I did not go with Pasei when she went to see the witch doctor in New York. When she came back, she said the witch doctor told her to take a dozen eggs and stand over them, saying, "Whoever picks up these eggs should pick up all the problems in my life." She was ready to do it.

I told her, "Don't do that. That is an act of evil. Why will you want someone else to bare your burdens? Bare your own burdens." I told her, "That witch doctor was an evil person to even suggest something like that to you. How will you feel if someone did the same thing to you?"

She said, "I was right, and she was not going to do it. Looking back now, I am sure she went ahead and did just what that witch doctor wanted her to do. After I left Uncle Murdock's house,

Persevu and I used to sleep in apartments that were being renovated. Most of the time, maintenance would leave the doors unlocked. Pevu had a technic of how he was figuring these things out. He would find the place in the day. Late at night, we would sneak in there and take a shower, talked until we fell asleep. I thought this was bringing us closer. We did that, and then whenever I braided hair, we would rent a cheap motel for some days. Pevu told me his friend was going out of town for a few days. So we could stay over at his friend's house until he came back. No problem, right? Wrong, big problem! We ran into Hector that day, and I said hi to him casually.

He asked me, "Why did you talk to Hector?"

"Hector is my baby father. What is wrong with that?" He got so mad. He started running toward me. I knew he was about to hurt me. The sucker came with a dropped kick, and my head hit the wall. I felt myself slowly passing out, and then everything went black. I woke up in a tub full of ice and water. I was cold. I got out, and he was right there telling me how sorry he was.

I asked the voice, "Is it time yet to leave?"

"No, it's not time," said the voice.

"Okay, I accept your apology," I said. Then we became like honey on rock once more (lovey-dovey). I wanted to hurt him so bad. But I couldn't.

Shortly after that incident, Pevu got a job and started working. And then he found a place. I did not help him financially. Now we don't have to park outside his ex-girlfriend's apartment anymore and watch her go in and out like we did every day, hearing stories of her all day long. I had a job, but I had my schedule changed and did not tell him. When we were done moving into his new apartment, he had a party. While the party was going on, some girl called and wanted to talk to him. He got on the phone and started whispering sweet nothing in her ear. I took the phone from him and hung it up. He started saying mean stuff because he was mad. I took the huge VSOP liquor bottle and was getting ready to hit him on the head with it when someone grabbed my hand and stopped me. I looked back to see who it was. "Hector."

"Why did you stop me?"

"Because I didn't want you going to jail for life. We have a son!"

"Please calm down." I went back in the room and lay down just like that, calmly. When the party was over, he came in the room and lay down next to me. When he thought I was asleep, he quietly got out to call her back.

All I could hear was, "She is sleeping."

I heard the voice saying to me, "You are now free." I didn't have to stay with him anymore. I have learned what I needed to learn from him. He came in, got dressed, and left. The next day, he asked me for money. I told him I didn't have any and lied to him, saying my job fired me. He believed me because of my change of schedule. Off seven days and work seven days. He told me to apply for welfare, but I told him that I did not qualify. How am I supposed to pay for this place? Everything I owned in his apartment went out his front door that morning. My panties went flying all over in the hallway as he was throwing my stuff. The neighbor helped put them into garbage bags and into my car. This girl was one of the people I never talked to because I did not think she was on my level, and I felt like I was better than her. She did not say a word to me as she was helping. That was one of my lessons. Don't ever look down on anyone because you never know what tomorrow would bring.

Hector showed up that morning returning my driver's license someone had stolen. Pasei also came to see me at the same time, neither one of them knew what was happening. They saw my clothes in the hallway. This happened about 7:00 a.m. I was more hurt than embarrassed. I had been there for him, and this is how he repaid me? All because he wanted his ex-girlfriend back. I slept in my car that night. He had seen me the next day and asked where did I sleep? I told him in my car. He felt bad. He knew I couldn't go home to my parents' house. He was just a user. He told me to stay the night, and I did. The next day, he was going to take his ex-girlfriend somewhere on a date. He started saying how great in bed she was, and he couldn't afford to lose her. As he was and walking away from me, I took the big butcher's knife from under the pillow and threw it, hoping it would stick in his skull. He heard it passed by his head and went straight into the wall were it got stuck missing him by inches. I had a nasty temper, and God had a lot of work to do on me. When he had seen the other knife in my hand, he ran in his underwear out the door. So I locked the doors and windows and took a long nap. He was trying to get everyone to open the door. But they didn't succeed.

His friend that I had a crush on came knocking on the door. He came in and we talked. I told him that I had a crush on him. But he was one of my friends' boyfriend. That didn't bother me. I asked him if he would sleep with me. He said, "In a heartbeat." He said, "Eve, you are one of the most talked about pretty girls around here." I already knew that. But it sounded better hearing it from him.

Then I asked, "So when can we hook up?" He said he and his brother were going to St. Cloud for a few days. I told him I was going with them. We let Persevu in his apartment; he seemed scared. "I told you! You didn't want to bring this side of me out."

"I can have a nastier temper than you. But the voice said to leave you alone, and you know it. You can date anyone you want to date now. I am leaving, and I am not going to bother you," I told him. I went with the boys, and we had four days of fun. It was a blast.

When we got back, Pevu was mad, and he came to me, saying, "So you let him fuck you?"

I said, "No, he made love to me. What is it to you? Go screw the chick you left me for." And I walked away from him.

CHAPTER FIVE

MOVING IN WITH SUE AND SAM

Su and Sam were living in an apartment north of the city. That was my first time living in the hood besides passing through it. When I got there, I was like, wow, this is cool. Everything was right there in walking distance. I walked to the liquor store every day with Sam who liked to drink. I started drinking right along with him. It was fun, not knowing this was going to turn into a habit that would classified me as an alcoholic for years to come. While I was living with them I kept to myself most of the time. It was fun observing everyone that went in and out. At least ten or more people came to their apartment every day. I called Sam my big brother. He was a talker. Now all the people that I thought I was too high and mighty to talk to before have been coming in and out visiting him. They were all very nice and down to earth. Seeing them now made me feel like a donkey for not getting to know them. I would never think of myself as high and mighty anymore. This to me was a valuable lesson. What you have or don't have should not have an effect on your attitude. Not because someone doesn't have what you have means you are any better than them. Thank you, my Lord Jesus, for allowing me to have experienced all these things. I know you want me be a better person. I had seen a different side of life.

I remember my parents telling me not to leave Jeff my ex-boyfriend because I was going to fall flat on my face. I told them, "Oh well, then that's what would have to happen to me."

I used to hear the voice saying to me, "You should not judge people. Now you'll live among them to know that they are also humans. You will come down to their level, and you are not allowed to have anything fancy. You will still get money but you are to give it all away and not buy anything for yourself." Okay, that is fine. I couldn't tell anyone anything about what was happening to me. Everyone that had seen me in Su and Sam's apartment was shocked. They would ask him where did he know me from and what happened to me. I looked the complete opposite of what people were used to seeing. It was going pretty much from nice things to rags. Some days I admit, it was very embarrassing, but I had to keep my head up because this was something the Lord wanted me to experience. If I told anyone what was really happening to me, people would look at me and think, "Who the hell does she think she is? She is crazy. God does not talk to anyone like that."

There was just no way I could tell anyone. So my life just had to go on. I had a lot of things going on with me in my head, in the spiritual realm, and physical world. By now, my battle with Mom was getting worse. She was chasing me every night in my sleep and trying to kill me. I would see her blowing red dust on me as I ran from her. By the time I woke up in the morning I would be so tired, and ready to go back to sleep for another eight hours. It was horrible. One night I fell asleep on Su's coach facing the wall, when I turned around I had seen my mother staring at me through the window. Her head was really huge. She was looking at me like I am going to get you. I could hear her thoughts. I told her not tonight, and I turned my face back to the wall and went back to sleep. I was tired. By now I started to realize the effect of alcohol and how it made you to temporarily not think about your problems so I started drinking a lot. I didn't want to think about a thing. I just wanted to make it to the next day; my life in the realm of the spirit was more complex and needed more attention than my everyday life.

Everyone from the spirit realm wanted me to fall asleep. First God, so he could reveal what was to come and how I should go about it in my dreams. Then my mother, so she could battle with me, one on one. But I realized the spirit of God in me is greater than the spirit that was within her. I either won the battle every time, or I would find a route of escape. Then it was the Ginas (the fallen angels) that wanted me to sleep so they could see which one of them would marry me, both women and men. They are also called Marine spirits. That Sandman was really busy with me, just my luck. Moving on…

Su was really nice to me. She had two little ones that were so adorable. I loved them very much. Her little girl would follow me everywhere I went. She was about two years old. But I got sad one day when Su told me that she was seeing some huge snake in her dreams trying to swallow her children. I never told her about my mom or the dragon. But when she said that I knew what she was talking about, I told her, "Su, it is my mother's dragon as we call it in Liberia."

She asked, "Your mom is a witch?"

And I said, "Yes. I will pack my things and move out because I don't want to put you and the children at risk."

She said, "No, you will not move out, now that I know, the children will be safe. Don't worry about us." Even though she knew now that my mother was a witch, I couldn't tell her the rest. She was a young girl probably a year or two younger than I was. But I could tell she was wise beyond her years. She did everyone's hair, so a lot of girls were in and out of the house. Su knew that I was a very private person, so she didn't get me involved with what she did. Every now and then, she would ask me to help her finish someone's hair when she was busy or had somewhere to be. She was a very good braider. The best I had seen, she enhanced my braiding skills. She could also cook her butt off. Everyone loved Su. I mostly hung out with Sam because I got along better with guys. Girls had never really liked me before. I can't blame them. He would take me everywhere with him. But whenever Romeo was in town, I would stay with him until he had to go away again.

This time when he came, he was not taking no for answer. He took me to buy me a cell phone so he could call me whenever he wanted. He just wanted to spoil me. But remember what God said? "Don't buy anything for yourself." I was not allow to but anything for myself. Yes I remember! I really wanted to go all out and get my own place and be by myself and buy all my fancy things that I was used to. I couldn't do that. He used to tell me, "Let's go meet you parents."

I'll say no all the time.

"Eve, I have money. I can give your parents some."

I said no. Because what he was talking about was not just a couple of dollars, he was talking thousands. I didn't want them to be scared. And if things didn't work out between us, I didn't want my parents in danger. I didn't know if he was going to do anything to them the day he would decide to get mad at me. Even though he was fine as hell, he was psychotic, and I could just tell. He went ahead after my refusal and still looked for them and found their address. He showed it to me. He was the kind of person that would pay money to get information out of people. He knew I had the gift of sight from things that would happened that I would tell him about. He told his brothers about me. At first, they were in doubt but later came to believe me and couldn't really make huge moves without consulting me first. It never clicked to me not to use my gift to help drug dealers maneuver their way through the industry. They had a lot of respect for me. He said, "Well, I couldn't be leaving you weeks at a time without money, so please take it." So he started to give me at least two thousand dollars a week. It was a lot of money.

But I couldn't spend it on myself. This one time I remember him giving me 2,000, and his brother also came to see me and give me 1,800 just to say thanks. I didn't know what to do with all that money. So I was like, I am buying a car.

Then the voice said, "I told you not to buy anything for yourself, remember?"

"You know what, you are just in my head, and I can buy me a car if I want to. I am sick of you constantly telling me what I can and cannot do. Nobody hears you anyways."

Then he said, "If you buy a car, you will be doing so in vein." I didn't listen. After Romeo left, I went to this guy I knew, and I bought an Acura Legend, not old or new just perfect, something to get me around instead of getting a ride from people.

As I was giving the money to the guy, there goes the voice again, saying, "This car will not last a week with you, and it will crash beyond repair."

I'm like, *whatever*. You know being really suborned. I didn't listen. So I bought the car. Everyone was happy. The next day, my sister Pasei called to ask me to let her borrow the car. And it was funny because I had just woke up from having a dream that the car crashed. So I told her no. I explained why. She didn't believe me. She said that I was just being selfish and didn't want her to use my car. I said no. That is not true at all. She hung up on me. I was scared to drive the car by the second day, so I parked it.

One of Sam's friend came to the house and told me that my car needed air in the tires and he could hook me up with some rims. He had offered to do that for me. I told him, "Okay, but you must be careful."

Su said, "No, because he was going to steal my car, and I won't see it again." He said that was not true. They all knew my boyfriend to be the biggest drug dealer in Minnesota at the time.

"He will bring the car back, won't you, Tarron?" I asked him

He said, "Sure!" So I let him take it. He took it that night, and a day went by, I didn't see him. Then two days went by, and I didn't see him. I didn't know where he lived.

Su said, "I told you Tarron steals cars all the time. You were stupid to give Tarron your car. You will never see your car again."

"I am not worried about the car as long as he is okay," I said to her.

Then three days went by, and I started to really worry. I didn't tell Romeo. He was out of town anyways. On the fourth day after calling his house at least one hundred times, there was a knock on the door. It was Tarron and his girlfriend. He was on crutches. Both of his legs were in casts. As soon as I had seen him, I was relieved. He was okay. He said, "Your car crashed, and it is beyond repair. I am so sorry, I can't afford to pay for your car, but I will try my best and make a payment to you every month."

I was like, are you kidding me? "You don't have to do any such thing. I am so sorry you got hurt. But I am so glad to see you." I hugged him and told him thanks for getting rid of the car. He was really concerned and was wondering if I was okay.

He said, "I crashed your car, Eve, you are supposed to be mad at me not happy to see me."

"I heard you." He was really glad that I didn't want to press charges. I told the guy that I bought the car from that it crashed; he did not believe it. So Tarron took us to Chaska and showed us exactly where the car crashed. We could see the marks in the snow.

John, the guy I bought the car from, said to Tarron, "Man, you were lucky to still be alive." Then he took us to where the car was towed. It was a big wreck. It was all crushed up like a can. I was even happier to see Tarron alive again at that minute. I told him thanks for saving my life.

When Romeo asked me about the car, I told him that it crashed. I had told him what would happen before it did. So he said, "Oh okay, do you want a new one?"

I said, "No, I will take the cab or call him." He thought I was nice for letting Tarron off the hook. I did not look at it as a hook; I looked at it as Tarron pretty much taking a bullet for me. Because I had disobeyed God by buying the car he allowed the witchcraft of my mother to go into effect. But God was still kind to not allow me to be the driver that particular day.

Su said, "Boy your mommy really wants you dead!" Sad but true.

I called her and asked her, "Why did I see you in my dreams trying to kill me in a car accident and now my car crashed? Are you a witch?"

She said, "No, I am not a witch, just how my hands are pure that is how pure my heart is."

"But why do I keep seeing you in my dreams trying to kill me all the time?"

"It is not me," she said, "It's my enemies in New York. They are using my face to make you turn against me."

So I asked her, "Why would they do that?"

"Because they hate me," she said.

So I said, "So what about the voices that I keep hearing saying to me that you are a witch? Don't forget what took place in my house for me to be homeless in the first place." As I was talking to her, I had a vision that I was in her house, and she touched me. She said that I was exposing her to everyone about her being a witch. Then my spirit left my body, and I fell to the floor and died.

The voice told me if I went there that would be exactly how I was going to die, and the cause of death was going to be unknown. She said, "Come over here so we can talk about it."

I said, "I would like to, but the voice told me not to ever come to your house again, that you are trying to kill me."

She said, "So what if I want to kill you? I am your mother."

"That does not give you the right to kill me," I told her. "I am a child of God." Not even knowing anything about God besides the voices I was hearing. I had heard of the Bible but never read one before. She got mad at me and told me she had to go. She started telling everyone that I was on drugs. Weed and alcohol are not even anything comparing to some real hard drugs out there that I could had gotten involved with. But she had to say that because of the work she had done against me in the realm of the spirit. She was sure that I was going to insane. Little did she know that God had my back. He protected me whether or not I knew his word or his name. He said in the Bible, "My sheep knows my voice," and I knew to trust and follow the voice that I was hearing; it never led me astray. I started having dreams of my sisters getting into car accidents as well. Of course, I did not keep my dreams to myself I told them. I was making them afraid of me not realizing that I was trying to save them. They all got in car accidents within that year. But they all acted like it was not a big deal. As for me, I had to stay away from my mother to protect myself.

One day, Pevu came over to Su's house. He drove his girlfriend's car. He did not come upstairs. He now knew where I was. The next day, he called me. He told me how bad he felt for the way he broke up with me. I was so happy to hear that he stilled cared about me. He had asked me how I felt about him; I told him that I was still in love. He was happy to hear that. He wanted to say bad things about his girlfriend. I told him, "Let's not talk about her." I was only focused on having sex with him one last time so I could completely get over him. But of course, I did not tell him that. He came over on the third day, and we went out in the stairways to talk. I had asked him did he still love me, and he said leaving me was the biggest mistake he ever made. So I asked him did he want to have sex. He said, "Where?"

I said, "Right here."

He said, "In the hall on the stairs?"

I said yes. And we had sex right there in the hallway on the stairs. And that was the end of him. He was happy, but I was relieved. Automatically for me, he was out of my head for good. He thought that he was going to sleep with me over and over again. Nope, I no longer had desires for him. Not even an ounce. Lovely, now that the ball was in my court, the only plan I had for it was to set it on fire and blow the ashes out to sea. I felt a sense of relief after one whole year, and it felt very good, like that; they will never forget you for the rest of their life. They will always think of what an idiot they really were.

One day, Nate came to the apartment saying Hector jumped him to fight on the basketball court. Nate was this guy whom I was dating at the time. Hector, my baby daddy, had just heard about him also going out with me and told him to break up with me. My baby father harassed every guy that I went out with. They all looked at him as a big brother. "Are you intimidated by Hector, Nate?"

He said no, but I felt like he was. Then he showed me marks all on his skin from the fight. "Hector did this to you? Do you want me to talk to him?"

He said no. And so we left it at that. Su saw the amount of traffic in the house and suggested that we moved somewhere bigger. She asked me if I could help her with half of the money. I told her that I would give her the money tomorrow.

She said, "Are you sure?"

I said yes. The next day, I gave her the money needed for us to move. The move was pretty quick. The new landlady moved everything along fast. She wanted the money, and we wanted bigger place. The new house was still in the ghetto not that far from the apartments we were in. I was busy at this time going from place to place with Sam. One day, we were going to the store to buy blunts and some cigarettes. We did not have the weed yet. He walked ahead of me and was almost at the store when I came around the corner and saw him and this guy talking.

All of a sudden, I had seen the guy pull a rifle out of his trunk and pointed it at Sam. I hid myself, but I could still see them. Sam reached in his pockets and gave him something. I knew he had $200 in his pocket that morning. "Great there goes our weed and brew money." But he had this trick where he would empty his pockets and still leave whatever he had there, and you won't know at all. Luckily for us that was what he did to the dude, and the dude thought he wiped him clean. After the dude left, I went up to him and told him how I've seen the whole thing.

He said, "That guy just robbed me."

"Did he take the money?"

He said, "Hell no, I did the trick."

I was like, cool. We turned around and went back home. I guess that is the way sometimes things run down here in the hood. Romeo came back that day, and I told him what happened. He thought that was funny, and then he asked me if Sam was scared. I said, "No, he handled it well."

We stayed together for about two weeks. At first, it was kind of strange to spend so much time with him because he was never around. He had a different place than the last one since I was in St. Paul. This house was over in North Minneapolis. I liked it. It was small and comfortable. He told me as a drug dealer on his level, you couldn't live in the same place too long. You would get caught up by the Feds or other dealers trying to get you. He would always leave around 5:00 every morning and be back before 10:00 in the morning. Then he would either take me somewhere for breakfast or he would make it for me. He was a neat freak. I was too scared to touch anything of his because I was the biggest slob ever. He would ask me, "Why don't you find something to eat while I'm out."

I would tell him that I wasn't hungry, knowing very well that I was starving and just didn't want to mess his house up. He would still make me something to eat anyways. I noticed he started to test me. One day, he went out and left a very huge block of money. When I was on my way to the restroom, I noticed the door opened to the other room. So I decided to take a peek. There was so much money in that room. It was some millions and millions of dollars in cash. I closed the door. When he came home, I asked him why he left all that money in the room like that. He asked me, "Why, were you tempted?"

I told him no. I told him that I was never starved for money, because my daddy had some, and he gave me whatever I wanted. So I don't get tempted by money so easily. And I always felt like I was not of this world, and where I came from, I was filthy rich there. Then he told me of a girl he used to date and how she stole from him.

"Honey, you don't have to worry about stealing with me," I told him. "Eve does not steal, baby." I liked him so much; he was really sexy, even though I knew deep down inside that he was very dangerous. I guess I have gotten used to living dangerously. That's funny.

Even though he was a drug dealer, he was not flamboyant at all. He liked the simple life. He told me he wanted me to meet some of his family members down in California. He bought my ticket, and I went down there for three days. I was treated like a royalty. I was picked up at the airport in a limousine. *This is great*, I thought. He had the driver take me to his family house. It was very beautiful. I had to behave proper because the place looked proper. We had a lot of fun, and I bought a lot of clothes at their malls out there. They said that I looked like a superstar. Everywhere we went, people would ask me, "Are you a celebrity?" I would say no. That is not something to lie about because the celebrities work very hard for every single dime they get. The everyday person does not think how hard those celebrities have to work just to produce the right things for their fans. So I was definitely not going to pretend to be one. But California was where they lived.

The places that I had seen looked spotless and green. Some of the places looked like heaven on earth. I didn't want to leave, but my three days were almost up. I was missing him. I had no idea that he send me down here just so he could follow me and we be in a different environment. I was so happy to see him that evening. I fell more in love with him and knew that he loved giving surprises. I hated surprises, but he didn't care.

That night we went to the reggae club. He didn't like to dance but he liked for me to dance for him. And I didn't mind. I loved dancing for him. Shoot I was so in love that I would had done anything for him. *See this is stupid Eve falling hard in love again because a guy was treating you nice.* I just loved his dangerous lifestyle; it turned me on badly. I remembered having visions of this Jamaican drug dealer that I fell in love with and got married to in Italy. At that time, I didn't know a thing about Italy nor did I know a Jamaican either. We had the most romantic time in California. But come to find out he only came down here to meet me because he was travelling back to Jamaica to handle some issues he had down there. He didn't know how long it was going to take. He always told me what he wanted me to know. He said there was going to come a time where things won't be all nice and lovely, and the less I knew the better it was going to be for me. I never asked him any questions. He was a man who knew how to handle his business so there was no reason for me to be nosy at all.

So I went back to Su's. Su's kids were happy to see me. They were so cute and full of energy. Being around them was a lot of fun. I had brought a lot of clothes for my sisters but I had them sent to the apartment Romeo was renting for me. He really wants me to move out and go live in the apartment, but I feel bad because I didn't want to leave Su and the kids. I felt that they needed me, and if I left, things were going to get tough for them. So I felt sad about leaving. That was what made me stay around.

Su had no idea that Romeo was renting me a fancy apartment in some nice neighborhood neither did she know about the amounts of money I was coming in contact with. The reason for that is what God had said, regarding me having to blend in so I could learn the ways of his people. He needed me to see people for who they really were, not for what I could do for them. I was very careful with that especially after my car crashed. While Romeo was away, I found means of keeping myself busy with Nate. This is really sad to think back and know that I had never been faithful in a relationship before. But anyways, c'est la vie.

CHAPTER SIX

MEETING MY HUBBY

While Romeo was away one day, a friend of my brother came to visit, and that visit changed everything. On this day, I did not know I was about to meet my future husband. I was home with Su chilling when the doorbell rang. My brother came in with a friend. When his friend and I had our eyes meet, right away it was love at first sight. My heart started pounding. There was something about this guy. I had to pretend I did not feel anything. They were only there for a brief moment. Then they left. I started asking myself, "Wow, what just happened?" This has never happened to me before. When they left, I felt like this guy took half of me with him. I couldn't wait for him to come back. Luckily for me, a couple of hours later as I was talking to Su, they came back. They went to get some drinks and smokes. I was so nervous and shy; I think he could tell that I liked him. Su told me that he couldn't take his eyes off me. I asked her, "Seriously?" That made me happy. We all went into the bathroom to smoke. After smoking, everybody left the bathroom, except for him. He stayed in the bathroom with me.

Then he asked me, "Are you Eve Dells?"

I said yes.

But I was wondering, *how did he know my name?*

He's said, "I have been looking for you. Do you recognize me?" he asked.

I said, "No, should I?" Then he told me where I previously lived and how he had been to my house before. I couldn't remember him. He told me, "Remember when you were going out with Persevu?"

I said yes!

He said, "Well, Persevu and I have mutual friends. I came to your house with some of our friends." Then he said something else again. He said, "Remember in 1997 on the soccer field in Brooklyn Park on July 26, a car almost hit you?"

I said yes.

"And you put your hand on your hip and said to the driver, 'See all of this pointing at your butt? If you hit me, your car would be ruined, and nothing will happen to me, so you better stop and let me go.'" I started to laugh. He told me he was a passenger in that car.

He said, "I came to Minnesota in search of you." And we were interrupted. Oh crap! My brother wanted them to go to the club. I didn't want to go. My brother didn't want me to go either; he just wanted to hang out with his friend, the love of my life, little did any of us know. I stayed home. Su went to bed and left me up. There was a knock on the door. I answered it. It was another friend of my brother named John Dells. "Uh-oh…"

John came to chill with my brother. I told him that my brother was not home. Instead of leaving, he decided to chill with me. John had a crush on me for a very long time. So I guess he looked at this as an opportunity to get to know me a little better.

I was sleeping on the floor in the living room, and he decided to lie down next to me. This was fine with me because John was very cute. So I did not mind hearing what he had to say. I knew I was not attracted to him. He got to the talking and telling me how interested in me he was. I was listening to everything he was saying, but my mind was on Chase, who by now is probably being hit on by other girls in the club. But I listened to John anyways. I think he could tell that I was bored. All I remember him saying was if I married him, I wouldn't have to change my last name because it was the same as his. Then I fell asleep. And I guess he stopped talking and lay there for hours. I heard some talking outside the house that woke me up. It was my brother and

Chase. I heard a key in the door and John and I both pretended to be sleeping.

When they walked in, Chase came right away and knee down next to me. I thought that was very brave. He started talking to me and asked me how I was doing, telling me what happened at the club. He continued where he left off from the conversation in the bathroom. He was on his knees for hours just talking to me all night long. I knew John was not sleeping, and I could tell he wasn't comfortable, but he never said a word. and Chase was not talking to him either. He was just whispering directly into my ear. A couple of hours later, my brother woke up to use the restroom, and Chase was still on his knees. My brother told him, "Man, you have some strong knees to be talking to her for so long." Chase just laughed and continued putting sweet everything in my ears. At this time, I had forgotten that I had a boyfriend, a could-be-dangerous drug dealer boyfriend.

Chase talked to me until morning. I was very wowed by this young man. He had me from hello. We hung out all day that day. My brother was off work. But what I noticed was he had a girlfriend, and she kept calling to talk to him. Oh and let's not forget a baby mama who was also calling him about some drama. I caught myself having an attitude. And he noticed. He started telling them, "Let me call you back." He stayed over at our house for two days. He said he had to go home and change his clothes. I told him I was going with him. I was attached to him already. After he changed his clothes at his house, we hung out a little bit. Then he said, "I have to go home now.

So I said, "No, my home is your home." I looked him in the eyes and boldly told him he was never leaving my sight again. As if we had been lovers in a previous life, it was very bizarre, but then again, my whole life is bizarre.

What am I doing? You probably wondered. I was in love. "You are staying with friends anyways. Stay with me at my brother's house. I will sleep in my room, and you can sleep in the living room on the couch." I could already tell that he was such a gentleman. The only pass he made at me was talking. He totally agreed.

It has been almost a week and I have run out of money. We didn't have anything to smoke or drink. I told my brother and Chase that I can get us money. I had told Chase about Romeo days ago. My brother asked me, "Is not Romeo out of town?"

I said, "Yes. But I can get us money from somewhere else." He and my brother bet me that I couldn't come up with any money. I said, "Watch and learn, gentlemen."

I need a toothpick. They got me a toothpick looking at me in awe as to why I requested a toothpick; I put it in my nose and gently started moving it around. I started to sneeze real badly. I did this for about three minutes. By the time I got done, my voice came from sweet and soft to that of someone who had a severe cold. I called up this guy, who could not even recognize my voice, and I told him, "It's Eve, and I am really sick." I told him that I was trying to get this car so I would be able to get to work but I needed money to add to it. He said, "But I thought you and I would go on a date and get to know each other a little more."

I told him, "You think I care for dating you if I can't even get to work?"

He asked me, "Well how much do you need?"

I told him I needed $700. "Today, like right now."

He said, "But I live an hour away from where you said you live." So I told him that this was a test to see if he will even be able to support me financially. I wanted to know if it was even worth going on a date with him. He said, "I will be right over. What is your address?"

My brother and Chase said, "He's not going to show up."

I said, "Yes, he will. And if he doesn't come, I'll just call somebody else. But let's give him one hour. Start timing him, gentlemen." Within forty-five minutes, he was calling me from his cell phone. I went outside to meet him. I made sure that I was looking jacked up.

He said, "Boy, you really look sick." He said, "You don't look like you want to eat anything."

I said, "No, I'm very sick."

He said, "Well, I will also give you lunch money then since you can't come to lunch with me." He gave me $750. I told him I will call when I felt better. And I never did call him back.

I took the money and gave it to my brother and Chase. They learned a lesson that day. Some women will dig for gold if they knew where it was and lie to get what they wanted. We had enough to drink and smoke until Romeo came back to give me more money. But doing all this time that I was coming across money like this, I still was not allowed by God to buy myself anything of value. And after what happened with my car, I was too scared to even attempt. So I had no clothes but rags.

Some people are so mean to you if you don't look like you have anything to offer them. They will just judge you by your looks rather than your character. I had to sit there and listen to people talk crap to me that wouldn't have even had the guts to have said anything to me before. I kept asking God, "Why are you are allowing this to happen to me?"

All I would hear was, "You need to be patient." Well, I did just that. My time was occupied by Chase. Some days it really was not that bad. He and I had so much in common until the days flew by when we were high of Mary J. But now, I could see that we needed a place to stay.

He couldn't live with me at the apartment Romeo was renting for me. I could not take him there, and I did not want to have sex in my brother's house, so I had to move. I called my sister Pasadena and told her I had a boyfriend that I was in love with and I needed a place to stay with him. She told me it was okay to stay with her. So we moved there. I threw everything away before moving to Pasadena's house. I wanted to start fresh. Chase and I bought one comforter that we slept on and covered with. Thank God he was skinny. He asked me why I didn't want to move to the apartment my boyfriend was renting for me, and I told him.

While Romeo was away one day, I decided to go to the apartment just to be by myself. As I was in there, I heard the key in the door, and I thought maybe it was the maintenance man because Romeo did not have a key to the door. When I looked, it was his brother. I asked, "What are you doing here, and how did you know where I live, and how did you get my key?"

He said Romeo told him where I lived, so if anything, he would watch out for me.

"Okay, so how did you get my keys, not even Romeo has it?"

He said he paid the maintenance man $2,500 to get him a set of keys. He had a stupid, mischievous grin on his face, and I could tell he was up to no good. He started coming closer and closer and telling me that Romeo thought highly of me, so he was going to get in my pants to find out why Romeo felt the way he did.

I started moving backward until my back hit the stove and I couldn't go any farther. He came toward me and grabbed me really tight. He tried to kiss me and started pulling my clothes off. I was so mad, and we started fighting, and I kicked him in the balls and punched him in the face. I told him, "No wonder you have always gave me the creeps. You want to be gangster. I'll show you, gangster fucker. You have fucked with the wrong bitch," and I grabbed the knife to gut him, and he surrendered and walked backward out the door. I told him the next time he wouldn't be so lucky. And he could tell I meant every word. I have been raped over and over until it's just had become normal for me. I least I know how to defend myself now. Chase was like wow you are gangster. That's what I talking about. So baby I don't feel like killing anyone that's why I don't go to the apartment and Su needs me here to help her out with the kids. Not long after the incident, Romeo came and asked me to come and see him.

I told Chase that I had to go because Romeo was in town. I could tell that he was sad. I told him Romeo was not the kind of person that took no for an answer. If I don't go, he would come, and it will be bad. I made sure he had his drinks and smokes and told him I loved him and I would see him soon. I was very nice to Romeo because I wanted to get in the game real bad, and then I wanted him to pay my way to go attend fashion design school in Italy. I hadn't told him about the Italy part yet. Romeo had sent a cab to get me from my sister's house. I was so happy to see him after sitting in the stupid cab for one freaking hour. He took me out to eat and when we got home he had a big fat blunt rolled up for us to smoke. But I felt like the number 1 rule in the drug game was never get high on your own supply. I felt as if he was testing me. I said I did not want to smoke. Even though I was getting high the whole time, he was gone with my brother and Chase. I wanted him to let me in the game.

I was determined to do what he did, not so much for the money but for the thrill. He asked me why I moved to my sister's house when he was renting the apartment for me to be in. I told him what happened between me and one of his brothers. He believed me and told me he would take care of it. As we were hanging out, I realized that I was missing Chase, but I was having a good time with Romeo. Being with Romeo, I was not the one to make any calls; he had the money, cars, and goods. Being with Chase, I had to think of ways of getting what we needed because he had just moved to Minnesota and was not yet working. I told Romeo that I was bored and needed to do something fun. So he asked me, "Do you want to take a couple of days and go to California to spend some time with my family?" I said sure though I was just there a few months earlier. He said, "Well, you can leave tomorrow when we wake up."

Oh crap, I thought to myself. *Maybe I should not have said that I was bored.*

That's a short notice I said to him. He said, "Do you have somebody else to report to besides me?"

I said, "No, of course not." I was thinking about Chase. *Oh my gosh, he will be so lonely. He didn't even know Minnesota. What would he do with himself?*

Romeo asked me, "What's on your mind, baby? You look like you are thinking hard.

I said, "No, I was just thinking I need to let my sister know."

"Do you need to feed her too? Is she a baby? Call her when you get there. You know I always tell you not to tell anyone when you are travelling." Romeo had a way of looking at you like "don't be that stupid and do what I say" in so many words. Next day I was on the flight to see his family. When I got to LAX, there was a limo waiting for me, and the driver came out with a dozen roses. Romeo made sure that I arrived and was greeted in style as usual. The limo took me to his family house. They were all very happy to see me again.

Two days later, a cousin of Romeo's tried to set me up. He brought some other guys and bought some champagne and told me to drink with them. I told him I don't drink. One of the guys came on to me, and I told him I had a boyfriend. Romeo's cousin was just watching to see if I would take the bait. I thought to myself, *Look at this dip shit*, looking at Romeo's cousin. I was not interested. This went on for a while until I got upset and told him that I was feeling disrespected, and I was going to tell Romeo what happened. I guess they thought because I was a pretty girl I had to be a gold digger. I would had probably dug all the gold out of Romeo's pockets if God didn't tell me that I was not allowed to buy myself anything fancy. The cousin told me that Romeo had a lot of respect for me, and he just wanted to know why, but now he knows.

Then he said, "Well, you brought my bag, and everything in it is correct."

I told him, "I am not a thief."

He asked me, "Do you know exactly how much you brought?"
"Yes, a lot."

He said, "But you did not take a penny of it." I told him that it was not mine. He looked like he had just gained some respect for me.

He asked me, "So I hear that you have premonitions and have been helping us escape some problems."

I said, "I just say what I see."

"You have been doing some good for us, so I would like to repay you." He took some money out of his pocket and started counting hundreds of dollars, and I stopped him and told him I don't take money for my gift because I didn't buy it. He looked at me and smile, and from then on, we became buddies. Romeo came to meet me a few days later and took me shopping, and then he told me how everything that happened was a set up to see if I would fall for it. I just told him to grow up and stop being a fool.

Though I was afraid of this man, I told him whatever came to my mind. And he loved it. I believed that turned him on about me because no one talked to him the way I did. Tell him like it is. Don't get me wrong I respected him very much. When I was a kid my dad always told me that no man has a mouth big enough to swallow you whole, so say the truth of what was on my mind at all times. And I have been doing that since then. Romeo took me around California, and we had a lot of fun. I haven't spoken to Chase in one week. I told Romeo I wanted to go back to Minnesota. "Do you want to go back tonight or do you want to go tomorrow?" I told him I would spend the night with him and leave in the morning. He never purchases any tickets beforehand. He would always buy it on the spot and leave right away. He told me he was going to stay in California for a few more days; he had to take care of some stuff. I told him okay.

The next day, I was at the airport, and my flight was running late. I went to find me some food when I met the lady from the show *227* (Sandra); her flight was also running late. I told her I admired her work, and she and I started talking. We went and bought our food together, and she asked me to come and sit with her. She introduced her husband to me. She was really nice unlike some other celebrities who you hear about being snotty.

When I finally got home, Chase was so happy to see me. I thought he was going to be mad. My sister was mad. She said I was being bad, and I needed to pick Chase and dumb Romeo because he was not good for me. Little did I know Romeo did not stay in California; he came back to Minnesota that very day.

Later, Romeo called me and told me he was outside, and he was on his way up to the apartment. "Oh shit, you have got to get out of here, Chase, leave now, go." I was not afraid for myself but for Chase because I knew Romeo would have him killed. I pushed him out the door after looking through the window and seeing that Romeo was still in the car. After Chase left, Romeo was knocking on the door. When he got in the apartment, he went to the window to look outside as if he suspected something. I didn't follow him. He said, "Come here. Who is that guy in the parking lot?" He was pointing at Chase.

I told him, "I see him around here with some other people that I know, but I don't know him."

He asked me, "Are you sure?"

I said yes. So he told me he was bored and was missing me. That was the reason he came back. Then I braided his hair, and he asked me to spend the night with him. He was purposely doing this to see if I would say no. I told him, "Sure, let me grab a few things." I went with him leaving a brokenhearted Chase behind, whom I did not tell that I was not coming home tonight.

What was a girl to do? My sister was so mad at me before she left. Romeo and I left also. The next day, I came back home late in the afternoon. I felt like crab. I didn't know how much longer I was going to carry on like this. Both the guys treated me like a queen. The only difference was one was rich and the other was poor. Being so confused, I called my mother and told her my dilemma, and she said choose the rich one. "If you choose the poor guy, you would always be poor, but if you stay with the rich one, you would have the best thing among your friends." Right away, I decided to stay with Chase, the poor guy, and not Romeo, the rich guy. I did not trust my mother for anything at this point. I couldn't go to my father with this because after my break up with Jeff I told my dad the next guy I introduced to him was the guy I was going to marry and stay with for the rest of my life.

Mom told me, "Your father wanted to talk to you about your son." I said okay. Daddy got on the phone and told me that my sister Anastasia wanted me to give her full custody of my son.

I said, "What did you just say, Daddy? Is she nuts? I am not going to give her full custody of my only child. You know how much she hates me. Why would I do that?"

He said, "Well, she said if you say no, than she will drive from Oklahoma and bring him back to you." I told my dad that was just fine with me. I will take him. I told him if I give her custody, she would use the child to make me miserable. And she would make sure he did not know me. I could not take that risk. My dad was the coolest dad ever. He was the only one in the family that told me positive things about myself. My mother and I never talked. She was always giving me strange looks as if there was something about me that scared her. Besides, Anastasia just took the boy some months ago only until I can get on my feet. That was not happening, I said to Daddy. Mom didn't say anything to me about this. Anastasia, I believe, is my mother's first and favorite child. Even though I loved my mother, but she and I were never close because of the vibes that I got from her. There was something sinister about Mom.

I did not hug her as much as I hugged my father because she was always surrounded by this dark cloud. Whenever I got closed to her, all the hair on the back of my neck would stand up. She too was nice to me and did whatever I wanted her to because of my dad. He would always say, "You know she is the most loving one we have." So anyways, I decided to do just the opposite of what Mom said. My dad told me he would inform my sister of my decision. I know when my sister took my son, she was trying to help, but there was no trust between us. So making that decision was not hard for me at all.

When I came back from Romeo's the next day, I went looking for Chase to his friend's house, and I found him. I asked him to come with me, and he did without fussing with me. Later that evening, he told me that all his friends were telling him to move on and find someone else. As jealous as I was at that time, I got mad and started to argue with him, and for the first time, he started screaming at me. Little did I know, Romeo came to the apartment that night and heard us from the door. He heard Chase and me arguing. He did not knock on the door but left a gold bullet from his gold gun that he always had with him. I was so mad and was about to leave the apartment when I had seen it lying there. I looked around, and there was no sign of him.

So I got back in the apartment, and I called him. I asked him why he would leave a bullet at my sister's door. He said, "Did you do anything to that would make me do that?" I just told him I was going to deal with him later. He loved me because I used to stand up to him unlike other people who just give him what he wanted when he wanted it. I hung up on him.

I told Chase, "Look, hear is the deal. I don't want to argue with you. I love you, and I also love Romeo."

He said, "You can't love two people at the same time, that's impossible."

"Whatever," I told him. "It's my heart, and I can do what I want with it." I told him that I was breaking up with him because my son is coming to live with me.

He said, "You don't have to break up with me for that. Looking at you, I bet you don't even know how to take care of a child." He said, "I can help, Eve, I know how to take good care of children.

I will be here for you 110 percent." I told him how scared I was. He was really supportive and made all my worries go away. So we worked out our problems.

I decided to call Romeo and tell him the same thing. He asked me, "Why are you always breaking up with me?"

I asked him, "What the one time you screwed my friend because she was trying to get back at me for fucking her man, that time when I broke up with you? You lucky I even took you back."

"Well, I don't know what to do to make you happy. You don't want my money, and I have to travel all the time so I can't spend that much time with you." I told him I did not want my son growing up around what he did even though I wanted to be in the game. But now that my son was coming back to me, everything had to change.

I went out and got a job, and Romeo who was now my friend asked me why was I working. I did not need to work; he would take care of me. I told him, "I can take care of myself. Thank you very much." He asked me to stop by the apartment he was renting for me so he could see me. He said since I did not want to live there anymore, he was going to stay there until the lease expired. I told him, "That's good." So I stopped there after work, and we talked. He was very much still in love with me.

"Not happening," I told him. Then I asked him, "Can I have ten thousand dollars?"

His whole face lit up, and he grabbed a box with five thousand dollars and said, "I only have five thousand right now. Come for the rest tomorrow."

So I asked him, "Why are you in a rush to give me ten thousand dollars?

He said, "Because we had been dating for two years, and you never asked me for anything before."

I told him, "I was just kidding. I didn't want the money." And I was testing him to hear what he would say. He looked so disappointed and sad. I kind of felt bad. I left after giving him the last time sex. Chase and I got our own place later that month. My son finally came, and Chase and I took him shopping.

I told him to call Chase daddy. He said, "I don't know him."

I told him, "Well, I'm going to marry him, so he will be in our lives."

Chase calmly told him, "You don't have to call me daddy. Call me Chase." He has been called daddy for almost twelve years now and counting.

After we moved, a week later Romeo's brother decided to take revenge and set him up, and he was arrested and sentenced to jail for ten years. He called me when he noticed the agents, but I did not hear my phone ringing because I was sleeping. I was sad; he was really nice to me. I had to go to my apartment and collect all his stuff. The brother paid the balance on the apartment. I went to the police station and asked them if I was in any trouble, and they told me that they had been watching him, and I had nothing to do with it. I told Romeo that he was being watched, and he said he had everything under control. One year later, his brother who betrayed him got caught and was sentence to twenty years. He too was set up by another relative of theirs. Funny how life goes, right?

Now Chase was at peace and said that he and I were soul mate. And we need to get our lives started.

We were both very much in love and didn't have any close friends. All the time, we had been with each other. But when a man has children before meeting another woman, it is always a challenge. The only problem that I started to encounter with him now that he was working was he and the baby mama drama. Oh my gosh! Whenever she called, he would sit there and talk to her for hours. If she even called during sex, he would stop and talk to her. Then he would want to continue where we left off. I had been patient for a while with this crap. But enough was enough.

One day, he was on the phone with her for three hours, and I just lost it and started screaming and cursing at him at the top of my lungs. "What is there so much to talk about two babies that you both has to be on the phone for hours every day?" I took the phone from him, and I asked her, "Girl, before I started to date Chase, did I not ask you if you were still in love with him and wanted him back?"

She said yes.

"Have you changed your mind because you did say you did not want him back?" He took the phone from me and told her he would call her back. When he got off the phone, he started yelling and telling me that I will not come between him and his baby mama. He would talk to her as long as he wanted to every day if he had to.

I told him, "If that be the case, get out of my life." I said to him since the apartment was in his name I would move out at the end of the month. No-nonsense kind of a woman I am not.

Did I have anywhere to go at the time? No, but I knew God would provide like he always did. We had it out. Later that day, he decided to apologize to me, and we were all good again. I was always busy working twelve- to fifteen-hour shifts at my job. So I was never home. While I'm at work, he and all his boys would be in the apartment drinking and smoking. By the time I came home, he would clean up, and there would be no evidence of this. I called his baby mom from work one day and asked her does he call her when I was not home. She said yes and told me all the things he would tell her. She knew everything about me that he knew. I was so hurt and felt like I had made a mistake leaving Romeo, but I would have probably been in jail too. What do I do now?

"Just pray" was the only thing I could think of. How can he still have feelings for this girl when he claimed she almost killed him several times? I came home from work in the mist of my problems and decided to take a shower. He told me he was leaving to visit with some friends. So I locked the door after him and jumped in the shower. I heard the voice tell me that he was back in the house, and he was hiding, and I would look for him but will not find him. So I got out the shower with soap all over me, and I searched the one bed room apartment all over. He was not there. I did not see him. So I went back in the shower, and the voice told me that he was still in the apartment. I thought, *Houdini was dead, what the hell.*

He was going to sneak out and try to scare me, but no matter what, I should not scream or I would lose my voice forever and not be able to explain my life story the way I was supposed to when the book is written. The voice also said that he was sent in my life to keep me drinking and smoking and slow me down from doing what I am supposed to do. After bathing, I decided to lay down for a nap. Just when I was getting sleepy, I saw him creeping, and *boom*, he tried to scare me just like the voice said, and I just put my hand to my mouth so tight I did not make a sound. I told him, "I knew you were here."

He said, "I just wanted to know if I could scare you."

I told him, "Good luck with that." He left, and I remember telling God thank you so much. He does not even know his purpose in my life, not knowing he was put in my life for a purpose.

"But what the devil means to harm you, I will also use for your good. The devil will use the ones closest to you to try and destroy you. Be strong. I am here. You need to write this book and tell the whole world what I have done in your life. They must know that I am alive and well and I am a God who hears and answer prayers."

What is going on with me? I thought. *I can't even tell anyone what's happening. They won't believe me, my Lord. Let alone, how am I supposed to write a book?*

I had my son, a job, a relationship, and then the supernatural to focus on. If it was not for the voice that kept telling me things before they happened, I would have lost my freaking mind. So I had to isolate myself completely from everyone I knew to be able to deal with this issue. People have all kinds of different spirits operating in them, and they don't even know it. If you are spiritually sensitive like me, the evil spirits would know this and just start attacking you. What I did not know was Satan had put a hit on my life before I was even conceived. "When she gets out, she belongs to me." And my life has been in danger since then. My mother made this deal with Lucifer after she and my father separated for twenty some odd years before having me. As the story went, her parents desperately needed her to be with my father. They told her they would disown her if she did not get back with my father. My grandparents believed in using witchcraft to get what they wanted from a person no matter how they felt so I heard. They were both dead before I was born. So my grandmother and grandfather who were very big time witches did all in their powers to get my mother and father back together.

Meanwhile on the other side of town, my stepmother whom my father separated from abruptly after having five children for him was praying desperately. She had just had my sister Cellia after being pregnant for thirteen months. She had to get out of the same area as my mother so she would be able to give birth to Cellia. Her womb was sealed spiritually so she won't give birth until it cause death for both she and the child. So I am sure you do understand her frustration. That is why she prayed the vigorous prayer. Her prayers went as follows, "Father, please let this wicked, wicked, wicked woman have a child that would be like you, who will expose her for who she really is. Please allow this child to tell the whole world how wicked this woman really is so they can know." Well, I guess in order for me to know just how wicked she was I had to see firsthand for myself, right? After all, she's my mother. How hard was that going to be, trying to convince me of anything about her otherwise? Everything I have been through it's only so God can use me as an example of what he can do in a person's life. He knows I will follow his orders and deliver the message to you just like it happened.

One day, Mom said she was going to Africa and needed money. I had one thousand dollars and decided to help her. That was a major, stupid mistake. As I was giving her the money the voice told me not to give it to her. "She is going to use that money to put a disease on you, and the doctors will tell you they don't have a cure."

I said, "Whatever. I am always hearing you, but I can't see you. What's up with that anyways? You would think that I would be so mindful of what has been happening to me, right?" Wrong, I wasn't, stupid me. One day when I went to see my mother, she told me that I was too beautiful and something needed to be done about my beauty. I just laughed and thought nothing of it. She on the other hand was very serious, and I was about to find out just how serious she was. She left for Africa and was gone for some months. By the time she came back from Africa, my face was ruined. My cheeks, one of my favorite parts of my body have never looked the same since then. The doctors told me that I had discord lupus, and there was no cure for it. That was my last straw with her. I had enough. My mom and dad meant a lot to me; this was when I said enough is enough. If I had $1,000, I would make sure I give them $500 of it, all the time. I had never given her a penny since then. My siblings get upset about this, but if they went through what I had to go through with Mom, they might understand a little better. Anyways, let's move on to the next episode.

Chase wanted to see his daughter for her birthday, so we put money together, and he took the bus to New Jersey. He assured me that he was not going to stay with his baby mama. She would kill him, he said. So I believed him. *Oh, what an idiot I was.* When he got on the bus, I kept calling him; he refused to pick up his phone. So I called his baby mama to ask her if she heard from him. She said yes she did and that she had been talking to him throughout his trip. She told me, "You know he is stopping here with me, right?

I said, "Really?"

She said, "I told you he was a liar." I wanted to be done with him at that moment, and I told God this is the man that I took all that beating from Persevu for? When you told me to be patient that you were going to send me someone that I would love whom I would need? What do I need him for? He is not worth it. Is this the man I fasted for three days? I don't want to be with him anymore. I heard the voice tell me, "No, be patient."

"Patience for what? Don't you see my heart is broken?"

"Now is not the time, wait," said the voice. I was mad at the voice but not for long because it had never led me astray. Thank God. These were the days that God was teaching me simple obedience. As you can see here, my head seems to be a little harder than a coconut, so God had to really work harder on me. Thank God. I'm laughing as I am thinking only he can accomplish such a task.

So I decided my son and I will go about our normal business. I would call Chase, and he sounded funny as if he did not really want to talk to me. So I stopped calling until he called; then I would talk to him. Chase is very easygoing, soft-spoken, and sometimes shy. So I felt as if her presence was intimidating him. I did not want to make him uncomfortable even though he lied to me. He stayed with her those two weeks he was gone, and I really missed him. I just kept myself busy by working and chilling with Su. I lost seventeen pounds in those two weeks because I refuse to eat, plus I had no appetite. I get very emotional when the people I love do such hurtful things just like anyone else. I am only human, you know.

Two weeks later, Chase came back. It was three weeks before Christmas. We worked out our problems and moved on. His baby mom called me at work one day after the incident and told me he was going to spend Christmas with them. I told her she was joking because he just left from there. She asked me did I know that. I said no. She told me that was his plan. I wanted not to believe her, but we had this weird connection. She told me all about him. By her doing so, it helped to know better who I was lying in bed with. It was really painful at times. I guess I tolerated his behavior because when I looked around me, all I saw was fake people. I was lonely, very lonely not for a lover but for someone I could count on. I was really attached to Chase and have been since the first day we met.

One week later, this girl we knew told me that Chase went to her house every day to call his baby mom. When I got home from work, I called the baby mom and asked her right in his presence, and she said yes this was true. He had just told me no before I called her. "Liar!" I screamed out. I slammed the phone on his head and went in the kitchen to look for a knife. He ran in the bathroom, locked the doors, and called 911. The police came, and he came out the bathroom. There was a jug of oil sitting on the counter, and I tried to reach for it to spill it on him. The cop grabbed me and slammed me into the wall. So I punched him in the face. They knocked me down to the floor while macing me at the same time. I scratched them really bad. They cuffed me. Chase was going to take care of my son, but I told him no. I told the cops to call Su to get my son.

I sent my son to Su's house. On my way to jail, I told the cop that he was going to die in a nasty car accident and his family was not going to have him around anymore. I was so angry and hurt at the betrayal.

What I did not know was he took me seriously. Later on after they booked me and everything, he came looking for me and asked me to rebuke what I had told him earlier. I asked him why should I. He treated me badly, he said, and that he was sorry for that. And he looked sincere about his apology. So I spoke life into his life and took back what I said. And I told him, "Rest assured nothing will happen to you." He must have been sensitive to the spirit. Whenever I say something, it happens. That was one of my big reasons of not getting into confrontation with people.

Don't want to say the wrong thing in the heat of the moment. I remember one time my sister Cellia called me, crying about how her husband stole her money out of her bank account bought the exact car she had been saving up for.

I told her, "Don't cry. Let him go. Within three months, he will get in a car accident, and he would be lucky to get out with his life. He is going to call you from the hospital to come see him. No matter what, you do don't go there, or you will also get in a nasty car accident as well. Let him be with all his bad luck. He has mistreated you enough." She asked me how I knew. I said, "Because he hurt your feelings, and you are my sister. I believe it was a month later she called me screaming how he got in a car accident and totaled the car. She sad he asked her to come to the hospital and she said no. I know I have a gift, but I only use it against evil. I believe everyone in this world should be treated fairly. I know I sound really naïve, but this is my belief. Oh by the way, I never used my gift for myself. Back to me and Chase situation.

I was in jail for four days, and this cop kept checking on me to make sure I was okay. I told him I was not a bad person, but the man had wronged me severely. He totally agreed with me. But he told me fighting was not going to resolve anything. I told him he was right. After I was released, I went home and told Chase that I was not going to bother him and his baby mama anymore. He was too drunk, so I couldn't even talk to him, so I left him alone to sleep it off. The next day, he was afraid to talk to me. I talked to him and told him, "I am not mad anymore. You did what you had to do. And I am glad you ran in the bathroom and called the cops. You saved me from going to prison for life. My temper would get me in serious trouble one of these days." Anyways, we worked on our problems and moved on. Just when I thought everything was okay, *bang*, he dealt my heart another blow. Two weeks after the cop incident, Chase did me wrong again. I find that as I am writing this now, the devil wants me to get angry with him all over again. "Satan, my Lord Jesus Christ rebukes you. Get thee behind me. The past is the past. Let it stay there. I have to live in the present where I'm at. Here we go!"

I came from work one day, and I decided to take a shower before napping. Before I went in the shower, he looked me in the eyes and told me, "You know I will always love you, right?" Don't you know while I was in the shower Chase had his things packed and ran away from me to go be with his baby mama on the East Coast again? That boy was quick. I did not know that he moved out. After I came out of the shower, I went to take a nap. I thought he went out to hang with his buddies. Oh no, that was not the case. Six hours later, my phone ranged, and it was Su. She said, "Eve, you sleep, girl? Do you know that Chase ran away from you and moved back to Jersey?" I asked her what she was talking about. She said, "Go and check his closet."

When I got to his closet, there was nothing in there. All I felt at that moment was a piece of glass shredding my heart into pieces. I could feel every little tear in my heart. I asked, "Well, where is my son and my car?" She told me my son was with her; someone we considered family had just dropped him off. And she said they were on their way to bring me my car. She thought it was a good idea when I found out for him not to be there. "Thank you," I said with the words barely coming out. Hurt was not enough to describe the pain I felt. My car came, and I just told the person thank you. And I took my keys right before I could close the door behind me. I was devastated.

I couldn't breathe. I was suffocating, and the apartment had gotten too small to stay in. I had to get out. I was so confused of how will he be so nice to me and do this? This man cleans, cooks, makes me bubble baths, massages me, and all that. With him by my side, I felt so complete. I have not done my laundry not once since I met him. We both have birthmarks under our feet. I was in love with him, and I thought he loved me too. With all this going through my head, I decided to go and buy some marijuana to smoke to see if that would help ease the pain or at least put me to sleep. I couldn't stop crying. To me, my whole world had just turned upside down. The last time I cried this hard was when my son Elijah died.

As soon as I got out of the apartment, there was a man standing right to the door. He was very tall. I asked him with tears in my eyes, "Can I help you?" while wiping my nose with the back of my hand.

He said, "I am here to help you, my name is Tray."

"Help me, who are you?"

He said, "I am your guardian angel."

"Really? And I am the queen of Sheba."

He said, "It's okay you don't believe me, but God had heard your cry and sent me to console you." There was a presence of calmness about him, but at this moment I did not really stop to think of anything but Chase." He said, "You were going somewhere?" I said yes and closed the door behind me and locked it. He walked with me. This man and I went on the stairs in the hallway and he talked to me and seriously consoled me. He was so peaceful and calm and very knowledgeable. He talked to me for what seems to be like hours. Then he told me that I should go back inside and get some sleep everything was going to be ok. I was in some sort of a euphoria. I had totally forgotten that I was getting out to buy weed to smoke. He walked with me back to my apartment door but did not come in. Before he left I asked him again who he said he was. He said, "Tray, your Guardian Angel." I told him yeah you said that already, whatever, can I get your number? He said he did not have a number. I looked at him and told him dude everybody has a number. So he said, "You're right, here is a number you can reach me at." He was smiling the whole time. I said good night and went in. When I got in I called the number to say thank you and all I heard was the operator saying, "The number was not in service check the number and call again."

I thought to myself, *Maybe he thought I was hitting on him so he gave me the wrong number.* I slept like a baby until 5:00 a.m. I woke up with extremely sharp abdominal pains. I was puking and having diarrhea all at once in the bathroom. I thought I was going to die. I remembered Chase had just left me yesterday. As much as I was in pain, I called his baby mama and asked her if he was there? She said, "Yes, hold on." One second later, he was on the phone. I knew right away they were having sex when my call came in. I told him if this was what he wanted; I will not bother him at all. This was my first time talking to him since he ran away from me. I told him I will not call over there anymore to disturb him. He said ok and that was it. I hung up.

This man and I were about to move to our new apartment in less than a week. "Nope." He decided to run away from me two days before Christmas and leave my heart in pieces. This was going to be my son first Christmas with me in my house. I had one hundred dollars saved under the mattress at the new apartment. I decided to go there and get it so I could buy his present. When I got there the money was gone. I flipped the mattress upside down to make sure. Only Chase knew where that money was. So I went back to the old apartment. I called him and asked him why he took the money? He said he needed it to buy his kids presents for Christmas. I told him but it was mine, not yours, he didn't say anything. I hung up on him. God, why are you allowing these things happened to me? What did I ever do so wrong that I have to feel this kind of pain?

In tears I called my dad and told him Chase had left me and he was not coming back. I did not tell him about the money because that was too embarrassing. My dad told me stop crying Chupee the young man will return he loves you very much. He will come back, be patient with so much confidence in his voice. I told him I had to go. I was in pain again my heart was falling out of my chest. I decided to get out the house to get fresh air. When I opened the door, guess who was standing right there waiting for me again. "Tray"! He said "you called "? I came because I heard you calling." I asked him who did you say you were again? He said "I am your Guardian Angel." I said yeah, about that. If you are my Guardian Angel what is hurting my feelings right at this present moment? He reached in his pocket and pulled out a $100 dollar bill and gives it to me.

"He said, "This is why you are crying right now?"

"I am impressed," I told him.

He said, "Come take a ride with me I have to show you something." He had an out of this world presence about him that when he was around I forgot my heart had just been shattered. He took me in all these places in Minnesota that I had never seen before. It looked like heaven and he told me that I was not going to be able to find these places on my own. Thinking about it now it was not Minnesota, was it? He had told me how I was chosen to do many things for God and that I was going to tell the world about God. He showed me how to solve all my problems. It was one of the coolest days of my life ever. By the time we came back, it was dark, and it seemed like we were only gone for a few minutes. He walked me to the door once again but did not come in. Stupid me I asked him for his number and told him the first number he gave me was the wrong number.

He just looked at me while smiling and said, "Sorry here is my number." I said good night. He told me he was always watching over me when I needed him to just call on the Lord, and he would come.

You would think someone who had seen Jesus all the time as a child and several different angels before would know that she had just been entertained by an angel, right? Wrong. I don't even know what to write here, that I am an idiot? I know! Don't blame me. I had a lot on my mind. I never did see Tray again after that. Maybe one day we will meet again. But I am sure he and all the heavenly hosts are watching over us.

I kept myself very busy at work putting in as many hours as I could. I lost seventeen pounds in two weeks. I was over at Su's house one day when her phone rang, and it was Chase. He wanted to talk to me. I had not called him and totally ignored him this whole time. I said, "Hello."

He asked me, "Are you mad at me?"

I told him, "No. But call me. I would be home soon." And I gave him my new number. There were a lot of people over at Su's house. I could not really talk.

He called me when I got home. Boy, did I curse him out. He said, "I thought you said you were not mad at me?"

I told him, "Did you want me cursing you in front of all your friends?"

I asked him, "Does your baby mama know that you are calling me?" He started telling me that he wanted me back and that he loved me very much. I told him I was not taking him back. He begged for a couple of days. I told him on a Friday, that if I did not see him by Sunday, New Year's Day, I was moving on with someone else.

He asked me, "Well, can you please pay my way back?"

I just told him on a Sunday, "Boy, walk if you have to." He came Sunday morning, and I and picked him up. We bought a lot of weed and drinks to last us a month. We did not answer the phone that month nor did we go anywhere. The only people I talked to were my parents. We took my son over there every weekend.

I had gotten a new job in the new neighborhood that was paying me good. One day I went to work and Chase called me all freaking out. He said that my mother astral-projected in the house while he was asleep and woke him up. I asked him how. He said that she tried picking up the keys and he heard them move. So he opened his eyes, and she walked over to the bed and sat down. The mattress sunk in. She tried to cross over him, and he yelled at her and told her, "Get out. Your daughter is not here!" That was the day he told me he believed me now about my mother and that she was a witch. I asked him do you want me to come home? He said, "No." Okay. This was my third day on the job.

Guess what? Remember the guy whose money I took when I first met Chase and I put the toothpick in my nose? Elijah? He was the supervisor at this job. "Oh crap." Man I've got to change my shift. He spoke with me briefly. I decided to work nights since he was the supervisor for the day shift. Why did this man come to the job when he was not supposed to be working? I was napping in the break room when I felt someone kissing me. It was him. I slapped him so hard. He tried to grab me and I got out the way. He said, "You did not expect to take my money and go free, did you?" I ran out and off the job and never returned. They called me to find out what happened and I refused to pick up my phone. I changed my number.

It was the weekend. It was time for Chase and me to party and drop the little one off to his grandparents. This was when Chase convinced me to go around my parents. My son went to use the restroom, and he said there was no tissue. So Chase checked and we were out of tissue. We took the little one to his grandparents' house. My mom went in the back and brought out tissue and said here you go; you out of tissue and you need this. The look she gave me was like "you know who I am." Chase and I looked at each other.

When we got back in the car, he told me, "Your mom is definitely a witch. I will not argue about that anymore." I was okay at that time with my son going there because the voice told me that she cannot harm him because that would be against the rules. And she had to follow the rules. She had never physically been in that apartment before. I told you. Everything was great with Chase and me. We were so happy. He stopped having intimate conversations with his baby mama. He demanded that he talked to the kids and told her they could not have any conversations if they were not pertaining to the kids. He finally stood up to her. When he came back here he had a burned mark on his face and all the clothes in suitcase were wet. He told me that she burned him purposely with her curling iron and soaked all his clothes in the bathtub. He had to run away from her and hide himself until he could come back to Minnesota. We laughed and cried and told each other everything that went on while we were apart. We bonded even more.

One day I had seen this commercial on TV about this design school in California, and I called them. Chase wanted to do interior design, and I wanted to do fashion design. We got the paper work, filled it out, and sent it back. It was March, and the school said we could come on campus to the start in July. While we were waiting to go, Chase started acting up again. He told me he was going to buy a pack of cigarettes around the corner. He was gone for ten hours. He started gambling and sleeping out. I kept telling him to stop. He was having fun I guess. He really got on my nerves, so while he was out, I had Su help me pack all my things, and I took them to my sister's house. When Chase got home, he was freaking out. He went everywhere looking for me. When he finally found me, he started to cry, and he told me how sorry he was for everything, and he wanted me to move back home. I loved Chased very much, and I hated to see him cry. I told him under one condition was I moving back home.

He had to change and behave himself and he had to move all my stuff back and put them away on his own. He agreed and did what I asked him to do. Then he told me, "Now I know how you felt when I up and left without telling you. It really hurt. How did you do it for the two weeks I was gone"? It hurt but what can you do you just got to take it one day at a time. We were ok again and it was time to move to California. We got our tax returns and bought us a lot of clothes to start off with over there. My best friend asked me, "Why do you want to take sand to the beach?" She was referring to Chase.

"You should not take Chase with you." I laughed because it was funny the way she said it. I told her the dream I had about being on campus and seeing Chase sleep with a friend of mine on what seem to be a bunked bed. She said, "See he is going to cheat on you when you get there. Leave him here." I couldn't. If I was going to get an education, I wanted him to get one as well, and I don't think I could do anything without him. We were very, very close. "California, here we come!"

We took the bus to California because we couldn't afford a flight. We had such a nice time on that bus. We were stopping different places and seeing and meeting all kinds of different people. We really bonded and went over our plans of what we would do once we got there. We were to go to school, stay focus, knock that eighteen months program out, and come back to Minnesota to continue our lives. When we got to California and it was time to get our bags, we came to find out that we were robbed. Someone stole all of our bags. *Are you kidding me?* We were devastated. What are we going to do? Our money was in those bags. We did not know what to do. We called the school to let them know that we were at the bus station, but we were robbed, and now we were stranded. They were expecting us, so they became very concerned. The president of the school got on the phone and told us if we could find a cab to bring us there, he would pay for it out of pocket. President Robert Wagner, I will never forget him; he was so very kind to us and made us comfortable there.

The only thing these thieves did not take was the overnight bag that we had. It was with us. Chase suspected that it was the guys that do the loading and unloading at the bus stop. But these things are all material things that you can't take with you once you are dead. As God would have it for us, our counselor told me that she had some clothes that she could not fit anymore that she could give me, but she did not know what to do about Chase. Chase said it was ok once I had clothes to wear he was going to be okay. So we told her we could work with that. The cab driver understood our situation and worked with us by driving us to the school on credit. When we got to the school, the president did pay for the cab like he said he would. *Wow. What a welcome*, we thought. Anyways, we are survivors; we can do this although we were a little scared of how this school thing here was going to play out.

We made a lot of friends. Then slowly but surely we started losing our focus. After the first three months, it was break time, and we went home to Minnesota. We had a lot of fun going out to the clubs and meeting up with some people we knew. But it was time to return to school. When we got back to school this time, we were not the new guys on campus anymore. We made even more friends and became very comfortable. Wrong move! Chase started to get worse, and I followed shortly after. By now, he had totally lost his focus. He was still doing his schoolwork and all but now he was hanging out all day after school, and I barely saw him. I was worried about him. I had to start making female friends, which was something I was not used to doing anymore. I have only had one close female friend Mennei my whole life. And here I am in California, and all these girls wanted to make friends with me. Some girls wanted to make friends with me to have sex with me, which I thought was kind of cool. I always wanted to explore that other side of me, and this seemed to be the perfect place to do that.

The devil will always find ways of taking you far from God's purpose for your life by bringing in all kinds of temptations. And being in California was like being in the middle of the soup pot of temptation. This very pretty girl came to me one day and told me that her roommate was interested in her, and she told the roommate, "Heck no."

She said to me, "Now if it was you, Eve I would jump at the chance because you are hot." I was shock, but I did not show it. I did not know how to respond to that. She was coming onto me really hard. All the guys and girls kept telling me the same thing. It started to get to my head. One day, Chase's friends and I had a surprised birthday party for him off campus. We had so much fun, and Chase was the life of the party. He knew how to party. I was drunk and tired and wanted to go back on campus to sleep it off, but Chase was not ready to leave. The pretty girl that approached me on campus came to me and said, "I'll take you back on campus." I said okay, not thinking anything of it.

When we got back on campus, I went to Chase's room instead of mine. She said she wanted to make sure that I got in the room okay. When we got in the room, she started to help me get ready for bed. After she helped me take my clothes off because I was so drunk, she asked me, "Do you think I am pretty?" I said yes. Then she leaned over and started to kiss me. It felt good, so I let her, and I started to kiss her back. She asked me for us to take a shower together, and I said okay. When we got in the tub, she started to bathe me. This girl did everything Chase did to me. She was good. After the shower, we went back to the bed, and it was a done deal. Then we heard a sound at the door; it was Chase trying to get in with his library card. We knew how to open the locks on any door with any card. So anyways, she got nervous and wanted to put her clothes back on. I told her no, that Chase was going to be happy to see her in his bed. When he came in and turned the lights on, he was surprised.

He had seen the both of us lying there naked looking at him. He did not say anything. He just politely took his clothes off and jumped in the bed, and she and I looked at each other and said happy birthday to him together. You think of how the rest of the night went. All I can say was we had fun. The three of us had breakfast together the next day. "My gosh, what a night!" And this was the beginning of our kinky life in California, living like there was no God. If God can change Chase and me, he definitely can change anyone. On campus, there was about ten of us were in our clique. One day, some of us decided to go off campus as usual to drink and smoke. Well, when we got back, everyone went their separate ways. There was only one of my friends who decided to hang with us. She said, "Now what do we do? I am bored." She said, "Eve, you are lucky, at least you and Chase don't have to be bored. You can just go to your room and have sex." Then she laughed.

Out of the blue, I told her, "We will only if you come with us." Her face turned red, and Chase's eyes popped opened.

She started saying something like, "I can't do that. Are you kidding me? You guys are my friends." And she walked away.

Chase was like, why did you say that to her? "She will never do that, now she will never talk to us again."

I told him, "Go upstairs, and make the bed in my room."

"Why should I make your bed?" he asked me. "Because I am going to get her to have a threesome with us, that's why."

He said, "Okay, I will, but I don't think you can pull this one off."

"This girl is very beautiful and don't seem like that type, Eve."

"What, am I ugly?" I asked him. So he and I made a bet. I talked to her and told her that I wanted her to have a threesome with Chase and me. She told me she would meet me in my room. I went back to my room where Chase was waiting. When he seen me by myself, he started laughing at me saying he had won the bet.

I told him, "No silly, she will come." Ten minutes later, she was knocking at my door. Guess what happened? It was her; we had fun, and I won the bet. Chase was having the time of his life hanging out with me. He always called me the bad girl who loved good boys. Because we did not know God at this time, there was nothing to be afraid of. God will pull you out of the deepest pit if he has to, no matter what. There was no Holy Spirit dwelling in our drunk and high-all-the-time bodies. We did not know that we were living in complete sin. It was all fun and games to us. In the midst of all the fun, I kept hearing this voice telling me to go back to Minnesota or I was going to die in California. And when I come, I should not blame him because he had already told me what to do.

One night, I went to bed and had this dream. The heavens opened up, and I see this huge figure dressed in a purple robe with two other people with him one on each side kneeling down. The one standing in the middle extended his hand to me and said, "Come to me." But when I looked around me, there were fireballs falling from the sky, and everybody was screaming and running around looking for safety. Blisters started forming on people; everyone seemed so helpless.

I told the figure, "No, I can't. I have to stay and help and find my friend and godson." I left and went on looking for people to help. The next day, I told my roommates whom were sisters the dream. They started freaking out.

"Do you know who you just seen?"

"It was Jesus."

"Je...who?

"Jesus," one of them said. "This is in the Bible." I looked at them like, what are you talking about?

There was a knock on the door; it was one of my smoking buddies. I told the girls we will chat later. They wanted me to stay, but they knew I was a smoker, so they told me when they go home on the weekend; they were going to tell their father my dream and bring back the Bible. "Sure, okay, whatever," I said. That Monday, they came back with this big book that I recognized from my nights in hotels and my dad. It read "The Holy Bible."

I said, "Oh yeah, this book, the sheets are really good for smoking weed in if you don't have zigzag smoking paper."

They looked at each other like, what?

"So what do you want to show me?" They opened the Bible to John 19:1, and it was highlighted all the way to verse 19, and they told me to read. This sounds like the dude from my dreams I told them. Then they told me these things about Jesus. They gave me something to think about. I remember when I was a child this man used to visit me all the time and carry me on top this mountain, and he would always tell me sit on his right side, and he would tell me a whole lot of things. They looked like they had seen a ghost. I told them, "Well, I don't know what this dead guy wants with me. But this is creepy." Not knowing this Jesus was the only way to my salvation. And this dead guy was the son of the God I have been hearing. I did not know he is more powerful than anyone in or out of this world and that he did not stay dead because death itself couldn't hold him.

After they told me, I started hearing the voice telling me everything they said was true and I should listen to them. I said, "Whatever, I don't even know them like that, and they seem too clean for me to hang out with. They don't even smoke or drink. What are we going to do together? They were good girls. I got a little annoyed with them. So I ignored the voice. Some of our friends started snorting cocaine, some were on crystal meth, and some were popping pills. We all were partners in drinking and smoking weed. It seemed like everybody was on something. Some would ask me to try some of the drugs they were on. I would tell them Chase told me never ever to try anything else besides weed and beer; he was absolutely clear about that. I hated making him mad. So I never did. But one time someone put something in me and my friend's weed; we didn't know, and we smoked it. Our lips were twitching the whole day. She said, "Girl, someone messed with us!"

Chase said, "Never ever smoke a blunt or joint that was pre-rolled from someone else." Now he tells me. Too late my lips are already twitching.

He told me, "Most drugs will ruin your life, and you would be seriously addicted to them." He said that once you were addicted to those serious drugs, you would either die or have to go to rehab to quit. Yikes, that does not sound good. We knew a lot of people that did all those others stuff, and their appearance drastically changed, and Chase would point them out one by one to me, so I could notice the difference.

Now there were strange things happening to me. At night, I would see dark shadows in my room, and they would be twisting my neck trying to turn my face to toward my back and my back toward my front. This was happening constantly, so I used to stay up as late as possible so they won't get me, but I would always fall asleep. I remember asking why they were doing this, and they told me if I lose my memories and go insane, then I would not be able to write this book. My life has been in danger by the dark side because of this book for a very long time. I remember the shadows almost choke the life out of me one day. If it was not Chase sneaking in my room in the middle of the night, I would have probably died, and no one would know what happened to me. They would say it was natural causes. I started getting very scared, and I told Chase I thought I was escaping my mother by coming here, but she is here, and she is still trying to kill me. I told him we got to go back to Minnesota. He said he was not ready to go back; he was having too much fun. I agreed even though I knew for a fact I was dying. Who was I going back to in Minnesota anyways?

My mom was trying to kill me. My two younger sisters were too young to help me. So when I heard the voice again, I would tell it, well, Chase does not want to go. I can't go without him you know that. We stayed on campus during that break because we were too broke to take the bus to Minnesota. We did not even have $1. I called my mom, and she said she had no money. She was lying, the voice told me. "She wants you to stay here and die." It was really tough for us. I remembered we had one pack of noodle, and we had not eaten anything that whole day. Chase cooked the pack of noodle, and he sat there and fed it to me.

As long as I ate something, he was okay, he said. How romantic was that.

One of our friends left her car with us so luckily we had a car to drive around but no money to buy gas. One thing about Chase, he would always think quickly on his feet. He said he had an idea. And every time he said that I knew it was something to fix whatever problems we were facing at the time. He is a genius when it comes to thinking fast on his feet. He said, "We know how to open every door on this campus, right?"

"Yeah, so?"

He said, "We have to do what we have to do." What are you talking about? He said we have to go in the rooms that had the most valuables in them and take what we can and sell it. That is the only way we will survive this mess we are in. I did not hesitate, and we robbed some of our friends on campus so we could survive. Hell, we made a deal with the guy in the bookstore to give us the most expensive books. It was an awful thing to do, but it had to be done, and I was his lookout. It was mostly books and CDs. Not that it made it right. All the people whose hair I would do for the money went home for the break. Not long after that, all of our friends were back. And they all came back with money. We were the ones that always used to hustle and get the drinks and smokes and stuff. So they were used to depending on Chase and me. Now shortly after school started Chase started to cheat on me. *Wow, not again.*

He started dating this so-called rich girl, ugly as a bat if you ask me. One night, he slept out, and I woke up in severe pain. My stomach started to hurt again. I recognized this pain when he slept with his baby mama in Jersey. So I woke up and went to the other building, woke my friend up, and told her that Chase was cheating on me right now. She said, "Is he not in his room?"

I said, "No, because I was sleeping there."

She said, "He loves you way too much to cheat on you, girl."

I asked, "What the hell love got to do with this? Let's go find the man."

She said, "It is four o'clock in the morning. Where are we going to find him?"

I said, "When we get there, I will know."

She said, "How?" I told her how I could sense him no matter where he was I would know what was happening with him. There were three dorms on campus with three levels. We searched everywhere, even the parking lot and the nearest store. So I said okay. It seemed he was nowhere to be found. My instincts are never wrong when it comes to Chase. So she said, "Let's go back to your room so you can get some sleep." I agreed. We took the back way to my room. Right before we got to my room, my feet got stuck to the ground, and I couldn't move.

She saw me trying to move, and I couldn't. She asked me, "What's wrong?"

I whispered to her and told her, "I can't move. My feet are stuck to the ground." She looked at my feet and saw that I truly was trying to move, but I couldn't. I told her he was in there. She said, "In Ana's room?" She said, "No, Ana is too ugly." She said, "I will knock on the door to prove you wrong." She knocked on the door, and we heard him jump of the bed and ran into the bathroom. The girl did not want to open the door, so my friend knocked super hard. She opened the door just enough so we could see her face. So my friend pushed the door open, and Chase was in there. I was disappointed.

I told my friend, "Let's go. I just wanted to know where he was." I did not say a word to him or his newfound bat. After them hanging out a few times, Chase started to ignore me and acted like I did not exist. It seemed like he was in some sort of a trance, and I did not know how to get him out of it. All my friends kept coming to me and telling me how they used to see the two of them all hugged up together on and off campus. My friends wanted to catch her off campus and beat her up. I told them, "No, now is not the time. Leave her be." He would sit with her in the cafeteria with her friends while I sat alone with a broken and confused heart as they looked at me giggling under their breath. At this time, I told all my friends I needed to be by myself. He had blocked his door, so I was not allowed in his room anymore. He took all my stuff out of his room when I tried to beat him up one night. I ripped his assignment that he had worked on for weeks, causing him to fail that class.

One day, this girl came to me and told me she practiced witchcraft and wanted to help me get back at Chase. She told me how she heard about what Chase did. I told her witchcraft was not a good thing. She said she was going to do something to him anyways. I told her she did not have my permission. She told me a few days later that she put a spell on him so his penis won't function anymore. I told her that was a mistake. I told her, "You have just pissed the devil off by taking an unauthorized assignment. Something bad is going to happen to you. Leave witchcraft alone." She was raped by eight guys later, and she remembered what I told her. She did not talk to me again because I told her prior that I opposed witchcraft. Not only was this going on, but the school told me I owed them $10,000. Where would I get this money from? They told me I needed a cosigner to get this particular loan. I called my eldest sister, and I explained the situation. So much was happening, but if I could stay in school, that would be great.

She said she wanted me to do a drug test first. I told her how I was making good grades and I could send her my grades. She said, "I know you are making good grades because you are a smart girl, but I want a drug test." She refused. Whether I was smoking weed or not did not have anything to do with my grades. She is not the one responsible for me getting an education anyways, so it was nothing personal. Right away, Chase walked into the room and heard our conversation. The reality sunk in that she had never done anything for me before besides bringing me to America and helping to bury my son after our mother killed. She had never made a phone call to me before to even say hi to me.

What was I thinking to even call her? I was desperate, that's all. I did not bother her again. He was so mad at my sister. He said he did not understand her at all. Then he said something that made sense to me. He said, "If she really wanted to help you, she won't request for a drug test, Eve. She had always belittled you since I have known you, so let it go." The realization of that fact was hurtful, but it was the truth. Chase left after that. I did not see him again for days, and my heart was just tearing apart.

One day, I was sitting on my stairs at five o'clock in the morning smoking a cigarette and the girl he was cheating on me with room door opened. It was him. He was trying to sneak out to go back to his dorm room. He looked left, and then he looked right, and there I was looking at him. He was shocked to see me so early in the morning. I just told him, "You better hurry up before the RA sees you." He slowly closed the door behind him and went the other way without saying anything to me. I could tell he was scared. He was very scared of me because he had heard stories and seen how bad I could be. I couldn't be bad to Chase. I had a soft heart for him. He was and still is my sweetheart.

Later on that day, I had a chance to talk to this girl one on one. I told her, "You know Chase is just messing with you, and he has no intentions of being with you, right?"

She said, "No, he's not. We are going to get married and have kids."

"Don't say I did not tell you," I said to her. "We are soul mates, and you are just a temp, Ana. When he comes back to me, which he will soon, you would be very hurt, and I will not be able to help you."

Then she asked me, "How did you know that we were going out anyways?" I told her I just did. She said Chase told her that I had ESP, but she did not believe it until now. I was in my room for one week and barely ate. I shut myself off from everything and everybody. *But it was time to get out,* I thought to myself. *I needed to face this problem head-on.* The next day, I told my closest girlfriend on campus to call the rest of the girls to come see me. When they came, they were happy to see me up and out of the room. "All I want all of you to do for me is to go back to your room's shower and dress in your sexiest outfits. We are going out."

"Where are we going?" they asked. I told them, "I don't know, but let's get dress and hit the road. Let's meet back here in one hour. Don't be late, or you will stay behind." One hour later, my girls were ready, and we left the campus not knowing Mr. Chase who did not have time for me had seen us and followed us.

Half a block off campus about fifteen to twenty low-rider cars were coming down the road doing their thing. Than they had seen us and started performing even more so we could be impressed. They stopped in the middle of the road to holler at us. These guys were so sexy looking. Then I saw Chase a block down the road. To make him jealous, I told the guys to pull over in the parking lot off campus. I asked them were they were headed. Guess who came running full speed up the road toward us? Chase! *Yes, my plan worked,* I thought to myself. He ran straight toward me, grabbed me, and ran back on campus without my feet even touching the ground. All my friends were yelling and screaming at him, but he did not care; he kept running with me in his arms. He was pissed. He did not stop until we passed through the campus gates where he knew he was safe from those guys. He knew that was the only way he could had gotten me to go back on campus with him. I was in payback mode.

If he had stopped just to talk, I was going to get in the car with the guys and be gone. He held my hand really tight and walked me up to his room like a child in trouble with their parent. I was calm because he was mad. When we got in his room, he cooled off right away. He started to plead with me and apologized for his behavior. He said he was done with Ana if only I could please forgive him. I looked at him for a long time, and I remembered finding this girl, long, jet-black hair coming out the crack of my butt in the shower in his room. And he told me it was one of my client's strands of hair. I got angry at the thought of that.

I told him, "If you want me to forgive you, you've got to do what I say."

He said, "Name it, and I would do it." She had given him a ring, a phone, and some other crap that was in his room.

I told him, "Pick up the phone, tell her to come to your room right now, you need to talk to her." Within five minutes, she was there.

He told her he couldn't see her anymore and to take all her stuff back; he didn't want it. She was so upset she started to cry and shake uncontrollably. I felt sorry for her, but I can't say I did not warn her. You can never claim something that is not yours. In the end, the owner most likely will come and take it from you. She took everything of her in tears as I sat there and watched her. I told him I was going to whip him with his belt twenty-five times on the rear for breaking my heart over and over again. He knew I was serious. He took all his clothes off and gave me the belt before lying flat on the bed. I told him for every time he screamed, I would add a lash, because he did not scream when he was screwing Ana. So I whipped him twenty-five times with his own belt. He couldn't sit for several days. We were like honey on rock again sweet as ever.

One night, he came in my room to hang out with me forgetting that Ana's cell phone was in his pocket. I heard a phone ringing, and I asked, "What is that? What the hell is that? Are you kidding me right now?" He did not have a cell phone, so it had to have been hers. "What in the hell? This was the reason you just got your ass whooped?"

He said, "She just gave it to me so I could make a call to my kids."

"Really?" I asked him. Then I changed my facial expression and acted like I understood, and it was nice of her for doing such a thing for him. I told him, "Oh okay, that's nice. Did you call the kids?"

He said, "I wanted to be here with you before calling them." It was past ten o'clock at night. He had no plans of calling the kids. He was lying to me again.

"Oh, okay, wait for me just one second. I promised one of the girls that I would bring them some change to do their laundry," I told him.

"Stupid" had to have been written on my face in bold letters. I kissed him and calmly left the room and went to this guy that had a crush on me. I left campus to go hang out with him. I did not go back to my room. *Silly boy, I'm just doing what you did to me*, I thought to myself. After hanging out off campus we decided to go back to his room. As we were hanging out in his room we heard the fire alarm start to go off. We did not even have sex. I asked him to help me make Chase jealous, and he was cool with it.

The guy said, "Oh man, what now?" I told him that was Chase messing with the alarm.

He said, "How will he know you are here?"

"He knows," I said. Chase had the same ESP connection I had with him. He knew where I was. But I did not tell the dude all that.

I said, "He wants me to get out of the guy's room. I was not about to do that."

He said, "But they will do a room search."

I said, "Yes, but they won't find me. I bet when you get out the door, you are going to see him standing at the bottom of the stairs waiting for me."

I had to think fast; they were already doing room search. I had seen his white blanket. I grabbed it and opened the bathroom door, lay down in the tub, and covered myself from head to toe with the blanket. I left the bathroom door opened so they won't think anyone was in there. With a glance if they looked they won't see me because of the white blanket. It was a false alarm. He came back to the room and told me Chase was the only one waiting at the bottom of the stairs. Chase begged me to stop so he won't catch a heart attack. He knew that I was about to put his heart through the ringer like he did me. You looked like shit, I told him. All he said was, "I love you so much, and I am sorry I don't even have that phone anymore." Sometimes, ladies, you have got to let the guy know you won't always be waiting around for him until he's good and ready before he tends to you.

By now, I was getting sicker but I was playing though. The voice kept telling me, "Go back to Minnesota. There you will meet a witch doctor who will help you, but she is not of me. I will send someone to you who is of me that will undo all your mother has been doing to you. The same way it started is the same way it will end." Then the girl Chase was dating went to the new president of the college and threatened them saying they needed to kick both of us out or she was going to find a different school to attend. She was paying cash for her tuition. Go figure. We got kicked out. And we could clearly see the president did not want to. He said his hands were tied, and this had to be done or he would lose his job. We just told him we understood. Not knowing at the time this was God's way of making sure I left California before I died there.

One of Romeo's brothers sent me some money and we bought our bus pass and left. It was almost a three-day ride, and I was clearly sick and dying. I could not stay awake for anything. Chase is so smart. With the little change we had, he decided to buy peanuts and water. He said we will need the protein, and we would fill up quickly. I remember sleeping on him the whole time. The only time I woke up was at the rest stop. I knew I was dying. But I thought I was going to die before getting to Minnesota. He was so scared, and I just told the voice, "Help me. I need you." When we got to the next rest stop, I had to use the rest room. When I left the stall and walked over to the sink, there was a very old woman. She said hello to me. Then she said, "I came to tell you that you will not die, but you will live to do God's work and write the book. She told me about Halle Selassie and how when they were kids they did some of the things they did.

I did not know who Haile Selassie was nor have I ever heard of him. She had searched a grace about her. She smiled the whole time, and she started telling me all these things about me and my future. She gives me a hug, and she got out the bathroom. I went to Chase who was waiting for me by the bathroom door and told him about the nice old lady in the bathroom. She told me stories of her and this dude named Haile Selassie and what they did together when they were kids. Chase, he was really nice to me. She told me that I was not going to die, but I was going to live. He had a puzzled look on his face. He asked, "Is she still in the bathroom?"

I said, "No, she got out first and left the door open so I could get out." He started to freak out. He told me he did not see any old lady. I said, "You saw her. She was just in front of me, and she went that way, pointing toward my right. He walked there and did not see her. He started asking everybody if they had seen an old lady anywhere. No one had seen her. I did not know what the big deal was. And my voice had gotten even smaller, and I could barely talk.

He said, "No one had seen her. Besides I did not see anyone come out of the bathroom before you. That's why I am looking around and to ask her about Haile Selassie. I think you had seen a ghost, Eve."

Oh well, I guess I did. It was time to get back on the bus. I was so sick. I was used to seeing ghost. What is the big deal? I thought to myself.

When we finally got to Minnesota, I was happy. I was relieved. But I have to stop with my younger sister and my mother lives across the street from her. When we got to my sister's house, I talked to her and saw my new niece and played with her. Then I told Chase, "Let's go say hi to Mom and Daddy." When we got over there, Daddy was so happy to see me, but my mother gave me a weird look, like "What are you still doing alive? You should have been dead by now." She and I knew what the look was for. She communicated with me telepathically all the time. I looked like death when I got back. Everyone that saw me asked me if I was sick.

I told them, "Yes, my mother was trying to kill me." That's when she started telling everyone that I was on drugs, and I was about to die. I have never heard about anyone overdosing on marijuana before.

CHAPTER SEVEN

MY TIME OF DESPAIR

Chase and I knew we had to get me to the doctor right away. We found a clinic in the Brooklyn Park area and made an appointment.

Some days later, we went there for my results, and they told me they could not find anything wrong with me. But looking at me and my symptoms, they could clearly tell that something was wrong. They tried to help me, but they did not know how. We did not know where else to turn. I remembered in California, the voice told me that after coming to Minnesota. One week later, I was going to meet an old lady who was a witch doctor, but she was not of him; he said, she would be the one to help me for now. It has not been a week yet. While Chase and I were sitting waiting for the doctors, we overheard the doctors talking about my case and how strange it was. So I went in to where they were talking, and I just told them that it was okay. I know you all can't help me with what is happening to me. I will just go home, and if it is meant for me to die, then I will rather die at home. They did not want me to leave, but they knew in their heart they could not help me, and I was running out of time. My condition started deteriorating rapidly. Something had to be done, and it had to be done right away. I knew in my heart if it was meant for me to die, God would have surely revealed it to me first before the time came.

A couple of days later, I ran into Persevu, and he said, "Look at you, you look like death. Your mother has really been busy with you! You look like her dragon has been sucking your blood. You need help, and you need it now. Here is the number to this old lady who I think can help you." At this moment, I had forgotten what the voice had told me. I was so weak I just wanted to get in the apartment and take a nap. Even if I didn't, I was still doubting myself, thinking maybe I was crazy. But before I could have a pity party for myself, there comes an even softer voice reminding me of the promise God made to me. A lot of crazy supernatural things were happening to me and very fast, back to back. Seriously when you are in the position of life and death, that's when your faith is really put to the test, by Satan. I kept thinking in and out of my head, *Please let all this be a really, really, bad dream.* I took the number and made an appointment for the next morning to see this old lady. When I got to her house, that's when I realized that I knew this old lady. Her kids and I went to the same school when they came to America. I had seen her around for a very long time. But I did not know she was a witch doctor. She greeted me, and right away, she said I need one hundred dollars and ten cents before she can work with you. I thought to myself, *Hmm that's a strange request.* But I went and got the money and came back an hour later.

She said, "Where is the man that you are with?"

I told her, "At home."

She asked me, "Why did he not come with you?"

I said, "Because he does not believe in stuff like this."

She said, "Go and get him, or I will not help you." My heart dropped. I was wondering what does he have to do with this. But I did not hesitate and went to Chase telling him what the lady had said.

He said, "Well, why does she want to see me?"

"Chase, I don't care. My life is involved. God said go to her to her. I am going, and you are coming with me right now, so get dresses and let's get going." I said it just like that. This is no time for questions.

When we got to her house, she took us in her room where all her stuff was. She asked him, "Do you want me to help her?"

He said yes.

She said, "The reason I am asking you is because you are her protector. And if you say no, then you both can leave right now, and she will die." He assured her that he wanted me to live and if she could please help me. She looked at him and smiled. She pulled out a little mirror and put some white powder on it. Ok, I thought to myself this is really weird. She chanted some stuff and looked in the mirror. That woman told me and Chase everything that had ever happened to us in our lives. She confirmed my suspicion of my mother being the one to kill my son Elijah in an African sign. She told me exactly what happened before my son died. She said, "Your mother ate the boy's heart, intestines, and all his vital organs."

How did she know this? I had never told anyone what Elijah showed me about his death in fear they would think I was crazy. He showed me that my mother killed him, and he showed to me that he had no eyes, intestines, or organs in his body. He showed himself like a deflated balloon. She went on to say that my mother had wanted me dead since I was a child. My father had warned her that if she killed me, he was going to destroy her. This was one of the things the angels told me about my dad the night they came to protect me from my mother.

Then she went on to say that when I ran away to California. At night, my mother came there to attack me, and I would wake up choking. How my mother had been twisting my neck so the front could go to the back and the back to the front. She said it was almost complete and that I was going to go insane and then finally commit suicide and die. She told me how my mother put a sweating sickness on me that made me have to constantly take showers and change my clothes. This sounds crazy, but it is all true. She had been telling everyone that I was about to die because I was on drugs.

Then the lady told me that I was destined to work for God to be his prophet. Chase started to cry, and he told her he thought I was just saying all these things, and it was all in my head. He never knew that this was actually happening. When he heard about all of his past things, I did not know about him from this lady; he started to cry even more. That was the moment he apologized to me. As the days started to go by, I started getting even sicker. I could barely talk. She told me to stay at her house. I said no because I had problems sleeping in strange places. And I felt a presence in her house that seemed gentle but would attack if need be. I did not want to see anything walking around that no one else could see but me.

She told Chase to keep a very close eye on me that no one should come in the apartment if they did not live there. Then she gave him this liquid in the bottle that looked and smelled just like poop, and I am not kidding. He had to bathe me with it and sprinkle it everywhere in the house. When we got home, I went to bed and did not wake up until three months later. The old lady, Grandma, as I called her, kept coming to the apartment every morning to chant over me. I could hear and see everybody. But the scary part was I could also see myself just lying there. I could not move. I was completely paralyzed from head to toe. I would see things that did not look like they were from this world. I could see my grandparents who were all dead before I was born. My grandfather was in the room crawling within the ceiling trying to kill me. I had never seen him or a picture of him before. Years later when I described him to someone who knew him, they said that was exactly how he looked, just like a gorilla. He was trying to help his daughter get rid of me. Why God? Why? What did I do to deserve this treatment from my own mother? I never once got mad at God nor questioned him. I trusted him completely. But every now and then, I would question my situation as to what could I have done so bad to my mother that she would work night and day relentlessly trying to kill me? That question was the one that I wanted an answer for. God was always right there talking to me. At one point, Satan told God that the only reason

I was being loyal to him was because he has been navigating me through all these struggles.

I would constantly tell God that was not true. "You know my heart, and it is pure, my Lord." This was a battle for my life, once again, talk about waking up in the twilight zone. Even at my weakest point when I could not take myself to the toilet, nor speak a word, my spirit man was strong and bold pleading my case at his most gracious holy throne. Lucifer and I met there occasionally. He would tell God all the things he believed that I should go through before being ordained a child of God by God himself.

God said to him, "She will do it all, and in the end, she will still have great love in her heart for me." I remember him walking away with the expression as if "we will see about that." Remember in the beginning God said that he wanted to bless me, but the people around me were not who they say they were. And he also said that I was going to struggle a great deal. Well, I did not know that this was going to last years and years. Satan wanted all my buttons to be pushed so I can deny God, our Heavenly Father. Satan always appeared in different shapes and form; he never sticks with one shape. One day, I asked God, "Why did you and Satan fall off?" He showed me a handsome fellow dress in white with the most beautiful voice, and he said, "That was Lucifer before he became Satan." But I noticed that God was not angry with Satan but rather grieving of how one of his precious one could go astray.

After reading the Bible years later, I come to understand that Satan was the prodigal son who has not returned home to do right by his father yet. I felt a deep sadness in my heart for God Our Father; one of his children has gone astray and has taken with him some of his brethren's to do evil with him to corrupt mankind for the sake of jealousy. One of the saddest moments for God was the day he ordered his disobedient son, one of his own creation band from dwelling in heaven with him any longer. This is why we have Satan going to the throne room over and over to plead his case trying to convince God that we are not worth his time and effort.

Let me tell you something, God he has a heart big heart. Can the one who created hearts, can he not feel love? Especially if we humans as small as we are have love for our sons and daughter, what more about him who had given these great gifts we go around showing off with. You can have all the sex you want, but if it was not because of God, we won't have the true beauty of life—the miraculous gift of life within us of bringing forward another human being into this world. Anyways, let us continue where we left off.

The forces of darkness wanted me dead, and the Holy one wanted me alive. This was when I knew darkness could never overshadow the light. Chase did very well by taking care of me. I remembered hearing him crying and talking to me telling me to come back to him. "He told me that you are supposed to have two children for me, a girl and a boy, Eve. I am supposed to married you remember? Don't leave me please." I remembered the look in his eyes when I came through. I had never seen someone so happy. He had lost a lot of weight. I could not talk to him because I lost my voice, and I was too weak to write anything. Little did I know at this time I had lost a lot of my memory. The old lady came over as soon as Chase told her I was awake. She was super nice and very overprotective of me. During this time, my sister Pasadena did not help Chase take care of me at all. Later when she was asked about this, she said she too was in a trance and had no idea what was happening around her. I did not believe her at all. I felt as if Chase was not in my life, and it was left up to Pasadena; my mother was going to kill me and promise to do something great for her, and she was not even going to realize that she had sacrifice me until it was too late. Although years later Pasei told me she was possessed and did not even know it.

Crap. If only I had that information years earlier, it would have helped a lot. Oh well.

The old lady said, "You have to gather your strength. This is only the beginning. Your mother is recruiting help from other witches because your spirit is too strong for her." She was right. I did see my mother gathering people as if she was about to go for battle. She started giving me this liquid to drink. It tasted nasty, but I could feel life coming back into me, and I wanted to live. *Wow, these things really exist*, I thought.

Chase carried me into the car early in the morning so no one would see me. He did not want people asking questions as to what was wrong with me. If any Liberian had seen me, they were going to know something was wrong, and it was going to be out there. And when you are in a physically weak state like this, you definitely don't want people around you that harbor negative energy; they will suck you dry like a cold orange on a hot summer day. Chase and I would stay with the old lady all day and at night after she bathed me; then, we would go home. One night Chase asked me to listen carefully, so I did. I can't hear anything I signed to him. He said it was a bird that came to the tree that was over the room window every night. He said he had noticed it every night for some days. He said, "Whenever the bird began to sing, I would act strange and confused as if I was going insane, possessed, or something. Remember the owl from the Ivory Coast that would watch me every night while I took a shower? I have not put two plus two together yet to realize witches deal with a lot of different kinds of birds." Chase put a lot of blankets to the window to lower the sound and lit several candles. He took such great care of me. I remembered him changing me when it was that time of the month and giving me sponge baths in bed, turning me and remaking the bed. I could see everything he was doing, except I was having an out-of-body experience and could physically wake up. This went on for three months.

The next day, Chase told the old lady about the bird. It was my mother. I had seen her before changing into a crow in my dream, and the crow had a funny hairdo. Grandma said, "Gamain, your dreams are not dreams. They are things that are actually happening in the realms of the spirit, and because you were born with the gift of sight, you are able to see them." She told Chase to take us to this farm. It was almost two hours away. But he did not complain because his future wife needed to be heavily guarded. When we got there, she bought four chickens, and when we got back to her house, she stripped naked with just her underwear on.

"You have to be naked to do most spiritual exercises involving the underworld," she said. The chickens were in the room tied up. Chase and I did not know what she was planning on doing with these chickens. She went into the closet and brought out a plate with stuff that looked like rocks, except they were not rocks. Then she said, "These are the people."

"What people, Grandma?" I asked her.

"The Ginas!" Most people from my country know what Ginas are. They are the fallen ones. They are the angels that fell from grace along with Lucifer. They are all over the world and some of these witches and wizards work for them or so they would like to think anyways. They only feed on blood, and I was just about to see witchcraft 101 live. She started chanting something to the Ginas. She was bowing down to them. She worshipped them as if they were gods. They all had names. After chanting, she told Chase to give her one chicken. She sliced the throat and poured the blood over the Ginas. Then she sliced the throat of the next and the other until all four were done.

Chase and I had seen the Ginas suck up every last drop of blood. I was shocked to see this. Then she told me she had to mark me so I would be a part of them, which was the only way the help she was trying to give me would be effective. She said, "Otherwise your mother will kill you." What choice did I have? I showed my arm. The voice told me that she was going to help me until I got a little better than he would instruct me what to do next. So I asked her where. I wish I had known about Jesus and his mighty blood at this point. I was robbed of my memory of the vital lost blood of Jesus Christ. If only someone could have told me earlier. If my mother did not erase my memory of my childhood, I was going to remember hanging out with Jesus all the time. What you don't know will hurt you.

She brought a sharp razor blade and a comb. She pressed the comb against my shoulders and started slicing me between the teeth of the comb. My blood was gushing out. Maybe she gave some to the Ginas, who knows, now thinking about it. She did this to both arms, and she put some black dust in the open sores and rubbed it really hard. Then she told me now I was part of them. After a few days, I was able to start talking but softly. She gave me a piece of soap, no more than two inches in length and width. She told me to bathe with it until it was all gone. It was crazy what happened next. As I started to bathe with the soap, I noticed that there was red mud coming off my skin. The tub started getting filled with this mud. I got out of the tub and got her. I told her to look in the tub. It was filled with mud.

She said, "Yeah, you are very beautiful, but your mother did not want your beauty to shine, so she put the mud on you so no one can notice you. When she said that, a light went off in my head. I used to have dreams of seeing my mother chasing me all the time and blowing out of her hands red dust on me. *Wow, my mother is a witch? How could she do this to me? Especially after all I had done for her. No wondered my whole life, she made the hair on the back of my neck stand up.* I had to wash the tub about three to four times before the soap was gone, and every time, it was filling with mud until the point of overflowing. This was real red claylike mud. Seriously, you have got to be kidding me. The water that finally dripped off me was clean and not muddy. What the heck? Grandma had told me to stay away from the mirrors because that was one of the ways my mother was tracking me. But on this day, she had me look in the mirror. I looked like I had been bleaching. I had my complexion back finally. Chase was happy.

I had gotten stronger as the days went by. I could walk and talk just fine. But the back of my head was still hurting like crazy. Grandma said that my mother took my spirit; she and her witch buddies were dipping it in and out of the river for the fun of it. But one day the back of my head hit a log that was under the water. It surely sounds right because it felt like someone hit me with a baseball bat back there. She used to put some green liquid from some leaves in my nose, and it used to soothe the back of my head. It made my mind not to be as foggy, and it did not hurt as bad.

When I got a little better, I started going out to the club with Chase. Grandma got mad one morning and told me not to go out at night. She said the witches were waiting for me to go out. I did not listen. How suborned can one person be? Me, I am very stubborn, which is good and bad. One night I went out, and they attacked me, and I became possessed. I knew I was in there somewhere, but I could not control my actions. I bit Chase's tongue and almost cut it off; he bled a lot. I busted all the windows on my car and flattened all the tires. I broke the apartment complex glass door with my high heels and sliced my hand. There was blood everywhere. And I had no recollection of this at all.

Grandma called me the next day, and boy she was so mad. She said, "I had seen you last night. Did I not say don't go anywhere at night? What is wrong with you? Do you want to get yourself killed?" I did not go out again after that. I knew better. But I would always hear them calling me to come out. I just felt like running out the door. It was tempting, but I fought it off and did not get out. Chase kept guard over me literally and never left my side for more than ten minutes at a time. It was as if I was in some sort of a trance, like a magnet pulling me. Shortly after my recovery, I became pregnant, and I had a dreamed it was a baby girl. Two months into my pregnancy, I had this dream, and this guy dressed in all black came to grab my daughter as she was playing. She put herself in a shield like a glass bubble and floated away from him. I woke up frightened. Chase woke up and thought something was wrong with me.

We both looked at my stomach, and it was in a ball under my breast. He said, "She is only two months. She should not be moving yet." I know, but she was in danger so she escaped. When I described the man to my sister, she said that was exactly how my mother's boyfriend used to dress and look. Another creepy thing happened around 5:00 a.m. I had seen my uncle Harold naked standing in front of my bed looking out the window as if the sun's coming up and he had to leave. He had astral-projected himself in the house. Right when he was turning to look at us sleeping, I quickly closed my eyes. I did not want him to know that I was awake. But he saw me, and to be sure, he walked to me and tried to open my eyes. I jumped and screamed; he ran out the door and slammed it really hard because I also scared him. He was there to keep watch over me for my mother. Chase jumped from sleep and saw that I was still in the bed and was very concerned as to who entered the house and slammed the room door like that. He called my sister's name, and I told him, "You know she never sleeps here." Then he walked to the front door leaving me in bed; it was locked. We lived on the second floor, and all the windows were closed.

"Who the heck was that, Eve?" I told him it was my uncle. He had been watching us all night. Chase said, "Man this shit has got to stop." The next day, I ran into him at the front door of the complex coming to visit one of his friends. I told him straight up; if he ever turns stupid to call himself coming to me like that again, I would shoot him dead. I told him if he did not believe me, let him astral-project himself there again. I never saw him again after that. My father asked me about the incident, and I told him. He never argued with me. My father knew I would never just pick on someone or curse them out for the fun of it. I was not that kind of person.

One night, my sister spent the night somewhere, different than she usually slept. This white lady came to the apartment. She was a ghost. Her cigarette scent was what woke me up. I asked her, "What are you doing here?"

She said, "I came to wait for your sister. She can hear me, and I keep asking her to help me, and she does not want to. I was murdered." I told her sorry about that.

"But I can't help you either. You have to leave. Your cigarette smell is really stinking, and I am pregnant. I had seen my mother's spirit come looking for my sister, and she did not find her. But she did not see the ghost. She passed right by it." *Weird, heck, my whole life is weird now that I am writing about it, ha ha ha.* Grandma came in my dream one night, and she went to the door. It seemed like she was putting something in the door. So I asked her, "What are you doing?"

She said, "*Shi*, go back to sleep." The next morning, I called her and asked her grandma I saw you last night at the door putting something there. She laughed and told me, "That's why I love you, Gamain; your head can see [meaning the gift of sight]. You are truly gifted."

She said, "In the next two days, your mother would be coming to your house to finish you off, but she will not see you." Then she told Chase to open the door when my mother knocks on it. She said that she would turn jet-black as soon as she enters. "Don't be afraid of her. That was why she put the thing at the top of the door. The war of the witches has just begun."

"Oh my gosh!" My mother came to the house with my aunty just like grandma said she would. Chase was looking through the peephole to see them. She stepped back and had my aunty knock on the door. Chase called Grandma and told her they were here.

She said, "Be brave and not afraid. She will not harm her." Then she talked to me and told me how I was going to be invisible to my mother. Chase went and opened the door, but my aunty refused to come in, and she took her slippers off at the door. My mother told her go in first, and she told my mother no. She was not going to enter the house. She told my mom that she was going to wait for her at the door. My aunty waited at the door with her slippers off the entire time, Chase told me. My aunty did not want to be a part of what my mother was doing, and I heard her say this to my mother in our dialect, which is Krahn.

When my mother came in, she turned jet-black and confused right away. She kept asking Chase over and over, "Where is Eve?" She asked him more than five times. I could hear her from the room where I was and desperately believing with all my heart on this voice that introduced himself as Jehovah God to me. I knew in me that this was not the day I was going to die.

Nope, not today, I said to myself. Then she came into the room calling my name looking around as if she was truly blind. I got up and out of the bed and stood right in front of her. I said to her, "Here I am, Mom." She could not see nor hear me, and all this was happening in broad daylight round about 8:00 a.m. She could not see me at all. "Wow!" I was right in her face, and she was looking right at me but couldn't see or hear me. She did turn jet-black like the color of tar. She started to panic, and she left. That was when she was really sure that I had a witch doctor helping me. She really thought that God was going to make me a sitting duck, so she could just waltz in, kill me, and waltz right back out. I did not know God's word said he will never leave me nor forsake me. After that, she told everyone how I hired a witch doctor to kill her. The news spread like a wildfire.

Anastasia, my mother's first child, called me to tell me that her mother was not a witch, and even if she was and wanted to kill me, so what? She gave me life anyways, so I should allow her to just sacrifice me. "Say what?" I was no shocked at her statement. If anyone in the family was to tell me some nonsense like that, it would be her. I just politely told her, "You have lost your damn mind. Why can't you offer yourself as a sacrifice since you love your mother so much?"

"Well she doesn't want me. It's you she wants."

"Yeah, um about that, I don't think I am ready to die, so if that is all you called me to talk about, then this conversation is over." And I hung up on her. My oldest sister is either a blind bat, or she pretends as if she does not know who our mother really is. My father stayed quiet in all of this. I think he knew that it was not in God's will for me to die. Grandma told me about this bench that was in the yard that all the witches in the neighborhood used to sit on every evening. That was true. My mom and her friends had this bench they sat on every evening. Grandma told me that her Ginas were going to remove the bench, and it was not going to be there the next day. Grandma told me that I had a comforter in my room that I had for years, and that it was not an ordinary comforter. My mother had it worked on to keep me in one place. So I won't succeed in anything I did. Grandma took the comforter from me and told me the Ginas were going to take care of it. My mom once again told my sister that I give her lappa to the witch doctor to kill her.

"How do you know what was happening in my home when you are not there? Witch, I tell you. That's who she is."

I was still having nightmares about my mom every night fighting hard to kill me. What did I ever do to this lady that she is so bent on seeing me dead? I am not going to die. I will live. One night, I had a dream. She and a bunch of people were chasing me. She threw fire like a laser beam at me. Someone gave me a mirror in my sleep, and I pointed the mirror toward the beam, and it reflected and hit her in the eye. Within that week, I heard she was having eye problems. I saw her across the street with an eye patch on the very eye the beam hit her in my dream. I am not the only one that has accused my mother of witchcraft. In Liberia, people accused her. In Ivory Coast, people have accused her. Even in Ghana, my cousin told me every time she walks the street, people would say, "There goes that big witch in America's niece." So see I am not the only one. People know her to be demonic, and she doesn't even hide it. She is very cocky with it. She said she is a man, not a woman in the spirit realm. Yikes! She said she had looked Lucifer eye to eye over and over and was never afraid. The nickname her friends have for her is the dead snake that still makes the children afraid. Lots of people bow down to her because they are intimidated by her. I boldly told her I am not afraid of you, and God will strike you dead first before you kill me. You will be strike by lighting on a sunny day before you sink your fingers in me. I told her if it was not for my trust in God, I was going to pay someone to shoot her in the forehead. But vengeance is not mine. It of God, so I will rest in peace believing he will take care of it all.

One afternoon, Chase and I were sleeping when I had a dream. I had seen Grandma going to her rental office to find out why they towed her grandson's car. I had seen my mother with other witches throw Grandma to the ground and broke her hand then they ran off before her Ginas got there. I jumped from sleep and woke Chase up. In a hurry I told him grandma was hurt and she needed our help right away. We rushed over there and saw her walking from the rental office holding her limped hand and crying. The voice told me that her time of helping me was over and that he was going to send his very own in the end to help me undo all my mother has been doing to me. Grandma asked, "What are you doing here?"

I told her, "Grandma, I just had a dream the witches attacked you and broke your hand. So we came to check on you." She was so happy to see us. She fell more in love with me that day.

She said, "I love you so much, Gamain, your head can see." We took her to the hospital even though she said no, but Chase insisted. They broke her hand so she won't be able to kill the chickens that she was sacrificing several times a week for the Ginas to give them strength in order to help me. She was about to be outnumbered, the voice told me. I was told in the spirit to take a seven-day fast. While I was fasting, I had seen a vision of Mom in a basket drifting down in a river of fire. She was crying, but there was no one there to help her. Grandma did not allow me in the room the entire seven days of my fast. She said now that I was better; I could not go to her room anymore because the Ginas did not like God, and they will not be a part of him. I was very okay with that.

"She did her part already," the voice told me.

Then grandma asked me, "Do you want to denounce God and work for the Ginas because they really like you?"

I told her, "No, that's nice that they like me. Tell them thanks for helping me, but my time with them is over, and I must go."

She was so sad and asked me do I love her.

"Of course, I do, but you know who I am, and you and I cannot work together."

I told her, "Thank you very much, Grandma, I will never forget you."

She said, "I know that, you love people way too much for that to happen." She told me, "Remember your sister is not for you!"

What sister? She was referring to Pasei. But it was one of those things you did not want to know the answer to. I remember her telling Pasei a parable, saying, "If you want to be a fool and get used like a tool, then that's on you, but if you think that you are not a tool, then don't be a fool."

You go, Grandma Rap tress! She was very nice and funny. My sister Cellia that I have not seen nor spoken to in five years showed up one day.

She said, "I heard you were dying, so I came to look for you to see if you needed help." She said, our aunty told her I was a dead person walking, that I was about to die any minute. She said that, "I have the number to a prayer warrior pastor that can help you." She had the phone card, and we called the pastor in Africa, and she introduced me to him. He helped me a great deal. He would confirm visions and dreams that I would have and would tell me where to find them in the Bible. He told me the voice I was hearing was the voice of the Holy Spirit. He said demons would also talk to me (I already knew about the demons), but I will know the difference because the Holy Spirit will always correspond with the word of God. This helped me a lot. Someone who believed me and assured me that I was not crazy. He showed me how to use the Bible to combat evil. He showed me all these Bible verses. And he had the gift of sight and would tell me all these things before they happened.

Finally, someone who understood exactly what I was going through. I talked to him for twelve years. Then she called another pastor who was a woman (Paula Atkins Haynes) and also made the introduction. She is also very nice, and her gift was different from the other pastor. What he didn't see in the spirit, she would see and tell me. I started to get stronger spiritually with their help. Things started moving faster. I was very happy with Cellia and, most of all, God for this divine connection. He kept his promise. The voice told me I was about to move out of the neighborhood and go far away from Mom. Pasei was angry that Cellia came looking for me. She was mad why Cellia had to give me the numbers to these pastors. I did not understand then why she was so angry. I am the most naive person on earth, seriously. I always think because people smile with me means they love me (stupid girl huh). I will not be nice to someone if I did not like them; they would know. But whatever, people are just not who they say they are anymore these days. For this, we all have to be careful; our enemies could be our best friends or members of our family. Not always the case, but it happens. We need to pray always for God to reveal to us and give us the spirit of discernment. Now looking back on this, I remember every time Pasei touched me when I was pregnant with my daughter at two months. The baby would start moving around and make me so uncomfortable. My love for my sister had blinded me for many years. The scales will be removed off my eyes later, and you will find out what I did about it. Keep reading

My sister Cellia told me about her place in St. Cloud that she did not want to be anymore and told me since I was pregnant I should move there. So I took her offer. But when I got there, the rent was three months overdue, and I did not have that type of money.

My sister gave me one month's rent, Grandma gave me a month's rent, and Chase put in a month's rent. We had a few hours to come up with that late three months' rent money. My sister said she had no idea that the rent was behind like that because she had not lived there for a while. She felt bad. But anyways, God worked his blessings again. At this time, the nightmares were increasing. My mother was hot on my trail. She was going all out to get a hold of me physically. God was too fast for her. And over time, I started reading the Bible and knew how to fast and pray. Psalms 23 and 35 works great against this type of evil. History is not going to repeat itself, Mother. My parents had no idea that I was moving. The move was very quick, almost overnight. I was having dreams of Ginas (marine spirits) trying to kill the baby that I was carrying. They were not Grandma Ginas (fallen angels).

These one were different. The fallen angels fell everywhere upon this earth. Some are under the ground, some are flying in the sky, some are in the water, ocean, lakes, river, some walk amongst us and etcetera. These spirits kept telling me that they were in love with me; I kept running from them in my dreams. If a Gina marries you in your dreams, you will most definitely have a miserable life. They are extremely jealous and evil. They will kill all you children if you even have any and anyone you get too close to for that matter. One night this female Gina came to me violently and started to attack me, and we started fighting. I asked her, "What the hell do you want from me?" She told me I was with her, man and she did not like that.

I asked her, "Chase is your man?" Then she stopped and took a look at a sleeping Chase next to me and realized that it was not the man she was fighting for. She left as fast as she came. I called my sister Cellia the next day and told her what happened. She told me the female Gina was looking for her husband, and it always used to attack her. She confirmed the description to me. *Man, what a life.* When it was time to give birth to my daughter, the attacks became stronger. I had angry Ginas on my tale, Lucifer and my mother and all those other physical issues and a home to run. And a very unsupportive Chase even bought me about 60-dollar phone cards a week to call Africa and talk with those pastors. The doctor told me that I was going to give natural birth.

After hours of labor, Chase noticed that the monitors were not the way they were supposed to be. He called the nurses and told them to come and check the monitors. It was the baby; her heart rate was rapidly dropping. The doctor came immediately and told me they had to give me a emergency C-section. I was calm. All I did was pray Psalm 23, which I knew by heart and believe that God was hearing my prayers. I was not afraid, and I did not panic because I knew God did not bring me this far for me to die now. Chase was calm, and he was also praying the Psalm 23 prayer. He held my hand throughout as I was getting cut open. Everything went well, and she came into this world a bless child. While her father was holding her, she started to smile, and he said, "Ooh look she recognized her daddy." When I turned and looked at them, I saw three angels over her. They were playing with her and making her laugh.

I told Chase, "Honey, it's not you she smiling with. There are three angels playing with her." At that time, Chase was still having a very hard time accepting my gift, and he was not supportive at all. He would say hurtful, mean things. So I knew I could not talk to him about my dreams or premonitions. When we got home, my sister Cellia had surprised me with a lot of stuff. She had a very rich boyfriend, and she told her friend that Chase and I needed help. They bought so many things for my son; they filled up the extra room with diapers of all sizes for my daughter. Chase and I did not have to buy diapers for an entire year. I was so proud of Cellia for coming through like this. She did not have to tell her friend to help me, but she did. They bought so much food until we couldn't keep up eating it. They also pay our rent three months in advance (sweet). But this guy was a piece of work, and he took my sister far away where I did not see or hear from her. It was hard on me because she was the only one in the family that I used to talk to. They kept disappearing and reappearing back and forth, not supernaturally of course. I won't hear from them, and all of a sudden, they will start calling again after months. I started to get used to them before their vanishing act.

One day Chase asked me if I wanted to get marry. I said, "Sure, why not?" It was a Wednesday, and by Saturday, we were getting marrying. He had been there for me all those times when I was closed to death that I didn't need to think twice about marrying him. Pasei and Jasmine were the only family there. I didn't know where Cellia was and did not know how to contact her. She probably would not have come anyways because she did not like Chase. Chase and I got married in our living room. I had on my jeans and a blouse, nothing fancy. At that time, Chase and I were smoking weed, and I was drinking very heavily. The day of my wedding, I was so drunk I couldn't remember anything. Pasei took pictures of us, but I have never seen one picture up till now and this was 2005. She said she misplaced them. *Yeah right, whatever.* I can bet you anything she gave them to our mother. That girl is the most devious person I have ever known. Cellia and I nicknamed her Devianna, short for devious Anna. I did not know Cellia herself needed a name like that too.

Chase got hired at the company he was working at as a temp, and the pay was very good. Things started going smoothly until stupid me. I had to mess everything up. My sister Pasei, that everyone was warning me about needed help with her daughter. Before I took her daughter, I had a vision that God told me to not allow Pasei to touch me or come near me. She was not who she said she was, that it would be the same as Mom touching me. So I told her what the Holy Spirit said. I told her to bring her daughter to stay with me until she could get on her feet, and she did. But that was not such a good idea. More crazy, supernatural stuff started to happen, and I had to constantly fast and pray. When things did not go as they had planned, she came and got her daughter, and they left. My mother wanted to use my kindness against me. This she had tried doing with me and my father before, using the love that I had for him to lure me into her deadly snare. When Pasadena took her daughter, she and I did not talk for a while.

When my daughter was nine months old, she had an asthma attack, and we took her to the hospital. While we were there, I also had an asthma attack. The doctor told me that he wanted to give me some steroids, but he had to do a pregnancy test first. I laughed at him and told him, "Doc, I cannot be pregnant. My daughter is only nine months old."

He said, "Okay, but let's make sure."

The nurse asked me, "Are you sure that you are not pregnant?"

"Dude, I am quite sure I am not pregnant." That nurse came back with a smirk on his face minutes later, and I knew right away that I was pregnant. I just lost it and started crying; he had to walk with me back to the room where Chase was. Chase was very concerned, and he asked what happened. I told him that I was pregnant. He knew since I found God, I did not believe in abortions anymore. What a horrible thing when you don't know God. I will forever be grateful. I am writing a tell-all book so the world can know that there is a God who sees everything and is always wanting the best things for us. I had twenty-four abortions in my life not knowing I was feeding the devil the blood he needed to by giving him my unborned children. The prophetess Annie who you will later read about told me this. I knew abortion was wrong when I found out about God, but I did not know I was assisting Satan and giving him a reason to attack me.

My first abortion was when my mother pressured me in the Ivory Coast to remove the pregnancy. Immigration, she said, were not going to allow the family to come to America if I was pregnant. I should not ruin my brother's and sisters' chances of a good life. She told me it would be evil if I kept the pregnancy. She had some girl stuck a stick in me, and the liquid from it burned through my womb and killed the twins I was carrying. My sister buried them after they dropped to the ground. I did not have the guts to do it myself. I was sad. I was living in darkness and did not even know it. What you don't know can harm you. Before this I never even knew what abortion was. After my son died a violent death in the arms of the one I trusted the most, I felt like any child I brought into this world, she would kill them too. I did not protect Elijah from her. If only I knew how to protect my child at that time. This is a woman that killed people for a living. I did take birth control to prevent this from happening, but I was reckless in keeping up with the days. I took the Depo shot, and it caused me to get very sick, I could not stop bleeding. I did not know any better. Now that I know what has been happening, I am so sorry for what I did and will never support abortion. I can't make up for what I did, but I can help a woman make the right decision tomorrow to choose life.

So I am pregnant, and by now, my stomach was showing. I had no friends, and I did not go around any family members because I did not want my mother to find out that I was pregnant. I did not want her to launch another attack on me. One day, my youngest sister Brittany called me from Georgia and told me she had a dream that I was pregnant. I told her, "Yes, but don't say anything. Let it be a secret." She did just that. But Cellia's boyfriend, the rich dude, told my sister Pasei that I was pregnant.

Not knowing at that time he was sleeping with both my sisters Cellia and Pasei. Gross! So Pasei called and asked me if it is true. I told her that it was not true, that I was not pregnant. I had to be very careful. By this time, I was suspecting Pasei to be working with my mother. One day, I heard the Holy Spirit (the voice) telling me that someone was going to pay me a surprise visit, and I should pray over some water and keep it in different places in my house. I did not know who this surprise guest was going to be. The Holy Spirit told me they would be sent to kill my son when he was born. I did everything I was told and was obedient to the Holy Spirit. The Holy Spirit told me that if I let this particular sister of mine know that I was pregnant, she would be there in the delivery room during my C-section, and the demon in her might come out and cause the doctor to make a mistake that would cost me my life. I was not about to risk anything. I had been unknowingly sacrificing my children when I was having all those abortions so they (demons) could feed. What you don't know can harm you; don't let anyone fool you about that. During my pregnancy, things got very tough.

After I had my baby that was when I called my mom and dad to tell them. The first question that came out my mother's mouth was, "Is the baby dead?" I laughed at her and told her the baby was alive and well and will be that way for years to come.

My father asked me, "Why did you not tell me?"

I asked him, "Why, so your wife can eat this one too?" He went quiet. Cellia and I made a three-way call to Pasadena.

I asked her, "Remember you asked me if I was pregnant, and I told you no." I said, "Well, I just had the baby, but you can't come over here because Mom is trying to use someone to kill my baby. So please don't come over here." She said okay. My sister Cellia was quiet on the other line bearing witness to what I was saying. About four days later, Pasadena called me and asked me how I was doing. I told her that I was ok. Then she asked me, "Where are you"? I told her that I was home.

She said, "I am outside in your parking lot."

"What the hell?" I have not seen this girl in about a year. I lived one-hour drive from this girl, and I just told her four days ago that I did not want her coming to my house. And now she is in my parking lot?

I called Cellia and told her what was happening and I quickly ran downstairs in the room to my children and started praying Psalm 23 over them as I poured holy water on them. Before I knew it, Pasadena was downstairs in my room. But I was done doing what I had to do for my children. I woke them up and took them upstairs. My son Cody, the oldest, opened the door for her without even asking who it was. Pasei was holding my son, and I saw his breath leaving his body and going into her. I started pleading with God and praying in the spirit. "God, you want me to be patient. Do you see what is going on?"

He said, "Trust in me." So I took my baby out of her hands and told her that he needed to go back and take a nap. The voice told me that I should not let her spend the night because she did not come alone. All the witches were with her, and if she spends the night, they would come out and jump on me. He said they would overpower and kill me. What I did not know was she was an incubator witch. A witch who transported in their body other witches and demons from one place to another and would get back in after their task was completed. That day, Chase was at work, and he came home about twenty minutes after Pasei got there. I noticed that my daughter was really afraid of Pasei, and normally, my daughter is friendly with everyone. Remember this is the child that moved in my stomach at two months along whenever Pasei touched me.

My phone rang, and I answered it, but there was no one at the end of the line. Then it rang again, and I answered it; there was no one there again. Pasei told Chase she wanted to wait until the time he was coming home before she got there. The Holy Spirit told me it was because he had a soft spot for her. "Make sure she does not spend the night. She left her car door open so the battery can die, and your husband is going to ask you if she can spend the night. Do not allow this to happen." She stayed and ate, and it was getting late. Something prompted Chase to go outside and take a look at her car. She left her car door ajar so the battery would die. He came back and told her that her car door was left opened and he needed her keys to make sure the battery was not dead. He checked the car, and the battery was dead.

She said, "Oh, it's okay, I will just spend the night." I was angry in the spirit, very angry watching my little sis trying hard to cause me such heartache by killing my son. Not again, not this time, not today, and not as long as I live. I cannot express enough how angry in the spirit I was. If Chase was not there, I was going to shred my sister physically into pieces. Once again, God spared my life.

I said to Chase, "You have jumper cables. Go and start her car. She has to go home. It's getting late, and I was very firm about it."

He called me aside and asked me, "Can't she just spend the night?" I told him she was sent to kill my baby, and since he was blind (spiritually), he needed to leave me alone let me deal with my family. Stay out of this and if you get me my way I will never forgive you and will spend the rest of my life making your life as misery as can be. He could see the anger in me. These people killed my son, and you now want to stand in my face asking me to do what? "Black man, step aside let me take care of this the way I know how."

Now go and start her car; she's got to go back to where she came from. After he started the car, I told her, "It is time to go, Pasei." I escorted her, and the whole time she was there, I did not laugh with her. My spirit was too strong for her to do what she came to do. God was present in my home that day, and the guidance of the Holy Spirit was very strong. She got in her car and left. She knew I was unto to her. My pastor from Africa, the lady, called me the next day. She was panicking and talking fast, trying to explain to me.

I told her, "Sis Paula, slow down."

She said, "Eve, some girl came to your house yesterday to kill your son, and she explained the whole thing that happened in my house." She was calling from Africa. She told me this very person was going to call me the next day and tell me how Lucifer and our mother wanted her to do something, and she did not do it; now they are mad at her. Pasei called me saying exactly what my pastor said she would say a day later. I went off on Pasei the minute she got done talking. I told her, "I don't know what in God's name I did in order for them to treat me the way they do. But I will not lose another child again." Before all this took place, Pasei called me and asked me for us to go to our mother's house and apologize to her for accusing her of being a witch. I said, "But she is a witch, why should I?"

"She is our mother, and the Bible said, 'Thou shall obey your mother and father.'"

"Yeah, I know, but not witches and wizards. I am not going to her house." I said, "Remember God told me not to ever step foot in here house, and if I did when I got up to heaven, I shouldn't blame him for my death. I am not going to do it. The spirit of obedience (to God) and stubbornness help me a lot to stay alive." She told me she was going because there where her blessings were.

She said, "I have to do what I have to do, Eve."

"You do that then." Coming back to where I left off about her visit, I told her, "From this day on, do not call my house anymore. Stay the hell away from me. You have deceived me and betrayed me bitterly. I don't know when I will forgive you for what you just tried to do to me." She was quiet and did not say a word. She and Mom knew very well of the power that laid on my tongue. If she had said one wrong thing, I was going to tell her something very horrible. Mom knew this all too well about me, and this is why she refrained from any physical confrontation with me. I did not talk to Pasei or see her again for five years. You are probably thinking and asking, "Well, if she had this gift, why did she not use it a long time ago with all that she has been through?" God wants you to see how he, God, should be glorified by what he has done for me. If he God can do this for me, he can do anything for you as well. Remember the purpose of this book in the first place was he wanted you to know that he was God and that he was alive and well and a God who answers prayers. I can never take glory away from my Father. This is why I have suffered a great deal. He trusts me to do what he tells me. Remember the bet he and Satan made? How can I, knowing all these things, allow myself to do anything else? I have thought of suicide many times and even tried it once after Elijah died. I cannot do it because that will make me an ungrateful little brat. Don't you think?

One day, I heard the Holy Spirit telling me to fast and pray and request the angels to come and protect me. I did. The next day, I called my aunty like I did all the time. She said, "My daughter, you are a child of God. The witches had grouped up last night and were coming to your house to kill you. But when they got there, your whole house was surrounded by angels guarding the whole place." I just laughed because darkness always underestimates the power of the light.

I told her, "Well, that's good. People, I am telling you. God is real!

My dad asked me one day if he could spend some time with me at my house. I really wanted him to. But I had a dream and saw my father lying in the bed, but when I took a closer look, it was really my mother, and she got up and injected something into my daughter and killed her. I told him no; he too was not allowed in my house because of who he was married to. Don't forget my mother is a shape changer. This was why God revealed this dream to me before the love I had for my dad would get my daughter killed. My aunty wanted to get to know me a little better I told her the same thing also. She too wanted to come to my house.

She was my mother's best friend even though she was related to my dad. I know I sound mean, but I had to do this; my life and kids' life were depending on it. I have learned that you can't play nice with witches, or this will get their aim accomplished. I also noticed they love to act like they are so nice, but behind closed doors, they did unspeakable things. I have been sent to let you know all these things, so please pay close attention. I am not saying nice people are witches. No, I am saying witches love to play nice during the day, and at night, they are not recognizable. I was constantly on my guard because I now have three children, two of whom my mother wanted to eat. Remember, she's not allowed to harm my oldest son because of the rules.

One morning after taking Chase to work, I came back home and was sitting on the bed taking my shoes off. *Boom!* Out of the ground of my bedroom floor came Mr. Lucifer himself with yours truly, my mother. He was angry with her and asked, "Why have you not brought me the girl and I have been waiting?"

She said, "I am trying, my lord, but she is too powerful for me." He said, "Than we have to distract her." He flew upstairs to my older son. Then there were two Codys. By the time the vision was over, I ran upstairs to my son and met him right where he was in my vision. I just poured the gallon of holy water on him and started praying.

He said, "Mom, what are you doing? Now I have to change my clothes before I go to school. Oh no you won't. You will go just like that. You had a vision or dream, didn't you?" he asked. Since that day, my son started acting like he had multiple personalities. But I did not let the devil distract me. I prayed and believed that God would help him.

Everything thing started to go well for us. Both Chase and I were working. I kept telling Chase for us to go to church and pay our tithes. He used to get so mad at me for saying that. He said that God new that he was poor and needed every penny for himself. This used to make me cringe and uneasy because I knew better. He would get mad at me for splashing holy water in the house, saying it was ruining his furniture. Every time I was fasting, he would get so angry, and that made me really concerned. When I told his mom, she said, "Well, not all pastors believe in holy water or paying their tides. I knew she was no different, and I couldn't talk to her. Like I said, the only supporters I had was Cellia and the two pastors in Africa.

We found this church that we started going to. I did not feel comfortable in the church; there was something not right about it. So I prayed asking God to help show me what was wrong. He said, "You don't belong in this church. There is a serial killer that goes to this church off and on, and the devil will use him to get rid of you." I told the unbelieving Chase.

He said, "You always come up with crazy things." One day we went to the church to attend the volleyball game they were playing. My back was turned toward the door when all of a sudden the hair on the back of my neck started to rise.

I heard the voice say, "The killer is here, and he got his eyes on you. Don't stay in this church." When I turned, there was this guy standing at the entrance of the door just looking at me. Then the voice said, "That's him." Every time I looked up, he was staring at me. I was so uncomfortable. I did not know what to do. I wanted to leave right then but, the voice told me wait when everyone was leaving before I leave. And I did just that. The voice of the Holy Spirit told me this guy killed a boy named Jacob Wetterling many, many years ago. Not to cause any pain to the Wetterling but if this man stood in front of me I would not recognize him right now. But at the time of Jacob's abduction this guy had to be in his late teens or early twenties. I remember the name because it was on the news when I was a child. I told everything to Chase who did not believe me of course. I told him I was never ever going to that church again and neither were my kids. He still went to the church but did not take my kids. After going there two or three times, he noticed the church was like a cult. We were the only black people in that church by the way. Not that it made a difference but just giving you an idea of how it was.

This lady came to do her hair at my house. As I was doing her hair, I asked her if she knew about the church, and she flat out told me, "You need to find another church to go to. The pastor of that church is very racist, and every black person living out here knows that. He preaches against Dr. Martin Luther King openly at his church. We were all outraged. If you know what's best for you, you will find another church to go to." Chase heard her saying this. He did not go to the church after that either. Somewhere in him, he believed me. The devil loves to go to church. Don't you know there, where the children of the light are; is where he is trying to eliminate them? Where better to find them than the church, don't stop going to church, just pray before you go? Sometimes the devil is the one in the pulpit. This pastor knew of some of the evil members of his church did, and he swept it under the rug. He is not a true man of God.

Now there was a problem. There is this woman in the neighborhood that was a witch. One day she came to me and, in a low voice, started asking me who I dealt with. I told her I know this man, and he was very good. Stupid me, I did not know that is not what she meant. She asked me for his number, and I wrote it down for him. When she saw that the name has a "pastor" title in front of it, she refused it and told me, "I thought the way you were always shinning you were dealing in the underworld." She got so mad at me and stormed away. I had just made a freindenemy.

She came to my house one day with her five-year-old son so I could babysit him. I said, "Okay, that's cool." While I was trying to take a nap, she came in shadow form and started to pull on my foot. I knew it was her, and she was testing me. She kept bothering me after I tried to ignore her. Like a pest that wouldn't go away. I called her name and yelled at her, telling her to leave me the hell alone and come get her son right now. Within a few minutes, she was knocking on the front door to get her son.

What the hell, man? I did not say a word to her, and she did not speak to me either. We were both mad at each other. This bimbo did not stop there. One time, I came home with my children and this chick was on some other stuff.

"Wow!" She saw me in the parking lot and insisted that I did her hair right there and then. The voice of the Holy Spirit told me that she wanted me to catch some disease on my hands. This woman did not even have any hair. She was so desperate. I told her I will be back as soon as I get the kids in the house. But she kept insisting. I yelled at my older son right in front of her and acted like I was so mad at him. He was confused but did as he was told and started walking in front of me.

When we got away from her, he asked me, "Mom, what did I do?"

"Nothing, baby. That woman is a witch. You watch and see what Mommy is about to do." We got in the house, and I told him to bring me the holy water. "Watch. She will run from me. She won't want me to touch her hair anymore." I washed my hands and told him to get her while I was standing outside watching. She started running like someone was chasing her. My son started laughing so hard.

She was screaming over and over, "Don't come near me. I don't want you touch me." "Forget about the hair," she said. My son was so amazed.

I told him, "Baby, that's the power of God."

Then he asked me, "Why would she want to harm you, Mom?"

"She can't help herself. She is working for Satan. People like that whenever they see a child of God, all they want to do is feed, and they will stick to you like glue."

Just when I thought things were getting better, they took a turn for the worse. When I told Chase what happened, he said, "Eve, everybody is a witch to you."

I said, "That is not true. This lady is a witch." He did not want to any hear of it. I started doubting little by little, day by day. I should not have let this happen. I slowed down in my prayer, and I stopped fasting altogether because I was tired of fighting with Chase every time I did. I could feel myself slowly getting spiritually weak and drifting away from the things of God and once again started to embrace the things of this world. As human beings, it is so easy to forget God once your situation improves. I started getting tired with Chase and his constant lack of support. Yes, he was working, but what good was the money when he was not paying his tithes? Even though I pay tithes but if he was not doing the same, mine wouldn't count because we were married. When you get married, you become one in everything especially in the realms of the spirit.

I decided with my super smart self (not) to cheat on Chase for cheating on me in California. I wanted to payback. I told him that I was going to, but he did not believe me. I did for three months. I also cheated because I wanted us to do the things of God, and he did not believe in all that at the time. I used to ask God all the time why would he let me date a man who was nothing like me spiritually. He was not supportive of my artwork; he was not supportive spiritually. It almost seemed like the only reason we got along was because we both smoked and drank. So when this guy came along and wanted to support me in everything, I thought I could leave Chase and be with him. Throughout my whole affair, I tried to leave Chase, but I couldn't. I loved him still and we had young children for one, and he was there for me when I was sick. He was really nice to me as long as there was not any spiritual talk. Three months later, I told Chase everything I did and the reason why. I could not get past all the anger of the things he did to me. That really hurt him. But at that time, I was numb to his feelings. He got stressed out and did not know what to do with himself. I realized that what I did was bad very bad! I told the guy that something bad was about to happened to me because whenever Chase and I do these things bad things always happened. I completely broke it off with the guy, hoping and thinking everything was going to be okay, not at all. Things turned out for the worse. I had just opened Pandora's Box.

I was a nurse aid at this group home, I went to work one day, and there was a cake in the refrigerator with my name on it. My supervisor Alicia told me this other lady that worked there brought this cake for me. She told me, "Eve, could you please not eat that cake. I feel like if you eat it, something will happen to you. I looked at her and told her thanks. I threw the cake out when I got home. Chase had a dream this very lady from the job wanted us to let our older son come to her house and be with her for some time. The Holy Spirit told me that this lady wanted my son dead. This is how evil these witches are. You have your children, and I have mine. Why will you want to kill mine? I told my supervisor to watch and see. She was very overprotective of me from the time I got the job. She told me, "I am not like this with everyone, but I feel you need me to watch out for you." Remember I told you how God always sent someone to help me. I told her the lady was up to no good, and she was right to suspect her. She got scared for me. I told her, "Watch, she will not be able to get me or my son, but she needs to sacrifice someone. Someone very close to her will die soon, and it will have something to do with water.

Alicia asked me, "Why water?"

I told her, "Because the lady was a water witch." A few months later, her granddaughter who lived with her went to visit her mom and drowned in the pool while there was an adult watching. My supervisor told me what happened. This very lady showed up in my dream before I even knew who she was. She killed her thirty-something-year-old daughter. The girl was a friend of my sister. I did not know the girl either but I saw the whole thing in my dream.

I told my sister, "I saw your friend dying, and her mother, father, and a sister were the ones that sacrificed her. Don't get involve now. It's too late. The girl got sick and died months later.

And my sister knew that her life was in jeopardy so she withdrew after the girl died. This gift is one that is very difficult to have. Knowing that someone's life is about to be over. It is hard to phantom every time. This girl picked up on the night, one night. After we did our midnight rounds, we sat down, and she was explaining to me about her boyfriend. All of a sudden, *boom*! This ghost came rushing to me, telling me to give this girl a message.

The ghost said, "Tell her she hears dead people, but she should not tell anyone, or they would put her in a mental institute where she will die." I ignored the ghost and was calm, so this girl kept talking about her boyfriend.

The ghost yelled at me really loud, and I jumped and said, "Okay, I will tell her, all right?"

My coworker was shock and looked at me like, what the hell is wrong with you? I looked at her and said you are going to think I am crazy for saying this, but I don't have a choice. Sara was her name. I told her there is a ghost of a woman in here right now. "Tell her my name starts with a B." "Ok I will", looking at the ghost. This poor girl must have thought something was wrong with me. This ghost in here was woman, and she is telling me to tell you that you hear other ghosts talking and you are getting afraid and want to tell someone, don't she said. Don't tell anyone or you would be placed in a mental institute where you are going to die just like she did. Sara started to cry and I looked at the ghost and told her see what you did now I am going to lose my job. The ghost left. I started apologizing to a crying Sara and asked her not to please say anything to anyone before I lose my job. She said, "No I won't I promise. That was my aunty I think she said Bernice. She used to hear ghost all the time, and they put her in a mental institute, and she died there."

"Is she still here?"

"No she is gone now. I have been hearing ghosts, and I wanted to tell my boyfriend because it's making me scared, and I don't know what to do."

"Well, your aunty said not to tell anyone. She said, 'Thank you so much, Eve.'" The next day, she told everyone of my gift. Now people were coming to me and asking all sorts of questions.

Anyways, back to Pandora's Box. I was lifting someone up when a loud noise a client's parent made startled me. I ripped the muscles in my hip. It made a really loud noise, and the supervisor heard it. I did not want to make an incident report, but she insisted. I was okay for a few, days until the same stupid witch came to the house to try me again. They were very persistent, those witches and wizards. She came at about 9:30 p.m. She had a hoody on so Chase could not make out who was at the door. She was not allowed in my house, and he knew this. Right when he opened the door, I was up the stairs already and a few feet behind him. She came in and shook my hand really fast and asked me to do her hair again at that very moment I told her no. She wanted micro braids and every stylist knows you don't do micro braids at 9:30 in the night.

"When will you finish?" She said okay and left. As soon as she left, I started feeling funny. My chest felt like someone was sitting on it. I couldn't not stand up; my legs went paralyzed, and I was in great pain.

"She came here with something, and that's what she put in your hands, didn't she?"

"Yeah." The two pastors called me the following day and told me how a lady came to the house to paralyze me. They prayed for me, but it was too late. She got me this time. I have not walked on my own for a while now. If I had not exposed my body to a man other than my spouse, I would have seen this coming and avoided it. I had made myself spiritually weak with my promiscuous behavior. I thought I was getting revenge on Chase all those times he cheated on me. I was wrong again! Having sex here and there is very dangerous not only for STDs, but it is very bad spiritually. Dwelling in everyone is a spirit, and if it is not the spirit of God, bet you it a spirit of Satan. But there is no such thing as an empty body. My pastor Annie Wolo Johnson said that the body is a vessel; it can either be used for good or evil depending on the spirit that is dwelling in it.

Chase asked me, "Are you ready for the long road ahead of us because of what you did?"

I asked him will he be there knowing how sorry and stupid I felt for what I did?

He said yes. *Boom.* Chase lost his job. *Boom.* I lost my job. *Bang.* We got in a nasty car accident on our way to the ER because of an asthma attack I was having, and the car was totaled. We got evicted from our home and lost everything in it when they changed the locks on us. Our daughter almost died and was hospitalized. We ended up in a shelter. I never even knew what a shelter was. See how one stupid mistake can turn your whole world upside down? All hell broke loose. Life is so much easier when both partners are faithful. The room we were in at the shelter smelled like piss so bad that you could smell it down the hall. There were poop everywhere, the mattress, the shower, the rug, and the walls. My daughter caught a vaginal infection, and the doctor told us to hurry up and find somewhere to live. They stole my clothes that I had with me. Wow! It was awful. Then the same witch again wanted to finish me off. She was a very skinny woman, but she looked like she was nine months pregnant. But she was not pregnant at all. Someone probably made her to get that an African sign. I have seen that before. Don't you know this bimbo tried to transfer that crap into me. I had a dream one night and saw her doing that. Are you for real, man? I woke up and started praying against it. I told Chase my dream.

He said, "You just need to let this go. She does not even know where you live right now." He was upset because of all the stress. Later that day, we went to the corner store for about fifteen minutes. Guess who came to the shelter looking for yours truly?

The witch! The girl that saw her there knew her from the old neighborhood. As soon as Chase and I came from the store, the girl said, "Oh did you pass by Gelina on your way back here? She was just here, and she waited for you a little bit but I told her to go, because whenever you left, you usually don't come back right away." T was the name of the girl.

I asked her if Gelina had her hands in her pocket.

T said, "Yes. How did you know?" I looked at Chase like you were just going off on me and now what I told you is happening. He did not say a word. He knew I was pissed. I just went in the house and told him that we had to pray. He had to get in agreement with me for God to forgive me for what I did. We fasted and prayed for three days. After the fast and prayer, there came a lady that was hired at the shelter, and she said that she wanted us out of the shelter and in a house. Her coworker was against that. So she went over her head and to the boss, and the boss favored us and gave us the house in a really nice neighborhood. We had to wait a few weeks for the house to be ready. CDI, the clinic that was giving me the steroid shots favored me and decided to adopt our family for the holidays. They gave us everything we needed and even more. The door I opened for Satan to enter was now shut. He favored us once again. God had sent this lady to help me and my immediate family. My adopted mom as I called her bought us a car and paid our insurance for six months. Then she paid our deposit for the new house. The shelter had a Good Samaritan program that paid our first month's rent. Everything was great. And it was time to move into our new home. It was a long road like Chase said, but he stood by me the whole time.

We loved our new house, and it was just big enough to suit our family. After being here for a year, I realized that everything we had just been through caused me to have situational depression. That's when I knew that depression was real. I started getting frustrated over everything. We had no income to pay the rent. My adopted mom had come through for us so many times, but I was not comfortable with someone paying my bills all the time. Chase couldn't go to work because he had to care for me and kids.

I started drinking heavily and found myself taking my frustration on Chase when I was drunk. This went on for some time. He was the one running the house by cooking, cleaning, and laundry. You name it, and he was doing it. I lost myself. I did not know how to take care of me or my children anymore. I had so much negative emotions in me. My mind was so cloudy. I had constant aches and pain in my body to the point it was unbearable, and I was bent over all the time. My back, hips, knees, neck, hands, and head were all hurting very badly.

Sometimes I couldn't get out of bed for weeks, and the only place I went was to the doctors. Depression does happen, but all these things had nothing to do with the depression. I started taking my sleeping pills several times in the middle of the day just to get a high off them, not to mentioned double dosing. I was tired spiritually and physically. I would say to myself, to whom much is given much is required. God has done so much for me because the devil did so much to me. I knew I had to go through all these things for the experience, some were my fault and some I had no control over. Like he said in the beginning you are about to suffer a great deal". If I did not, how could help God's children understand something I have no experience of? Plus God is involved, and with him, anything is possible. He knows that I cannot praise him from the grave, so he was going to heal me eventually and make me whole again. I believed that with all my heart. Chase would express to me how worried he was, and he would even go as far as hiding my prescription sleep medicine. Nightquil didn't do anything for me. I would drink a bottle of that on the spot. Not to mention that I was also smoking weed and getting drunk like crazy. It was awful. But it helped with the pain mentally and physical for the moment, I would forget my troubles. I was in another maze, and I couldn't see my way out. I had stopped praying and fasting. Like I said, I was tired. God knew my heart and everything in it. At some point, he was going to show me a way out, and I had hope when there was no reason to have hope.

All I could think about was all the hardship I had been through. It all hit me at once. I had no family that I could turn to besides my elderly aunty who was already in her late seventies. I couldn't bother her with my problems. I did not want her to worry about me. My adopted mom only came around to help financially. She had her own home to run, and what she was doing in my life was more than enough. Besides she knew nothing of the supernatural. I just wanted to curl up and die. But I knew that if I took my own life, God was never going to forgive me because he had done so much for me to feel his presence in my life. If that was not the case, I was going to be selfish and probably take my own life. After all, we as human beings have some selfish tendencies. This was around the same time I started hearing a voice. For one week in a row, I kept hearing this voice telling me that Chase had to leave and go back to his family in New Jersey. It said that if he did not leave, I was going to lose him forever to death. It kept saying, "Now is the time." Everywhere I looked, I would see "Now Is the Time" on TV, billboards, magazines, etcetera. I started to get scared. I did not want to say anything to him, but I now am aware of God, so I get scare if I don't do what I am told.

I told him, and he said that he was not leaving me, and if it was his time to die, then let him die. I begged him to go. And he refused. One day, he had a dream and seen his dead grandmother bring him three watches and told him to choose one. He did not know the meaning of the dream, but when he explained it to me, I knew what it meant. It was confirmation to what the voice was telling me. I believe it was a familiar spirit which can also be send to one by another human being like a witch or wizard. Little did I know a demon called Asmodeus had entered into my home! Someone had sermon this demon to do this to me I found out later. Someone who knew I was sensitive to the spirits. Cellia's betrayal did more to me then she will ever know. Anyways I felt as if I had no choice but to call his family and let them know what was happening and told them that it was serious. They thought it was because I did not want to be with him anymore, so I was making an excuse. I told his mom, "If you let your son stay here, if anything happens to him, do not hold me responsible because I am giving you a warning about what I was hearing." They panicked and asked him to leave. He pleaded with me not to do this. He was so very sad. *I could not be with him anymore,* I thought. He has suffered enough taking care of me. He did not know how to help me with what I was going through and it was frustrating at times for him. When I met Chase he was an unbeliever and for years I would pray and ask God why he sent an unbeliever in my life and insisted that I stayed with him. I would tell God if you want me to be with him you have got to help with his unbelieve and make him a believer. Even though it took years Chase is now a believer. I divorced him two months later after he left. He was shocked. He knew that I loved him very much, so he could not understand what was happening. After that, I decided to marry a pastor friend of mine hoping that he was going to help me find the Lord so I could be this Godly person. He had helped me deal with a lot of the supernatural things that I was going through before. I thought since Chase didn't know anything about the things that were happening to me, it would be best after leaving him to be with this pastor. That was one of the biggest mistakes of my life, and it cost me to lose a great deal. He was worse than ten of the most awful guys I have ever dated put together. He frustrated me to the point where my depression got severe, and I shut down mentally and physically.

I had so much respect for this man before, and I remember Chase used to tell me all the time that "This pastor friend of yours is not really who he says he."

This man was my worst nightmare. If I had been a weak-minded person, he would have made me to turn against God completely. He used to tell me how I was not fit for the kingdom of heaven and how I would never be good enough to work for God. It was because of him being a pastor that I decided to date him in the first place. This guy told me that it was my fault, that my son was autistic, and that God hated me for that. Guess who was the cause behind this? Cellia, my precious sister! She would call this pastor and tell him everything she knew about me, and then add some lies to that. He got frustrated because he was in love, so he allowed to the devil to get the best of him. It was like he was insane, and he hated to hear my voice reasoning out. How could Cellia betray me like this? She told the dude that I was worthless and no good. When I confronted Cellia about this she denied everything forgetting the fact that there was no way he could had known all these things he did. She did not own up to what she did. She told people the reason she does not want to be bother with me was because I am rude. The real reason was because she knew I cover her butt a lot of times and she ended up betraying me. When I told her lets squash the whole thing she refused and I was thankful for that. I did not want to have someone around me who have betrayed me several times already. I pray for myself that the love I have in my heart for people does not end up being the death of me.

This pastor was all the way in Africa, and she was my sister, so he believed every word that came out of her mouth. This is the time, she did this before with Pevu, and I did not say anything. I remember she would literally walk around in the house naked, and Pevu would get turned on. She always pretended to be innocent, she was far from innocent. She is very devious. I was very hurt by Cellia's behavior. She had a lot of thing to tell Jeff about me also until we broke up then she became good friends with his girlfriend. She is a snake, a coward, and people like that are not worth ten minutes of my time. Jasmine warned me for years about Cellia but I was too busy doing my own thing to notice who all was digging a pit for me to fall in. I will always keep her at an arms reach because I believe I am allergic to snakes. Especially vipers!

Before I persuaded this pastor, I asked Cellia if she was interested in him. She said no, and I made her swear it three times. She told the pastor, "Eve made me say I swear to God, but what she didn't know is I said that I swore to Gog not God. There were too many things he couldn't had possible known that only Cellia knew. She too has been exposed to me as a devious person. I don't think she can help herself that's just who she is. When I confronted her a year later, she said it was all a lie. I cursed her out. I was drunk. She has a lot of recording of me cursing her out. I cannot stand devious people especially in my own family. So I already know when this book comes out and she is not in favor of what I wrote about her she will tried to discredit me by playing the recordings for the public. "Cellia, honey, I really don't give a damn. You can tell the whole world how I always cursed you out. Please don't forget to tell them it's because you are so damn devious, and you have been too busy pointing your fingers to everyone else instead of yourself." I personally never heard the recording, but the spirit would always tell me that she was recording me and that she had more than one because she wants to use them as bargaining chips for the day I get rich. The best thing to do to a blackmailer is to tell the truth.

Everyone in my family had dreams regarding my future at one point or another. They all know that one day the whole world will know about me. They have all experience at one point the power of God in me and all the gifts I have been given. My sisters would always ask me, "I don't know why God favor you so much and do anything you ask him to do."

"It's my heart. He is a God who searches hearts at night. Why do you think he trusts me enough to make a bet with Lucifer? Please don't get me wrong. It is not because of a man I can't stand my sister. It's because of her devious ways. I know she was really nice to me at one point until I got something she wanted. I told you the good things about her now; here "lies" the bad side of her.

I used to tell Chase everything that was happening while he was in New Jersey. Chase would calm me down on the phone every day. He would remind me of the great person he felt that I am. Chase was gone for nine months. He kept calling me every day, asking me if he could come back home, and I refused every time. I wanted to see what I was capable of doing without him. I felt useless when Chase was around since I got hurt.

Seriously, he did everything. For a long time, all I did was eat and sleep and gained one hundred pounds. He made me breakfast, lunch, and dinner and brought it to me, even if I was in bed. He was putting in a 110 percent into the relationship and because of all the chaos in my life I couldn't see that. He wanted me to forgive him for everything he did to me in the past, and he would say that nearly every day. Not a day will go by without him telling me how much he loves me. As I am writing this book, he is busy taking care of our children and home. I resented him for a long time. I had no friends, so it was easy to take all my frustration out on him. I have learned not to do that anymore because he too is only human.

Chase is the calmest person I have ever known besides my father. What he had to go through with me only God could have sent him my way. I thought I was going to be ok without him. I was wrong, very wrong. It was already hard keeping up with our autistic son and Cody my eldest son was constantly on the run and going into placements. I couldn't do it on my own. I needed Chase to come back, but I was too stubborn to tell him or agree for him to come home. One day, I had a dream my kids were taking from me. In my dream, there was a winding road that led to the house. In this house was a woman who took care of a lot of children. The only problem was I saw a man who helped her up keep the grounds. This man in my dreams was molesting the children. I stripped him of everything and told him to go to church. In my dream, he was punished for what he did. I did not know why my children were taken from me until months later. I was so stressed out I started drinking even more than usual because of the people I had gotten myself involved with. I had stretched myself thin and very thin.

On two separate occasions what I did all the time backfired on me. I had a couple of beers and took my sleeping pills and almost died. If it was not for my daughter I was going to die, and I would have made the enemy happy. She was the one that called 911 both times to tell them that her mommy won't wake up. This daughter of mine is truly a Godsend. The police took me to the hospital. In the hospital, they were so mean to me and treated me like crap. They looked at me like some animal that had no right to live. I felt so bad, and I told myself over and over, "They don't know you or what you have been through." This man came to ask me if I was trying to kill myself and when I explained to him how much I love God and what I have been through he told them to release me, and he was super nice. I believed that God sent him to talk to me and be super nice because of how sad I was by the way the staff at this hospital treated me. This is the same hospital that the nurse left scissors in my daughter's crib. My daughter was only nine months old. I remember Cellia telling me not to go to this hospital when I have to give birth with my last son. This hospital has a bad reputation on how they treat black people. It is truly a scary thing when I think about all the stories I have heard concerning this hospital. Unfortunately, it is the only hospital in the area. Anyways, I know for a fact that no bad deed goes unpunished. The day will come when they will learn to treat everyone fairly.

My sleeping habit became worse during this time. The doctor said it was my depression which I never accepted to begin with. I had this severe sleeping problem for fourteen years. I would sleep a little bit, but the smallest sound would wake me up, and I wouldn't be able to sleep again. Not only that I was constantly battling if not my mother then demons in my dreams day after day. So I was suffering from lack of sleep really bad. There were shadow demons all in the house, and I could see them in my sleep and when I was awake. They would just wait around until I fell asleep; then they came over me and started doing things to me. By the time I woke up, I would feel like someone had beaten me up and my body would feel like I had bags of sand hanging on me. The dragon egg my mother put in my throat when I was six months pregnant with my son was seriously hurting and bothering me. My hip started hurting really bad. I could feel something walking around in my head and under my skin in my face. I saw in my dream something like a big worm in my head. I was in a huge mess that only the power of God could deliver me from.

Social Services came and took my kids from me. They had my kids for three weeks what seem to be years. That was the first time they were ever out of my sight. I thought I was going to lose my mind. I called the pastor guy that I was dating to tell him and the first thing he said to me was, "So what, I don't give a fuck they are your kids not mine!" That very minute, I broke up with him. I was very disappointed in his behavior. I called Chase, and he got on the flight back to Minnesota. He stood by my side until the end. That's when I knew that I loved him with all my heart and I was a jerk by letting him go. When he came, he told me that he had seen my sister Pasei, and he had the chance to talk with her. He told me how she missed me so very much, and she said five years were too long to be without her sister and best friend. He said that Pasei was in the things of God and was now wearing only white color clothes. I asked him and you believe her, he said yes. I cursed Chase out so many times over the years for telling me to reconcile with Pasei.

But at this moment, I had no energy left to fight, not with him and definitely not with anyone. He went on and on for weeks trying to speak on her behalf as to why I should forgive her. He told me, "You have no friends, and all the members of your family are now estrange from you. I think you need Pasei to help you out. It might help you get well to be around your best friend again. The two of you were so close. "He told me that Pasei and her daughter were struggling really bad, and since I had a house, I should allow her to come stay here with me so she can do something better with herself. I told him that I was not convinced and that I know she did not change. The dreams and premonitions I would have about did not show she changed.

I told him, "I will only do this because you need to learn firsthand that Pasei is who she is and that will not change." I called her, and she was happy to hear from me. I was also happy to hear from her. Her voice sounded so different in my ears. With all that, I was still skeptical that she did not change. I went against all my instincts and told her that if she wanted to move to Minnesota, she could stay with me. She said she had to put it in front of God, and she was going to get back to me. I thought to myself, *Which God?* Hey can you blame me? Moving on! After a week she said God was not permitting her to move to Minnesota she was not going to come. One day I connected her on the phone with this pastor friend of mine. (a different pastor) I guess they fell in love he always respected me for my gift and told her to move in with me. All of a certain she said God told her to move to Minnesota. That was my first question mark on her.

Chapter Eight

MEETING PROPHETESS
ANNIE WOLO JOHNSON

One day I called my sister Anastasia after giving her such a hard time during our family conferences to tell her that I was not going to be a part of the conference anymore. It was because of Cellia's betrayal against me. My father's other children were being treated unfairly, and I was standing up for them. But when Cellia betrayed me, it made me weak to even speak on their behalf. I told Anastasia my opinion about the land my father left behind and how it should be divided the way our dad would had wanted if his will wasn't forged. She was happy to hear me say that I was not going to be partake in any more family conferences. I was not taking her side, and I let her also know that. I just decided to withdraw and let them handle it among themselves. She went on to say that her pastor had prophesied that I was going to make peace with her. I also knew that I was a torn in her flesh. When someone gave me a reason to go after them, all I do is give them everything I got. My intentions will be to devour them. Remember, I only go after people who treat other people unfairly, and this act I must see with my own eyes and not by word of mouth.

Anastasia and I had not been in each other's lives for fifteen or more years. We knew we had our difference so we kept away from each other. She started making attempts to keep in touch with me. It was weird, but I thought to myself, *our father just died maybe she feels now is the time for her to be to me the older sister she should had been.* My dad and I had already talked about how he was going to let go of this world the next time he got sick and go on into the afterlife. For many years he promised me that when he entered into the afterlife he was going to destroy any and everything that was keeping me in bondage and keeping me from living the life God has destined me to. He told me that he was holding on to this life because he felt that he had to continuously pray for me. I said no you must go, that he was not much help to me in this physical life but; when he enters into the afterlife he was going to be able to help me a great deal from beyond. He and I had that understanding between us. My dad and I Before he could believe that witchcraft existed he was already in too deep and there was not anything he could do. He also knew that he could not take his own life because that is both knew that my mother had already overpowered him a very long time ago in this world. against God's will for mankind. He thought he was protecting me because of the deal he and my mother made. Mom was not to kill me as long as daddy was with her. My dad never told anyone about our conversations. All my mother's children knew how much my father adored me. That was not a secret. My father appeared to me in a dream a couple of days before he died and told me he was ready to die and move on into the afterlife. I called him after I awoke from sleep and told him the dream. He was thousands of miles away in Africa but he would still telepathically communicate with me. He basically told me good bye and told me he loved me more than I knew. I was happy that it was time because I knew that he was going to keep his promise to me. The day my father in Oct. 2009 I did not sleep at all that night. My cousin called me early in the morning to tell me my father was dead. My beloved sisters Anastasia and Jasmine all decided that it was not time for me to know so they did not tell me. Jasmine made a prank call to me once to tell me daddy was dead but when he actually died she didn't call me. Anyways that week I seen my father in the spirit and he went and checked on all his children to make sure they were ok. My house was the last house he came to and when his ghost arrived I was in bed and it was night time. He stood over my bed and told me to move over so he could lie down. I said but daddy I am so tired. I was very drunk and tired that night but my spirit was very much alert. So my dad decided to jump into my body and I jumped right off the bed. He was in me for a whole month and I thought I was going to go insane. It was the weirdest feeling ever. He had thought me so much within that short period, knowledge that was not of this world. He must have kept all his good deeds receipts from Earth for him to have been granted this huge favor from beyond. After he came out of my body he hung out with me in my house and told me all these things to do so that I would be free in the realms of the spirit and free of my mother. I was not scared having my father's ghost in the house with me. My step mom told me to tell my dad to help out his other children too that I was not the only child he had. He told me that when his work with me was done he would go and help them. He loved watching my TV. He acknowledged that I was never crazy and my mother was evil like I said she was. He said don't worry her time is up she will be coming here very soon. But you must make sure to stop drinking because you will die in a car accident if you don't and all this would be a waste. He told me not to worry to do all the things he said and always pray. He said that when the day came to go to the afterlife he would come and get me himself but for now it was not my time and he left. I saw the hard work my dad did to help set my spirit free. I was very proud of him and gain a lot of strength spiritually and physically after that. Thanks daddy. My father is God in Heaven but my daddy is Cyrus.

Because Anastasia was so determine to be nice to me, I gave her the chance and answered all of her phone calls. Something I normally would not do not just for her but for anyone out of my circle of trust. She kept telling me about the pastor at her church. She invited me to the church to attend the delivery service that occurred on the third Friday of every month. She expressed to me how very important it was for me to come. She said that I would benefit from it a great deal. After missing a couple of those services, I decided to attend.

I heard the Holy Spirit saying to me, "Go. The same way it started is the same way it will end." Since my car was too old to drive the distance, I rented one and went there on a third Friday. We drove for one hour to get to the Faith Healing Ministries International that night. As soon as we got there with the children, our youngest son who is autistic was really behaving unruly, and Chase had to take him out. Unfortunately, they were out the entire time. It was time for the delivery service to start. Right when I was having doubts as to why I should trust Anastasia to come to a church that she invited me to, I had seen a vision. It was Jesus. His heart was bleeding, and there was light illuminating from his chest. I heard the Holy Spirit say, "The blood of Jesus." I felt peace and calmness come over me right away. The Prophetess Annie Wolo Johnson was at the altar. She gave the congregation a simple delivery exercise to do. As she told us to breathe in and out, I started getting a feeling of euphoria. It was wonderful. She said, "Some of you in here tonight are going to started coughing and throwing up. What's in you must come out." I started coughing out of nowhere, and I had to run to the bathroom because I had vomited. I felt as if I was floating. I had never felt such anointing in my life. I am extremely sensitive to the spirits, good and bad.

The Spirit of God was definitely in Faith Healing Ministries International Inc. that night. I looked at her from the distance, and all I could sense from her was anointing, power, from up above. For Jesus himself to be there, it was amazing. She told people to come up to the altar so she could anoint them. I see her make the sign of the cross on several people before she could get to me. As soon as she came close to me, I felt myself going down to the floor. The anointing that was in there knocked the demonic spirit that was in me to the floor. All I could think was, *Oh my gosh this is real. She did not even touch me. The demon that was in me was fighting and did not want to get out.* It was being much stubborn. I could feel it holding on with all its might. But the anointing in her did not give it a chance. It did not want to get out. She came down to the floor as I was shaking uncontrollably. She told the demon, "You are going to get out of her tonight, no other night, but tonight. You do not belong in her. Get out in the name of Jesus." She started to rebuke it in the name of Jesus and praying. *Wow.* Jehovah God is great.

As stubborn as it was, she was even more stubborned; she did not let up until it departed from me. I knew something horrible had left my body. I had been possessed for years. I knew there was something not right about me. It was as if I had split personalities. This demon was the one that would say completely the opposite of what the Holy Spirit would tell me. It was the one that fought hard for me to have doubts even when the truth was in front of me. It wanted to take me over completely and then I would have been working for the devil. I had twenty-four abortions in my life and never gave it a thought. After I confided in the prophetess about what I have done, what she told me changed me forever. Even though I didn't have any more abortions after Chase told me never to ever have anymore. I had one abortion for him and that one almost killed me. The voice told me that this was my last abortion and if I ever to attempt it again I would die. I don't believe in abortions anymore since God started to communicate with me. I feel so horrible for what I have done. I did not know any better. Some people may hate me for this but, I can't take it back what's done is done and I can't erase that. I just have to be a better person from here on. I must tell the whole truth of my life and this is just one of the most awful one. The prophetess said, "Whenever you have an abortion, you are feeding the devil your unborn children."

Every time I got pregnant, there was a voice that would tell me, "Hurry up go and abort it." It was a different voice. I now only hear one voice, and I finally have a peace of mind since my delivery. There is not a war in my head anymore. The demon that was in me I believed now was placed there so I could go away from God's purpose for my life.

It was the one that would tell me, "Forget about all those things the other voice tells you. There is no such thing as God. Now I know that if there is no God, there should be no demons either, and my experiences with both would be a lie when I know for a fact it is not. This demon was easier for me to follow because all the things it wanted me to do seemed fun, not knowing I was slowly but surely killing myself spiritually. It made it seemed like following God was a lot of work that was not worth it. How did it enter into me? I can think of numerous ways. Was it the only spirit dwelling in me? No, not at all! There were more. The spirit of tobacco and alcohol were there and also had to go. When you go through a powerful delivering with an authentic person of God like I did, you are bound to be purified.

She told me, "As time goes by, you would see yourself drastically changing. That has been happening more and more every day. For someone who did not want to get out of bed at all, I now can't wait for the arrival of a new day every day. I am up at the crack of dawn, and now I am happy to have life and life more abundant. The thief does not come except to steal, and to kill, and to destroy. I have come that they may have life and that they may have it more abundantly. John 10:10 "God is super cool". I can't wait to get to God purpose for my life. I have never wanted anything so much. I am so very pleased with God for sending such a powerful woman of his.

God told me, "I sent her to undo all your mother has done to you." I couldn't believe it when I heard that.

"This is the person I have been waiting for the last decade and a half, God? I have looked high and low and cried for days and nights wishing you would send the person that you promised me. This is her? Thank you, my Lord." There seem to be many so-called houses of God all over the place, but this particular house of God; he is actually residing in it.

The miracles did not stop there. My sister Anastasia was so proud to see me go through the delivery. I was so proud of her too. That within itself is a miracle. She and I both gave our testimonies. After the service, I told the Prophetess thank you very much, and we went home. There were a lot of people, and I did not want to say anything about my experience to her. I wanted to be sure she was the one. Within three weeks to the next delivery service, I had a dream. God told me to go to the church, and the Prophetess Annie was going to touch my neck so the dragon egg that my mother shoved down my throat would go back to where it came from. I did not say anything. I decided to go to the next delivery service a few days later. I asked Chase to come with me, and he refused, making excuses. I was going rain or shine. When God says go, you don't say, "Let me think about it. You go." On my way there, Lucifer wanted to take my life in a car accident, but God refused. I got there safely. The prophetess once told me that Lucifer was a natural loser. His name should be spelled "Loserfer."

I told God, "Show me another sign that this is the anointed one you have sent to take care of all these problems that have plagued me all these years." When I got to the church, once again she did it. All my secrets that I had with God she started to say them. There was no way she could have known. She spoke of 777 and how God had made this promise to someone here tonight.

Then she said, "The Holy Spirit is leading me to do something I normally don't do." She told everyone to come up in line because someone came to be touched by her tonight. It was me, and I was in the back of the line. Everyone went up, and she was touching them in the hands. When it was my turn, instead of her only touching me in the hands, I put her hand on my neck like God instructed me to in my dream. She knew right away that the Holy Spirit told her this because of me. She touched my neck, and I was so happy because I believed in my delivery. It does not stop there. There are more miracles; keep reading. One day, I was sick of all the shadow demons that were in my house, and in my life, that made sleep impossible. Remember the shadow demons from the beginning of my story? They have been following me for about fourteen, almost fifteen years, and I have not been able to sleep. This had me tired always. Prescription sleeping pills was the only choice for years. It still did not help. There were several near-death episode of overdose. As a mother, sleep is very important to keep up with your children. This proved to be a challenge and the little bit of sleep that I got were filled with dreams, revelations and nightmares. I plan on revealing all the dreams in my second book as I am lead. The doctors told me it was depression, but I knew that was not it. How do you tell your doctor, "Hey this is witchcraft?" I couldn't, and I did not know what else to do.

The Prophetess Annie was my last option for help. So I asked her. She came over two days later with her spiritual entourage. They prayed and anointed the house our home. She told me to get Chase so she could talk to him; he refused. He was mad; he did not want her in She said to me, "He is going to leave and will not be able to come back into your life until he is ready to change. And she left. This happened in January. *Wow!* She anointed the house with the blood of Jesus. I had never dwelt anywhere so peaceful my whole life. The shadow demons left. Even Chase kept saying there was a dramatic change in our atmosphere. I wasn't screaming and jumping out of my sleep anymore. I slept every night like a baby and woke up revived. Wait there is more. Chase left because we could not get along at all. We kept clashing on everything. It was March of 2011 when he left and Pasei had just arrived in my home in February a month earlier. The prophetess warned me to not allow Pasei to stay in my house but I told the prophetess "well she is here now and I can't just kick her out. She also said there were going to be consequences if I didn't tell Pasei to leave. He went back to New Jersey. He did not want to go but the girl he used to date and would still talk to on the phone bought him a ticket. Obviously they discussed it prior to that and that's why she bought. When I found out I told him go back and find out if there where you want to be and if that be the case I won't bother you for anything. If you decide Minnesota and being with me is what you want to do I will pay for you to come back but you must leave all your trash and drama in Jersey.

Around that time, I got frustrated about my money situation. I had lawsuits that were pending for years, and nothing was happening. I knew the devil did not want to release my funds and had a strong hold on my finances. I told her my concerns on April 7th. I did not tell her I could not think clearly nor could I even remember what I ate the day before.

My memory was fading rapidly. I knew it was because of the book. My mother told me I will not write this book as long as she was alive. I asked Prophetess Annie Wolo Johnson to please pray for me. She prayed right there on the phone. On April 11, my settlement money started coming from everywhere. Every time I checked my account, there were funds from unknown sources in there. This has never happened in my life before. I had cancelled Chase's ticket because I was mad, and it was nonrefundable the lady told me. I canceled the reservation for the shuttle to bring him home. I had not yet received all this money. So I had no extra money to buy a new ticket and neither did he. After we had a heart to heart on the phone I decided I will let him come back. We have been through so much. Pasei did not want him to come back at all. I did not care what she wanted because she was not the one that took care of me all those days when I was sick. None of my sibling came to my aid when I was not well. They all gossip about me behind my back instead of coming to help me. To them I was never ever going to mount to anything. Chase and I decided to call the ticket agent. When we called the ticket agent, she said she did not cancel his ticket; she felt like he was going to come. Something told her not to cancel his ticket she said. Amazing! When we called the shuttle to ask about the cancelled reservation, the guy said he did not cancel his reservation; something told him not to. Chase came back as a changed man. Chase quit smoking marijuana after sixteen years.

Chase is now delivered and is in the things of God and wants to do the things of God. This has been the biggest issues in our relationship for years. God once again showed to me what his anointing could do. Prophetess Annie Wolo Johnson is highly anointed no doubt about that. For the stronghold that has been on my life to be removed by the anointing place on her life was wonderful. My sister Anastasia have completely redeemed herself in my book. We are now working on our relationship and trying to get it to where it is supposed to be. She had seen a great light at Faith Healing Internal Ministries in Brooklyn Park Minnesota where everything started. She did not hide the light but rather showed it to me. Matthew 5: 15-16 Nor do they light a lamp and put it under a basket, but on a lampstand, and it gives light to all who are in the house. 16: let your light so shine before men, that they may see your good works and glorify your Father in heaven. I am truly grateful to her and to the Prophetess Annie Wolo Johnson.

My life was a jigsaw puzzle, and now it is coming together rapidly. I can't wait to see what's next. I have my memory back that was the only way I could have written this book. I have been seeing the number 11 for the last four years and did not know what it meant. The prophetess told me it means completion. "Whatsoever you have been going through is complete," she said. Amen to that. Right now it is December 10 2013 and I am still seeing the number 11 like crazy. Chase said it is an awakening of what's to come. I went to see the prophetess at her house one day to chat with her. When I got in her parking lot, the Holy Spirit told me that she was going to give me water and that the water was the blood of Jesus, and I was to bathe with it according to her directions. I did not say anything to her about this. The Holy Spirit had made this woman a mind reader, a hidden camera, and intercessor and so on. The Holy Spirit had made her way more than the CIA. Seriously!

As I was about to leave her place, she said, "Oh wait, the Holy Spirit said that you are here for your healing." She went and got this water from her altar and brought it to me. She said it was water from the Dead Sea. She told me to bathe with it while calling upon the blood of Jesus. The water would spiritually turn in the blood of Jesus. I followed her directions. There was this huge cyst that had been on my face for a year that was killing my self-esteem. On the second day, it popped and left a large indentation in my face, and that was the end of it. She told me I was covered with the blood of Jesus and that I have crossed over to the light once and for all, that I should not allow fear to come in me ever again.

The reason I named this book "777: The Lost Blood" is because of the Father, the Son, and the Holy Spirit. In 1999 God told me when I see 777 know that he was God and he would give me all my hearts desires.

The lost blood is the blood of Jesus Christ that was lost and now is found thanks to God almighty. I have found the blood of my Lord and Savior Jesus Christ! I have found the most powerful weapon in the world to go against those forces of darkness.

Thank you, Father, for being a God of your word!

God is awesome!

Chapter Nine

THE RETURN OF PASEI

Shortly after meeting the prophetess, Pasei came to live with me in Minnesota. The minute she walked through the door and I laid eyes on her, I knew right away that nothing had changed. She looked strange to me. It had been five years since I last saw her. I also know that she was shocked to see me in the situation that I was in. She has never seen me this big before. I gain about 100lbs since I hurt my hip and couldn't walk Brittany also came to live out here and stay with me for two weeks before she found her place. I had a full house meanwhile I was writing this book. Brittany kept telling me, "Don't let Pasei move here to you," over and over. She told me she did not trust Pasei. Even though Brittany would cave in at times when the heat was on, but you could count on her to say it like it was. I remember when we were younger whenever I got dressed to go out, everyone around me would tell me I looked great. I would call her to come over. If she told me to change my outfit, I would change so fast, and my friends would get mad. She would tell them I'm not letting my sister get out the house looking like that. I would never wear that outfit again. That's the kind of girl Brittany was but people change. Now she throws me under the bus any chance she gets and has said some of the most hurtful things to me. I told her Chase said Pasei has changed and got mad at him. In the end, the decision was mine.

When Pasei found out about the prophetess, she told me that She did not trust her. She told me that the prophetess is from the underworld and that I was stupid for letting Anastasia encouraging me to talk to her. Pasei wanted to start her ministry right away. Her best friend allowed her to use her basement in the cities, one hour away from where I lived. On the weekend, she would go there. Now here is the thing. Pasei has a dominating behavior, and when she wanted something, she was going to get it rain or shine. But this behavior worked on her friends and not me. Brittany would always remind me that Pasei would use my love for her against me and that I needed to be aware. I was still drinking and getting high like crazy. Pasei wanted me to be a part of her ministry. But here is the thing she did not believe that Jesus was the son of God. She said Mary was raped by a Roman soldier and that was how Jesus was conceived. She said Jesus is the name of a demon and that I shouldn't say the name because it was demonic. She was only wearing white clothing and said she was pure and God anointed her to deliver this message to the world. She said God told her to only wear white. Matthew 7: 15-20 said Beware of false prophets, who come to you in sheep's clothing, but inwardly they are ravenous wolves. 16: You will know them by their fruits. Do men gather grapes from thorn bushes or figs from thistles? 17: Even so, every good tree bears good fruit, but a bad tree bears bad fruit. 18: A good tree cannot bear bad fruit nor can a bad tree bear good fruit. 19: Every tree that does not bear good fruit is cut down and thrown into the fire. 20: Therefore by their fruit you will know them.

She started to make me uncomfortable in my own house. She would not even call God, God but call him I AM. She tried very hard to convince me to join her ministry. One day, I heard her praying in the room with the door closed. I realized that my son was in there (youngest) while she was praying. I opened that door so fast that she almost jumped. I told her never ever have any of my children in the room with you behind closed doors. She knew even though I was very lay back that I only needed to strike once, and that's it for whomever. She said sorry. She had seven gallons of water in the room that she would constantly pray over. She said she wanted to bathe me with them. Here is the thing. I had this dream before Pasei's arrival that my mother had a bucket of water that she was trying so hard to bathe me with.

When Mom came close to me in my dreams, heavens opened, and there was a man dressed in white on a white horse, another dressed in red on a red horse, another dressed in black on a black horse and there was one more, but I did not get to see him. My mother screamed really loud and said, "Now we are all going to die." And I jumped from my sleep. Now Pasei wants to bathe me. *Yeah right.*

I told her, "You better start drinking that water, girl." She was disappointed and was not too happy with me. She opened up a prayer line where people could call in and hear the word of God as she preached. I volunteered to read the Bible for her. I am a good reader. As soon as I got done with the reading of the scripture, she immediately said it is one thing to read well, but it is another thing to read and have understanding

She was talking about me. I did not respond. She always made me look bad so she could appear to be the good one. She always went behind my back and said a lot of things that were not necessary. Her whole sermon she gave that night was solely about me. Making me to look bad and that she was my savior. What I did was not be a part of her prayer line anymore. Brittany was on the line that day. She was livid. It goes on. Pasei knew I was writing my autobiography so she also decided to write a book. Here is the thing; her book talks about how Jesus is not real, how there is no power in the blood of Jesus, how people should not eat meat or salt. She said everyone in the ministry should wear white and that would show how pure they were. She was determined to get me to believe all this cocka mimie. I can't stop laughing right now as I write this. It's just too funny. I'm sure out there somewhere is someone whose diet is consistent of cocka mimie BS, but I only eat the truth. Hello now! Pasei was getting very frustrated with me not wanting to believe a word from her mouth.

She asked me one day, "Why didn't you want to join her ministry?"

I told her, "If I join your ministry, fire would come from heaven and devour me because God will no longer have a need for me. What you are asking me to do contradict everything God has thought me over the years. You are latterly asking me to denounce my *God* and my *Lord* and *Savior Jesus Christ* that I cannot do. Denouncing them meant denouncing my own existence. Don't forget that the devil told God at the end of my struggle I was going to denounce he God. She was angry. For everything strong man or woman who is born an opposer will be sent by Satan to try and fight them for the anointing God has placed on their lives. Pasei was determined to follow all the non- sense that she was saying. Her problem was she thought because I was getting drunk and smoking weed that my spirit was drunk or high. My spirit is attached to God and it does not get drunk or high. This is what she came up with later. She said that she and I should sleep in the same bed head to head so all the information in my head can go in her head and all the information in her head can transfer to my head. Tell me something. Is this Godly talk or demonic talk? In your opinion as the reader, does it seem like this Bimbo has changed? This is witchcraft behavior. This girl knows for a fact since we were kids whenever I slept next to her I would have nightmares all night and get severely sick the next day. She knows even our mother forbid her from ever sleeping in the same bed with me. Chase, do you need more proof." Okay, here we go. This person you brought into our home is not who she claims to be.

After I refused this, here is what happened next! I went to bed very drunk as usual. I heard the Holy Spirit waking me up. "Eve, wake up! Eve, wake up! I'm tired. Please leave me. Let me sleep I said. Your daughter is not in her room where she belongs. Your sister is doing a transfer of spirit with her in her room."

Say what? I jumped to my daughter's room; she was not there. When I went to Pasei's room, there lays my daughter head to head with Pasei's daughter. I tried to wake my daughter up, but she was sound asleep. I was livid. She was too heavy to carry with my hurting hip. I asked God, "What should I do, Father?"

He said, "Pull her, and turn her around." So I did, putting her feet to where her head was. I knew Pasei was a deep sleeper, but I tried waking her up anyways. She did not wake up. I asked God again will my daughter be safe laying here?

He said, "Plead the blood of Jesus over her, and pray Psalm 23." I did and even added extra prayers, and I walked away believing God will answer my prayer and not let me daughter suffer this fate again. After all he was the one that woke me up. The next day, I asked Pasei how my daughter ended up in her bed with her and her daughter? She said maybe my daughter sleep walked into her room.

I told her, "I'm her mother. If she was a sleep walker, wouldn't I know?

She said, "Well, Eve, I don't know how your daughter ended up in the bed with us." I wanted to leap across the table and ring her neck, but the Holy Spirit said no. The Holy Spirit told me that the demon in her was a very powerful demon that feeds of anger and that it will transfer into me if I did that. *Blasted!* I told her if anything happened to anyone of my children like it did Elijah, I will buy a gun and shoot all my mom's children in the head and every one of their children. I meant it because I wouldn't be able to bear the thought of losing another child to witchcraft.

I said, "Since you are pleading innocent, I best don't see a darned thing, no one will be left in this family to tell the story." I walked away from her. I did learn something important from Pasei, and that is how to do a dry fast. A dry fast is when you go for days without food or water at all. She said when you do that anything you ask God for, he will do. I kept that in mind.

One day, the Holy Spirit told me that I should pack up all of Pasei's things and take them to my auntie's house so she can get them from there without returning to my house. Pasei was spending the weekend with her friend. During this time my auntie called to speak to Pasei, and I told her Pasei was not here.

She said, "Your mom has been calling me. She said it is very important that she speaks to your sister immediately." The Holy Spirit told me it was about me and that my mother's spirit is in my sister Pasei. This is their last chance to kill me or one of my children. "Your mother wants to strike you one last time. You must kick Pasei out immediately without any physical confrontation." I called Pasei and gave her the message.

Her exact words were. "I'm not calling that witch. What the hell does she want from me?"

The Holy Spirit told me that she was lying. "She's only trying to gain your trust. Do as I say. Kick her out now and shortly after your mother will die an untimely death because she would have lost for good." I did not need to be told again. At 5:00 in the morning, I had my son Cody packed all her things, and we drove one hour to the cities where my aunty lived. When my auntie saw me, she was frantic because it was very rare for any member of my family to get a visit from me. She asked me why did I bring all my sisters' clothing to her house?

I told her, "Aunty, she is working with Mom, and the both of them want to kill me or my children." My exact words to my aunty was, "Watch your friend is about to die a sudden death."

She said, "But she is not sick."

I said, "It does not matter this was her last attempt on me and my children's lives, no more. I said this to my aunty with conviction because I knew for a fact that God was with me." On my way home, I called my mother because I knew she was not yet aware about what I have to done to Pasei. She was happy to hear my voice on the phone in a creepy kind of way. I asked her did Pasei call her, and she said yes boastfully as if they got me now. She said me and Pasei talked for a very very long time. She thought she had the last laugh.

She said, "I heard you sister now lives with you, like you idiot."

I said yes. And left it I that. I had to lie which is something I hate to do but I felt that I had no choice. I wanted to know what she had to say to me. Mom plain blank sounded happy as if now she was going to live long because she and Pasei were about to kill me. Don't forget readers that this is the same Pasei that asked me to set our sister Cellia up so she and our mom could kill her. She is not innocent and I am not painting a picture of her that doesn't exist. She has done other things that are unspeakable but those things don't have anything to do with me, so I am not going to write about that here. Pasei is demonic and as much as I love her we will have to be like oil and water for now. Once you are a witch you will have to confess and except Jesus Christ as your Lord and savior and denounce witchcraft and the devil. She feels her powers are strong and she wants to remain this way. Greed, envy, jealousy etc. will make you do things that are not Godly. This is why we must always examine ourselves, our actions and our motives for everything under this sun. I will not have anything to do with the underworld. Am I trying to tarnish her reputation, no of course not I am telling you facts. Things that happened within my family that I am not proud of but is the truth. If I was not asked to write this book you would had not had known the story. My family is not the first or last family to experience these things, it's happening worldwide. Extreme evil within the family called family secrets. If you don't expose it then you are a part of it like or not. My mother's children are going to say that I am a liar when this book comes out but I am willing to take a lie detector test at the drop of a dime. The million dollar question is, will they? When Pasei found out what I did, she was furious with me. She called me and cursed me out real good. I was calm and told her, "Pasei, I had to do what I had to do. I will not let history repeat itself." I said, "Now Mom is about to die a sudden death."

Anastasia called me to ask me why did I kick my sister out.

I told her, "Because she and Mom are working together to kill me or my children, and I will not allow it." I told her how God told me to kick Pasei out. I told her mom is going to die a sudden death now that I have done this. She was not too happy with me. She said are you still on this mom is a witch thing? I said yes I am and I stand by my word.

She sounded mad at me. She said, "Just who do you think you are? You claim to hear the voice of God. I think you are hearing demons and not God. Why did you change your name to Eve instead of Evelyn, your birth name?"

I told her, "Because God calls me Eve and not Evelyn." I was surprise to even hear her ask me anything like that. And I could hear in her voice that she thought of me as the scum of the earth and me changing my name to Eve happens to confirm that in her thoughts.

She said, "Eve is the greatest manipulator of all times."

I said, "Well, she is back to make amends for all the wrong she did."

She said, "You are no woman of God. Saying this in a very stern voice as if it was the devil himself trying to convince me that God couldn't possibly consider someone like me to be called his daughter. I knew right away that it was the devil wanting to implant the spirit of doubt within me. I couldn't allow that to happen. When someone brings fire to you sometimes all you need to give them is water in return. You don't always have to fall into the devils trap when you can just step right over it. Pasei is the real woman of God."

I told her in a very polite calm tone of voice, "Yeah sure if you say so. That's your opinion, but I know who I am. I do not need any validation as to who I am to my Father in Heaven. There is no reason to argue about that. In the end, we shall see the false and the true." She said what I did to Pasei was very wrong. "Again, *Anastasia*, you are entitled to your own opinion."

She said, "Well, Pasei is the one wearing white, not you."

"And what does that mean anyways wearing white? White is a color even Satan wears. The makers of the movie Constantine knew that when they dressed Satan in white. That is just too funny to hear her say that. It made me to feel bad for her in a way that I knew how far behind and spiritually blind she was. But she is not alone there are many more people out there such as herself. A lot of people are asleep spiritually and it is really a scary thought when you are the one awake looking in on all the sleepers. My prayer for the world is that we all wake up out of this slumber we have been in for so long. If the veils between us and the spiritual realms were to be removed; some of us will pluck our eyes right out of the sockets and our hair out of our scalps when we see what truly surround us. We are at war and there are demons all around us doing things to us that we cannot see. This is why we must always pray to God for his angels to take charge over us. It says so in psalms 91:11. Satan can quote the Holy Bible backward, and he comes as the angel of light sometimes, doesn't he? It says so in 2 Corinthians 11:13-14 For such are false apostles, deceitful workers, transforming themselves into apostles of Christ. And no wonder! For Satan transforms himself into an angel of light. " Anastasia was not too happy with me. I told her, "Got to go! Scooby doo, 'bye, 'bye!" I hung up. Mom died a month later, a sudden death. Before that, I did a four-day dry fast asking God to rid me of the Goliath in my life. I did not think I could do it but God gave me the strength and I did it. When I went to sleep, I saw a giant skeleton come and lay over my house holding it as tight as it could, like a bear hug. Then I saw my mother planting ant domes with red sand all around my house I did not know what that meant but I knew it was not a good thing.

In my dream, I got on my knees right away and started praying to God. The heavens opened and out came fire that looked like volcano lava. It started pouring down on my mom and the skeleton, and they started running away. Jesus came dressed in all white with a white long robe and white beard. As soon as I saw him, I dropped to my knees and bent my head down at his feet and said, "*Lord*, who am I that you find me worthy to show your face?" He stretched out his arms, and I went to him. And he hugged me. This happened in June, and it was the same month my mom died. He is a God who answers prayers, and he is alive and well. Whenever the light shows up, darkness will disappear, no doubt. Faith is the key.

Of course, Pasei called me when Mom died, but she totally ignored the fact of what just happened between us. T. D. Jakes said, "Once you reject someone, don't let them come close to you again because their only aim will be to harm you." This is still the case with me and Pasei. To this day, I refused to be close to her. She just got pregnant by Cellia's ex-boyfriend and a current boyfriend of our family friend. She told me that she did not let me know she was dating him because I would have been angry. All these while wearing white. She started drinking and doing unspeakable things. I told Brittany to let Pasei know that if she continues to wear white, I will expose all her dirty secrets to everybody. I learned recently after not being in contact with her almost a year and a half that she is no longer wearing white I am not sure how true that is however. My prayer for my sister is that she truly turns to God one day and not ends up like our mother. Our mom has an older sister who knows that our mom is a witch but supports her a hundred percent because she loves our mom dearly. I am not going to jeopardize my eternity to be with God because of love for man that will make me knowingly turn away from God.

This girl has tried all her life to steal my destiny, but God refused. I once had this dream about my dad telling me about this book I have never heard of before to buy it and study it. I told Pasei the dream, and she got the book behind my back and hid it in my house all those months reading it without telling me a word that she had it. God told me one day, "Go to your sister's room right now while she's in there, and walk straight to her table. There you will find something." She knew I wouldn't just go in there. But today I did. There in her bag on the table was the book. She asked me, "How did you know?" I told her God just told me to come in here; there was something he wanted me to see. She was speechless and wanted to lie saying she told me. "Shut the hell up I don't want to hear a peep out of you!"

There is so much she has done to me, you know. Everybody was right when they told me not to trust her. Of course, all these things happened when she was still living with me. I found out later that people on Facebook would tell me how my sister sent them pictures of me telling them it was her. I am disgusted with my sister's behavior. Mom was right when she told me Pasei was the one that had the same heart as her. She said that she was going to turn over her witchcraft to Pasei because Pasei was just like her. All I can say is "Wow, thank you, Jesus, for everything." This is not everything I know about my dearest sister Pasei, but this is where the story ends about her behavior. Let's see what God says.

CHAPTER TEN

THE CONCLUSION OF MY STORY

It is Friday, June 17, and I am sitting in a delivery service that the Prophetess Annie Wolo Johnson is leading at The Faith Healing Ministries International Inc. After praise and worship, she started to pray for the people in the church. Then she said that there was a witch that had been troubling someone in there for a very long time. This witch had even gone as far as telling this person that they were going to die. "The Holy Spirit is telling me to tell the person that the witch is going to die. Witches, you need to repent before it is too late," she said.

If I had not seen this prophet of God in action before, I was going to ask myself, "Did I tell her any of these things? She is truly a woman of God, and no one can convince me otherwise". She did not call anyone's name, but right away, I knew that the Holy Spirit was sending me a message through her like he has been doing since my very first encounter with her.

She said, "Exodus 22:18 The Bible said, 'Suffer the witch not to live.'" She said, "I am going to pray a dangerous prayer here tonight." She started praying, and she said, "For all of you that are here tonight at this delivery service, if there is a witch in your life stopping you to do God's will and they do not want to repent, let them die. If it is good for you to suffer, then it is good for them to die. The saying goes like this, "What is good for Paul must be for John."

As she was praying that prayer, I felt my sister Anastasia praying for our mother to live. So I said to God, *Why is the prophetess praying for the witch to die, and I'm sensing my sister praying for it not to be our mother?*

All of a sudden, the prophetess said out loud in a stern voice that, "You who are sitting in your seat praying the opposite prayer, stop now before the Holy Ghost fire burn you." Right away, I felt my sister back off on her prayer for our mother. Even though she was praying silently, but the Holy Spirit revealed what she was doing. A few days before that was our mother's birthday, June 15 to be exact. My sister Anastasia called me to tell me our mother went into a coma. She was really sad. I told her that she needed not to worry about that. She told me how she and her friend were praying for our mother to get out of the coma and be okay. She sounded like her whole world had just been turned upside down.

I told her to prepare herself because she was about to take a trip to Africa. She told me that there would be no need for that because she believed that Mom was going to be okay. On June 16, she called me back and was very happy that our mother was now responsive and out of the coma. She expressed to me how God was a God who answered prayers. "Yes, he is," I said. I told her that I was happy to hear her sounding and feeling much better. I guess this is good news, isn't it? She was so happy. Right after I got off the phone with her, I heard the Holy Spirit tell me that even though she is out of the coma, she is about to die an immediate death. So I ran to Chase and told him of my conversation with Anastasia, and then I told him what the Holy Spirit had said to me.

He said, "Well, let's wait and see." So on June 17, when the prophetess Annie Wolo Johnson prayed that prayer of not letting the witch to live unless they repent, I knew something was about to happen because of what the Holy Spirit told me.

The prophetess is a woman of very few words if not I was going to ask her if she had a vision as to who that witch might had been. But The Holy Spirit had already told me anyways. I was waiting to see what was about to happen. My mother wanted to kill me or my children for a long time so she could live. She must kill a direct immediate family member every ten years to insure her own survival. It was no secret; she did not hide it and neither did I. I remember this phone call mom made to me three years ago in October telling me that I was going to die before New Year's Day. Out of the blue, I had not talked to her in years and didn't even know that she knew my number. She told me that I needed to die. Can you believe this? She had the nerves to call me and tell me that I should die so she could live. I waited until she had finished talking, and I told her unless we served the same God that is the only way that I was going to die. I also said there was not enough space in all of America for her and me to live at the same time. I said to her I will not die, but I will live and declare the works of my LORD. On New Years' day. "I will call you and wish you happy New Year. But When I make that call, you better make sure you pack up all your things and move back to Africa immediately before the years end or you will die. If you don't, you will die a miserable death here in America." She said okay.

On New Year's Day, I called her and wished her happy New Year. She got so afraid she could not say a word. She was in shock. "My God let me live," I said to her as I was laughing. Now you have to move back to Africa before he shows you his wrath. That year, she moved back to Africa after living in America for sixteen years. She told everyone that my father was in a hurry to move back home so he could make peace with his estranged brother before he died. I believe one of the reasons my mother tried so hard to eliminate me was because of the anointing God placed on my life. She was hoping that I would use my gifts for evil and not for good or killing me was the other option. Either way they would have won if God did not intervene. I knew what took place between mom and me. Daddy going back to Africa was the last of her worries. She was in such a hurry to go back home, and people kept asking me what she was running away from. Why not run? Her life depended on it. If you are a deadly witch, who has confidence in yourself and your dark powers, you too would be sure of killing the person that you want to see dead the most. So when she failed, she knew that everything she had ever done to me was about to backfire on her. If at any point I had disobey God and went to my parents' house when he told me not to, I was going to die and my story was going to end up in the breeze like so many others before me. Disobedience is extremely dangerous. I believe it's more dangerous than swimming with sharks, than jumping off a plane, and playing Russian roulette. When God says no you don't ever say yes. People with the spirit of the anti-Christ will hate this book and gave me a hard time because they don't have the spirit of the LORD in them so everything I have written here will agitate them.

Before they left, my father pleaded with me to come and see him. I could both know not because of my mother. She was expecting me to show up and see my father so she could try and kill me one last time. The Holy Spirit brought back to my memories that God forbid me from ever going into my parents' home. My mother got on the phone as I was talking to my dad, and she said, "Well, come let me give you my blessing before I go back home."

I told her no; whatever blessing she had, she should give it to whichever siblings of mine came to wish her a farewell. Since they wanted to show her motherly love.

She said, "Well, you are the one I put the curse on, so let me remove it."

I told her, "You could not have put a curse on me because I am a child of God. But when you release a curse you released it on you and those that believe you are their mother not I. You are just a vessel God used to bring me into this world, but you and I you are not my mother. I thought I clarified this a long time ago. As long as you practice witchcraft, you and I cannot have any kind of relationship whatsoever." Oil and water cannot mix no matter what, and that's how we were, mom and me.

I never did see my father until he died years later. I was really hurt when I got the news of his death. I drank myself into oblivion that day. Here is the most hurtful part I have come to find out. My brother told us on the family teleconference that our father had a bladder infection and was not well. Anastasia was called and told that our father was sick. What should they do? They asked her if they should take him to the hospital, and she said no. I had spoken with him at that time but he did not tell me. When I called back my mother wouldn't let me speak to him anymore. When I spoke to him she was not home. We have sisters that are doctors, nurse practitioners, and nurses. What was she thinking making a decision for all of us by not letting anyone know that our father was sick? Then she tried to cover up the cause of death. Then it hit me that the only reason she would not allow our father to get to the hospital so he could live was she must have life insurance out on him. So while on the conference, I brought this to their attention. She denied it at first, saying that she would need a death certificate if that was the case and she did not have life insurance out on on our dad. She lied plain blank, and I cannot stand it when people lie like that. If you are brave enough to partake of something, you should not deny it when questioned. You must be able to stand by the decisions you make. And if you don't have evil intentions, then you most likely won't be making decisions that will cause you embarrassment when questioned.

Anastasia was found to be a liar by our other siblings. I had put her on the spot to tell the truth. She got all flustered and said yes she did have a death certificate and life insurance on our father. Then she said that there was no will for our father. I told everyone that was a lie also. I told them that there was a will but that it was forged because our father refused to write a will. She denied all this, and again she was found to be a liar because there was a will, and it was clearly forged. According to the will, my father left all his possessions to Hamilton. That is a big lie right there again. Our father was a righteous man who would find no pleasure causing such havoc among his children. When my other brother (Junior) requested to see the will in Africa, they came to find out the envelope the will was in was tempered with. They had already opened it to see what was inside. That was stupid knowing that the envelope was supposed to be sealed until the children were all present. Why Anastasia and Mom even bothered opening it, they wrote the will out anyways. I spoke of how unfair and corrupt what she, Anastasia, Mom, and Hamilton were doing. They were not happy with my boldness, but I don't like injustice. It just doesn't fit in my suitcase, so I can't take it with me when I go anywhere.

I told Anastasia how everything you do in life has consequences. Greed is something one must never be a part of because whatsoever you are greedy to maintain is the one thing you will find yourself losing in the end. And it would be one lesson that would pierce your heart in terms of emotions. But anyways, where were we?

Back to my mother, a name I have to call her so you can all know who I am referring to. Well, Friday was the delivery service, and my mother died a sudden death on Saturday. I expected it, but I don't think any of my siblings did. I got a call that night, and someone told me that my mother was dead. I started giving praise and thanks to God immediately. He had saved me from the hands of the witch once and for all. He took care of my goliath. Because she was the one that gave birth to me, it was easy for a lot of the spells she did to get me, she had everything she needed, toenails, hair, clothing etc. I did live at home at one point before I was truly aware of who she was. Now the wicked witch was dead. It was ironic when the call came in. I was playing Monopoly with Chase and our oldest son. As soon as the phone started ringing, I told them right away that my mother was dead and that I needed to answer the call. Not even knowing why the person was calling me, I had a gut feeling. They looked at me in funny way.

After answering the phone, I went back to them and said my mother is dead, and then I fainted in my son's arms. I couldn't believe that God did this wonderful thing in my life. The next day, I went to the church and gave my testimony. I stood in front of the church and told everyone my mother just died. The church members started to sigh, and I said, "No, no, no please don't be sad but be happy for me. I am not sad, and if I stood in front of you to say that I was sad, then I would be deceiving you. But rather praise the Lord here today with me because he had done a great thing in my life." I briefly explained why I was not sad. After the service, everyone started to tell me how things were going to get better with me now that she was dead. They saw the wonderful working powers of prayers. The prophetess was sent to help me in the end like God had promised ten years ago. I suffered in the wilderness for fourteen years waiting for God to deliver me, and he did. I kept my faith through all the darkness.

It was a tough thing to stand in front of a group of people to tell them you just got the death news of your mother and how relieved and happy you are. It was not something my siblings would forgive me for especially Anastasia. But like I told the church that day, it was not about how they felt; it was about what God is doing in my life. I couldn't say because they would be sad so I won't give God the glory. I am not the type of person that will suppress God to make man happy. I told my aunty that I would not have anything to do with the death and burial of my mother. I did not take part in anything they did because it would be deceiving, and I am not a deceiver. Besides my mother once told me the day she died it would be because of me and if I shared a tear she would hunt me from the grave for the rest of my life. She told me not to even give a penny towards her burial when she died. I kept that in mind also. I had told Anastasia that I would gave her the money but the Holy Spirit brought back to my memory the conversation I had with my mother prior to her death. Oops, I almost bought myself a ghost. My siblings are all at odds with me still, but I know now that since our mother is dead, they too will see the light. I don't hate my siblings. I pray that one day we will all live in harmony mother and fathers' children. My brother and sisters from my mom side will not be happy when this book comes out, but I cannot put their happiness in front of Gods' orders. Writing this book is something I was told to do since 1999 and the year is now 2013 in one month it will be 2014. Everything God told me would happen did happen word for word and writing this book is one of the things that were on the list he told me about.

The moral of my story is no matter what you are going through in life, put God first and he will surely deliver you from the hands of darkness. Do not judge people on their past when they are struggling to be a better person for their tomorrow. Judging them will not encourage them but rather discourage them. If you can't help build someone up you should not be the one to tear them down either. Life has a funny way of turning around. I believe people can truly change. I myself am changed person. My dad loved to tell me parables, stories, and sing songs to me all the time. There is a song he used to sing to me when I was a child that stuck with me all these years. "The way I used to walk, I walk like that no more. The way I used to talk, I talk like that no more. The things I used to do, I do those things no more. There's a great change since I have been born." Today, I am proud to say I don't drink or smoke anymore because God has done it for me. If he can do it for me he can do it for you too. One of the keys to life is perseverance. Always push forward and never give up. Jesus Christ had saved me through his mighty blood, and I am proud to say I am on team Jesus. The Lost Blood of Jesus Christ has been found. This is the most powerful weapon you can use to fight the kingdom of darkness. Jesus Christ our Lord and Savior is coming back soon. Let us all repent and give God the glory.

The Lord revealed to me through a dream something troubling that I must share with you before I go. In my dream it was a sunny day, and people were going about their business normally when all of a sudden the sky became dark, and there was the sound of thunder; then I saw in the sky our God, and he had lightning, and he was angry. He said out loud with a voice like no other, "This is not what I created you to be." He struck the ground with lightning, and the ground started to split open rapidly. People were falling through the cracks, and the ground started freezing all of a sudden. People were dying all around me. I got on my knees and started to pray, asking for forgiveness for all when all of a sudden it was quiet, and it seemed to be a whole new land where the sand looked like gold. But there were two men who seemed to be like twins that were opposing the goodness that came to the earth. When I told Prophetess Annie about this, she told me to look in the book of Exodus 19. There I read about what I had seen in my dream. But except this time the Lord is coming back, and we have to be ready. We are asleep spiritually, and we need to wake up now before it is too late. Demons did not leave the earth they are amongst us. Jesus removed demons out of people during his time here on earth but that does not mean they all left when Jesus left. This is one of the reasons he send back the Holy Spirit. We are an unbelieving generation and this has to come to an end. We must believe and have faith. Faith is the substance of things hoped for, the evidence of things not seen. Hebrew 11:1 There are more demons roaming the earth now than there was doing Jesus's days because there are more people on the earth. That means that there are more people for the demons to possess and live in. If you are an unbelievable pray and ask God to give you faith. Ask also for wisdom understanding.

Many people have made fun of me and looked down on me over the years telling me that I was never going to accomplish writing a book. I have been the laughing stock of friends and family and the black sheep for years. Nobody wanted to believe that when my mother and father forsake me God was there to take me. I am a high drop- out who got my GED and tried for college but did not succeed. Am I a professional writer, no of course not, but I will do my best! I believe God has been with me all along and he did not give up on me like everyone else did with the exception of Chase and our children. I am showing to God that I appreciate and love him with all my heart by doing what he had asked me to do. God loves to be glorified and proving that he is God and through him all is possible. I believe God is using me as an example to show his mercy and goodness in the land of the living. I pray that you take away with you after reading this book a lesson that may stay with you all the days of your life. My mistakes and sorrows don't have to be your mistakes and sorrows. My achievements against all odds can also be your achievements against all odds only if you believe in yourself, have faith and don't give up. Whoever you are remember mankind loves you but God loves you the best whether or not you are a believer, you just have to want to believe. Fear is something one never wants to face but once faced is no longer a fear. Embrace yourself and the life that lies ahead of you! This is only the beginning. Thank you and may the love of God be with you!

"THE GREAT BOSS"

The Great Boss is no other than God himself. Who else did you expect? On an extremely hot day, he will quench your thirst. When you feel that you are in hell, he will soothe your soul. The pay is remarkably high. He will bless you in many ways. You can get a hold of him at any time, night or day. Whenever you pray and call his name, he will answer. But be aware, you cannot cheat him; he is always watching. You may call on him for good and bad situations anytime, anywhere. He is the creator of heaven and earth, remember?

He will make sure that you are healthy, happy, and full of life. God will make you whole. Whether your needs be great or small. He is such a fair boss that he gives all his employees a direct line to reach him. Call him, you'll see. This call will not be connected by any means if you are not who you say you are. You cannot fool him, he who has clean hands and a pure heart. Can you understand this? There will be no prank calls or bomb threats made to his office...ever again! The last time that happened, angel Michael had to clean the house. You will always have one partner (guardian angel) with you at all times; just listen carefully to that little voice in your head that tells you to be good, besides the mandated reporter the Holy Spirit! He has to report back to heaven.

You get to see things other employees don't get to see. Work time you can share your spiritual knowledge with each other, and make great teamwork to carry out the word of God to the four corners of the earth. God is a God of goodness. Deuteronomy 11:1 says, "Therefore thou shall love the lord thy God, and keep his charge, and his statues, and his judgments, and his commandments, always." Everything you desire is at the tip of your tongue and fingers. Say it, and then reach for it. The power of life and death is in the tongue. Proverbs 18:21 said death and life are in the power of the tongues, and those who love it will eat its fruits. Brothers and sisters, please examine yourself, do your best, and let God do the rest. Amen!